Shattered Justice

Critical Issues in Crime and Society

RAYMOND J. MICHALOWSKI AND LUIS A. FERNANDEZ, SERIES EDITORS

Critical Issues in Crime and Society is oriented toward critical analysis of contemporary problems in crime and justice. The series is open to a broad range of topics including specific types of crime, wrongful behavior by economically or politically powerful actors, controversies over justice system practices, and issues related to the intersection of identity, crime, and justice. It is committed to offering thoughtful works that will be accessible to scholars and professional criminologists, general readers, and students.

For a list of titles in the series, see the last page of the book.

Shattered Justice

CRIME VICTIMS' EXPERIENCES WITH WRONGFUL CONVICTIONS AND EXONERATIONS

KIMBERLY J. COOK

 RUTGERS UNIVERSITY PRESS
New Brunswick, Camden, and Newark, New Jersey, and London

LIBRARY OF CONGRESS CATALOGING-IN-PUBLICATION DATA

Names: Cook, Kimberly J., 1961- author.
Title: Shattered justice: crime victims' experiences with wrongful convictions and exonerations / Kimberly J. Cook.
Description: New Brunswick: Rutgers University Press, [2022] | Includes bibliographical references and index.
Identifiers: LCCN 2021047983 | ISBN 9781978820357 (paperback) | ISBN 9781978820364 (hardback) | ISBN 9781978820371 (epub) | ISBN 9781978820388 (mobi) | ISBN 9781978820395 (pdf)
Subjects: LCSH: Victims of crimes—United States—Psychology. | Judicial error—United States. | Restorative justice—United States.
Classification: LCC HV6250.3.U5 C629 2022 | DDC 362.88/0973—dc23/eng/20211
LC record available at https://lccn.loc.gov/2021047983

A British Cataloging-in-Publication record for this book is available from the British Library.

References to internet websites (URLs) were accurate at the time of writing. Neither the author nor Rutgers University Press is responsible for URLs that may have expired or changed since the manuscript was prepared.

♾ The paper used in this publication meets the requirements of the American National Standard for Information Sciences—Permanence of Paper for Printed Library Materials, ANSI Z39.48-1992.

www.rutgersuniversitypress.org

Manufactured in the United States of America

This book is dedicated to the brave women and men
who participated in this research project.
(* indicates pseudonym)
Penny Beerntsen
Ginger Blossom
Janet Burke
Tomeshia Carrington-Artis
Andrea Harrison and Dwayne Jones
Debbie Jones*
Regina Lane
Karen M.
Michele Mallin
Sean Malloy
Millie Maxwell*
Peggy Carter Sanders and Christy Sheppard
Yolanda Thomas
Jennifer Thompson
Ida Mae Wilhoit and Guy Wilhoit
Krissy Wilhoit and Kim Wilhoit
Nancy Wilhoit Vollertsen

In Memoriam
Debra Sue Carter
Morris and Ruth Gauger
Jacqueline Harrison
Noreen Malloy
Millie Maxwell's father
Jacquetta Thomas
Kathy Wilhoit

Contents

Shattered Justice

Studying Victims Who Experienced Exonerations

TOMESHIA WAS twelve years old in 1987; she was sleeping soundly in her bedroom in the first-floor apartment her mother had rearranged. Normally, her mom put a stick in the window to keep the room secure, but she forgot to insert the stick after putting the rest of the furniture in place. Tomeshia was awakened by the sound of someone coming into her room through the window; it was an adult man, a white man. She was frightened as he held a knife to her throat, so she tried to remain quiet. He raped her. After he left, she fled her room and told her mother. The police came. She was taken to the hospital, where they poked and prodded her body in ways she never knew about before. Her mother believed that the crime against her child, a Black child in the American South, might not be taken seriously, especially since the intruder was a white man. Her mother insisted that the police follow through with an investigation and arrest. Two years later, after a stalled investigation with no leads, during an unexpected run-in with a small group of people, Tomeshia froze; she thought the man who raped her was among them. This set into a motion a series of events that would consume many more years of Tomeshia's life and cause an innocent man to be incarcerated for seventeen years and the actual perpetrator to remain free. No one knows at the beginning of a criminal investigation how it will end; and few ever expect it to become an ordeal that steals nearly two decades of everyone's life.

Studying wrongful convictions and exonerations usually centers on the legal system processes that fail to produce accurate outcomes and mostly focuses on the wrongly convicted defendants. It is necessary to examine the causes of wrongful convictions and the process of exonerations as well as the consequences of wrongful convictions for defendants and their families. The legal process inflicts trauma on exonerees and their families.

Often missing is a systematic examination of the process and consequences of wrongful convictions and exonerations for crime victims whose lives are marred by violence, who depend on the system to redress that original harm

and yet endure a process over which they have no control and little influence. They take their primary trauma to the legal system seeking answers,
accountability, justice, and resolution. Instead, like most victims of crime, they
endure a secondary trauma associated with investigations and trials. Resolution, if present, is a by-product of another uncontrollable ordeal. In wrongful
conviction cases, and often decades after the crime, these victims endure postconviction claims of innocence and experience tertiary trauma. This research
examines wrongful convictions and exonerations based on crime victims'
experiences.

Part 1 (chapters 1–4) explains the research topic and methodology,
introduces the research participants whose experiences are included in this
book, and documents their primary and secondary traumas. Chapter 1 introduces the research questions, explains the methodologies and ethical principles that guide the research, and briefly introduces the research participants.
Chapter 2 explores in detail their recollections of the original crimes. The
recollections of the crimes never left their memories, and the exonerations
brought those memories to the surface with new light, due to new information that emerged during the exoneration process. Readers should be aware
that these recollections exist through the lens of post-exoneration reorder-
ing of information in their cases. Many of the stories are graphic; I chose
not to spare the reader the details because the crime victims cannot evac-
uate those memories from their experience. When these participants learned
that postconviction innocence claims were under way, they inevitably returned
to the original harms they endured. For the readers to understand the
victims' experiences, the original crime is a starting point for the wrongful
convictions, the traumas, and the brokenness that resulted. It is the primary
trauma.

Chapter 3 explores their experiences with the original investigations
and trials. Here participants describe the investigations that unfolded in
their cases, including eyewitness-identification processes, other elements of
the investigations, and court. For the homicide victims' family members, the
original trials were opportunities to learn how their family member was
murdered and ultimately stitch together some sense from the trial process.
For the rape victims, testifying in court often resulted in cross-examinations
by defense attorneys that added scars. Ultimately, they hoped for closure or
resolution, only to realize later that it would be elusive. These secondary
traumas remain vivid in their lives as they attempt to make sense of the
exonerations and wrongful convictions.

These experiences harm their families too. Chapter 4 explores the impacts
on families. Most were having ordinary life experiences when this violent
crime exploded in their lives. Some described their families as strong
and resilient, others as abusive and difficult. How families rallied or failed to

rally around the original victims largely reveals their strengths and their limits. In the wreckage of the original crime and then the exonerations, families of the victims inevitably were left to pick up the pieces, again. How families coped with the exoneration shadows how they coped with the original crimes.

Part 2 (chapters 5–8) presents victims' experiences with the exonerations in their cases. Chapter 5 explores victims' experiences of the post-conviction process and exonerations. Typically, exonerations occurred many years after the original crime, when these participants' lives had continued with marriage, raising children, military service, divorce, education, and so on. Exonerations launched these participants on a journey of reflection on their victimization experiences, traumas, and efforts to discern how it was possible that such a colossal error occurred. Some participants blamed themselves, which stems from cultural misunderstandings of exonerations that place blame on survivors rather than the system (this is particularly apparent for rape survivors who participated in flawed eyewitness-identification procedures). Some participants felt deeply betrayed by the system that they believed should have provided accurate information and compassionate support, which is the cultural lure of the legal system. All of the participants experienced grief and anguish when the system acknowledged that the wrong person was convicted for hurting them or their family members. In two of the wrongful convictions included in this research, the exonerees were family members accused of killing fellow family members (the Wilhoit and Gauger families).

The book then leans into a more analytical effort and presents a grounded theory of tertiary trauma of the wrongful conviction and exoneration experiences for original crime victims and survivors. As with secondary trauma that results from the legal process, tertiary trauma is a by-product of an adversarial system ill equipped to aid victims in their traumatic experiences. Chapter 6 identifies sources of the tertiary trauma: their experiences within the system they depended on for redress and accurate information. Some victims found system officials who were helpful (i.e., victim centered), but others were disappointed by the lack of concern or information they received. Crime victims often believe the cultural lore that the legal system invariably offers compassionate treatment, support, and ultimately accurate resolution for the crimes they endured. Yet these participants experienced crippling, though misdirected, guilt and shame for their role in the wrongful convictions and/or a deep sense of institutional betrayal when the state produced this additional harm in their lives. It all resulted in compounded grief and persistent extreme anguish.

Chapter 7 illuminates the elements of tertiary trauma based on variations in their cases and the social context of intersectional analysis. Elements include frustration and confusion, betrayal and deception, misplaced guilt and shame, and powerlessness. Intersectional analysis reveals how institutional sexism and racism cocreate and contribute to tertiary trauma. This grounded theory connects legacies of gendered mistreatment and systemic racism as experienced by these participants.

Chapter 8 explores how these crime victims and survivors describe their grief, loss, and coping. When the crime occurs, victims grieve their losses that include the lost family members and the lost sense of security within their lives. Grieving unfolds based on their understanding of what happened to them and their loved ones in the original crime. They experience interwoven strands of anger, denial, bargaining, and possibly acceptance as they move on with their lives. The exonerations unravel and shatter whatever progress they may have had and require them to examine anew the crimes they experienced and the legal system failures in their cases. Ultimately, they continue grieving by having to begin again with dramatically different information. Sometimes they receive information in which they can have confidence (as in cases with DNA identification of the actual perpetrators). Sometimes they are left with an open wound that cannot be closed or resolved (as in cold case homicides). Woven within their new grief process are recurring frustrations and a lost sense of confidence in the legal system.

Part 3 (chapters 9 and 10) presents findings on how these participants describe their journey into healing, finding community, often with each other, and reforms they advocate to address the needs of other victims in cases that result in exonerations. Chapter 9 presents their experiences of moving toward healing through restorative justice. Jennifer Thompson started the nonprofit organization Healing Justice, shaped by her personal belief that crime victims and their families, as well as exonerees and their families, are harmed by wrongful convictions. They are all victims of the actual perpetrators and of the flaws in the legal system. Jennifer's experience is an example of reconciliation and redemption given her meeting the exoneree Ronald Cotton and sharing a public platform with him for many years as their shared experiences raise awareness and shape policy reform. Chapter 9 discusses how restorative justice techniques, particularly the circle process, are powerful and promote healing and community among victims and exonerees, separately and conjointly.

Chapter 10 offers ideas for system reforms that these original crime victims suggest, combined with an exploration of current policy reform efforts to reduce wrongful convictions. The chapter is organized around ideas that may prevent wrongful convictions, moves toward ideas that help mitigate the harms of wrongful convictions, and ultimately ends with ideas for repairing the harms, if possible.

CHAPTER 1

Introduction

GINGER BLOSSOM AND her twin brother Gary Gauger's parents were murdered on their family farm in April 1993. The killing was gruesome. Morris and Ruth Gauger, both in their seventies, ran the farm and a rug import business in northern Illinois. Morris also had a motorcycle repair shop on the farm and often welcomed visitors looking for motorcycle parts or repair services. Ruth ran the rug business and spent a lot of her time in the rug barn. At the time they were killed, Gary was in his early forties and living back at home with them while his life was in transition. Ginger Blossom was living out West and working with her husband as a ski instructor. Gary was questioned and submitted to the interrogation, where detectives claimed he confessed. He was charged with capital murder, convicted, and sentenced to death and then exonerated in 1996, after a federal investigation into an outlaw motorcycle gang revealed the actual perpetrators. Interviewing Gary Gauger, who participated in prior research I did with Saundra Westervelt (Westervelt and Cook, 2012), was a heartbreaking experience. Among those most painful moments of my time with Gary was when he broke down during our conversation while describing his grief over losing his parents (see Westervelt and Cook, 2012, pp. 74–75). It was not lost on me that Gary and his twin sister Ginger were, first and foremost, murder victims' family members. The police and legal system turned them into something else: death row inmate and family member.

Each person whose life experience includes direct involvement in a wrongful conviction and exoneration has a unique and consequential story to tell. Hearing those stories can promote understanding, acceptance, and perhaps resolution and healing. Exonerations may generate significant public attention for the exonerated person and for the attorneys involved. We typically see the celebratory release from prison, with media coverage of the event and a retelling of the case and its flaws, and ultimately the triumph of correcting a miscarriage of justice. Celebrations are welcome: the relief after decades of stress, trauma, and frustration fighting a system that is reluctant or refuses to acknowledge its own mistake is palpable. As a society, we celebrate the transformation of the Central Park 5 into the Exonerated 5 in the wake of the much-celebrated Netflix series *When They See Us* (2019), by Ava DuVernay. We follow what happens next for the exonerees: do they receive compensation, are they able to build a good life for themselves, can they be made whole again? As scholars, we learn about, document, and research their life experiences (Kirshenbaum et al., 2020; Shlosberg et al., 2020; Westervelt and Cook, 2012) aimed at expanding awareness of how harmful wrongful convictions are to those who endure them. We acknowledge the traumatic impact on their families, and their attorneys, and others who advocate for the wrongly convicted. Yet we seldom go beyond a passing acknowledgment of the original crime victims in these cases.

This book explores the harms generated by wrongful convictions for the original victims of the crimes that resulted in the wrongful convictions. The phrase "original victims" centers the genesis of the legal system's involvement, which often is rendered to the shadows of wrongful conviction research and policy, to include rape survivors and homicide victims' family members. Typically, scholars, lawyers, and policy reformers focus on the wrongly convicted and exonerated former prisoner as the victim of these miscarriages of justice, and certainly that is true. Usually, the concern does not go beyond an oblique reference to the victims of the original crime. Our previous research explored how exonerees rebuild their lives after being released from death row (Baumgartner et al., 2014; Cook et al., 2014; Cook and Westervelt, 2018; Westervelt and Cook, 2008, 2010, 2012, 2013, 2018). In that research, several exonerated death row survivors were also surviving family members of the (presumed) murder victims.[1] Several exonerees expressed their concern for the family members of the murder victim, knowing that the family members were not getting justice. Expanding the circle of harm (Thompson and Baumgartner, 2018) to crime victims is inclusive of the exonerated original defendants who are victims of this miscarriage of justice, *as well as* the original crime victims throughout this research. The present research places the voices of original crime victims and survivors squarely in the center of concern. Readers will notice that I use metaphors of *parallel tracks* and *conjoined harms* between the original victims and the exonerated individuals. While research has illuminated many aspects of wrongful convictions for exonerees, very little research has highlighted the other parallel track: original victims and survivors. The parallel tracks are conjoined in that they connect to the same events: court dates, hearings, news reports, and other moments that impact both the wrongly convicted and the crime victims/survivors. This book sheds light on the less examined parallel experiences of original victims.

To date, one research project has examined the experiences of victims/ survivors of the original crimes during wrongful convictions and exonerations (Irazola et al., 2013; Williamson et al., 2016). Williamson et al. (2016) show that victims experience extreme disruption during and after the exoneration process. For example, victims reported that the exoneration process can be worse than the original crime; as one victim reported, "It was harder going through the revictimization than it was through the rape. . . . Now you have the same feelings of that pain. You have the same scariness. You have the same fear. You have the same panic, but now you have this flood of guilt on top of it" (Williamson et al., 2016, p. 160). Factors that complicate the experience for original victims include the media coverage of their cases, family dynamics where differing views of the exoneration can damage family relationships, and the reality that "you're never the same after an exoneration" (Williamson et al., 2016, p. 161).

QUALITATIVE RESEARCH METHODS AND TRAUMA FRAMEWORK

Replicating feminist qualitative methods used previously (Westervelt and Cook, 2012), the current project explores these research questions: *How do crime victims experience the original crime, the original investigation, trial, and conviction, and the exoneration process? What impact does it have in their lives? How do they cope with these experiences? How have they been harmed, and what do they need to repair those harms?*

According to Judith Herman (1997, p. 33), "Psychological trauma is an affliction of the powerless. At the moment of trauma, the victim is rendered helpless by overwhelming force. When the force is that of other human beings, we speak of atrocities. Traumatic events overwhelm the ordinary systems of care that give people a sense of control, connection, and meaning." Citing the *Comprehensive Textbook of Psychiatry*, she reports that traumas are often accompanied by feeling of "intense fear, helplessness, loss of control, and threat of annihilation" (Herman, 1997, p. 33). All participants in this research experienced the depth of trauma that resulted in being overwhelmed and helpless and suffered a lost sense of personal control over their bodies and their lives. Therefore, this research methodology applies a trauma-informed approach to the process of conducting the research interviews. Drawing important lessons from trauma research, Reeves (2015) offers critical insights for trauma-informed care, including the importance of trust, collaboration, safety, and comfort, as well as control in the hands of the participant. These factors form the basis that Bath (2008, p. 17) identifies as the "three pillars of trauma-informed care." Complex trauma results in survivors often feeling stressed and uncomfortable in unfamiliar surroundings and in social situations where they may feel trapped or unsure of themselves.

It is vitally important to acknowledge that the experiences of trauma for the research participants in this study are broader than the one single event of the violent crime they endured or that caused the loss of their family members. In fact, the traumas for these participants are complex and recurring, where the participants have no control over when or how the traumas resurface in their lives.

Trauma research (Herman, 1997) usually is framed around discrete life events that have beginning and ending points. For these participants, however, the original crime is the first step in a series of traumatic events that continue to unfold over decades of legal procedures, similar to the "continuing traumatic stress" experienced by exonerated death row survivors (Westervelt and Cook, 2018, p. 309). Furthermore, the sense of grief and loss is a common theme in the lived experiences of these participants. The grief and loss form a shape-shifter—when survivors embark on the inevitable grief process, they do so with an understanding of the event that produced their loss and trauma. When that understanding changes, unavoidable in an exonerations process, the process of resolving grief begins anew, with fresh wounds inflicted. Those fresh wounds may include a misplaced sense of shame and guilt for those who provided eyewitness identification that DNA later revealed as flawed, for example.

Following the definitions used by Irazola et al. (2013, p. 14), "The term wrongful conviction is defined as a case in which a government entity has determined that the originally convicted individual factually did not commit the crime. The term exoneration refers to the process by which a government entity, by way of a pardon or judicial order, concedes that a convicted person is indeed innocent." Original crime victims are survivors or direct victims of the actual perpetrator of the crime that was the subject of the wrongful conviction. The exonerated person is referred to as the "exoneree" or "original defendant" throughout this book and is rightly designated as a victim of a miscarriage of justice.

Researching this topic is a delicate process; the people who have endured these extremely painful situations are not easy to find, and reaching out with cold calls to invite participation is too intrusive (see Westervelt and Cook, 2012). Contacting most of the participants was facilitated by Jennifer Thompson, who is also a participant. Thompson is an internationally known advocate for repairing the harms of wrongful convictions. The book *Picking Cotton: Our Memoir of Injustice and Redemption* (Thompson-Cannino et al., 2009) documents her experiences as a rape victim in the wrongful conviction case of Ronald Cotton in North Carolina. The book marked a major turning point in the field of wrongful convictions by featuring the profound impact on original victims (documented in later chapters). Thompson has devoted her life to policy reform and to assisting others who have experienced exonerations. I used a convenience sampling technique to connect with a population of survivors, often from Thompson's contacts. In 2015, Thompson launched a nonprofit organization, Healing Justice, an organization based on peer support and restorative justice that hosts healing retreats for people impacted by wrongful convictions and exonerations and develops policies/practices for professionals working in this field.[2] It is the only nonprofit in this field that addresses the needs of the original victims as well as those of the exonerated former inmates and their families.[3]

Given the diverse population involved in this research, their complex trauma is compounded by additional traumas that result from generalized sexism (and the harmful impact that has on women), institutionalized racism (and the perpetual harm that inflicts on people of color), and the chronic challenges of poverty (and the harms that relentless despair and frustration generate for the poor). For the purposes of this research project, and to adhere to the good ethical practices of research (Newman et al., 2006), I used these guidelines:

1. Reach out to invite participants through a trusted relationship that we both share (this often meant Jennifer Thompson facilitating the contact)
2. Having an initial phone call to explain what the research interview would entail and how it would be conducted, providing ample time for the prospective participants to ask questions and receive answers before deciding to participate
3. Ensure that the prospective participants would be in control of the process: to reveal or conceal their identity, where and when we would have the in-depth interviews, what questions they wanted to answer, and so forth
4. Explain in advance the audio-recording technology I would be using to capture their words and experiences and provide an opportunity to proofread their transcribed interviews for corrections
5. Explain in advance how the process would unfold after the interview was completed and answer any questions they may have about what's next for this project
6. Remain available and in contact with the participants with updates and information on the project as it unfolds
7. And ultimately ensure that they would receive a copy of the book upon publication

In an effort to gain a holistic understanding of their ordeals, I replicated a four-pronged approach used previously (Westervelt and Cook, 2012) to conduct this research. This detailed knowledge of each case aided the in-depth interviews insofar as the participants were not required to explain who was whom or when and where specific events occurred. Had they been expected to do so, it would have circumvented, and muted, their individual stories by focusing more on the case and less on their lived experiences. On the other hand, some of the documents reviewed prior to meeting these participants may have included oversights, errors, and misrepresentations, in which case the in-depth interviews were opportunities for these participants to remedy those gaps. The four prongs included

1. reading as much of the legal materials available on each of the exonerations with a special emphasis on the victims' documented harms and participation in the original case,
2. reading as much of the media coverage of the original case and then the exoneration process with a special emphasis on victims' experiences,
3. in-depth interviews with the original victims in each case, and
4. follow-up contact as desired by the participants.

Of the people I contacted, one original victim declined to participate due to continuing legal claims in her case. Two other eligible participants were interested in contributing, though, sadly, the budget for this project had been exhausted by that time. I aimed to achieve a diverse sample in terms of gender, race, and region. I confirmed this sample with the National Registry of Exonerations (NRE).[4] The NRE is widely recognized by scholars, lawyers, and advocates as the most dependable list available in the United States. The number of cases expands daily, and assuming between one and four victim-survivors in each case, I assume a population size of two to eight thousand original victims whose cases have resulted in exonerations, once removing the cases where no crime occurred (Henry, 2018, 2020). The recruitment process resulted in twenty-one in-depth interviews with original victims and murder victims' family members in cases where criminal convictions were reversed based on claims of innocence by defendants.

During the institutional review board–approved informed consent process, the participants had the option of using their actual identities/names in this research or having their identities concealed by choosing a pseudonym. (Table 1 and Figure 1 display the participants and basic information about their cases.) Most of the participants (eighteen) chose to have their actual names used, but three elected to alter their names to preserve their identity and privacy. The choice to reveal their identities was deeply personal. For example, Jennifer Thompson has become an internationally known advocate in the field of wrongful convictions; her story is widely known, and it would be nearly impossible to conceal her identity. Others had already participated in media coverage of their cases, so they decided that concealing their identity in this project was futile. Furthermore, the toll their ordeal has taken on these research participants matters to the broader questions

Victims/Survivors in Exonerations

Research Participant	Crime[a]	Victim/Survivor Status	Race/ Gender	Age at Victimization	State	Year of Crime	Exoneree's Race/ Gender	Contributing Factors[b]	Year of Exoneration	DNA	Actual Perpetrator Identified?
Penny Beerntsen	Rape	Direct victim	WF	36	WI	1985	WM	WID	2003	Y	Yes, but not prosecuted
Ginger Blossom	Murder	Victims' daughter	WF	41	IL	1993	WM	FC, OM, PFA	1996	N	Yes
Janet Burke	Rape	Direct victim	WF	20	VA	1984	BM	WID	2011	Y	Yes
Tomeshia Carrington-Artis	Rape	Direct victim	BF	12	NC	1984	WM	WID, FMFE	2007	Y	Yes
Andrea Harrison[c]	Murder	Daughter	BF	3	NJ, NJ	1987	BM	FMFE, PFA	2006	Y	No
Dwayne Jones	Murder	Boyfriend/partner	BM	Mid-20s							
Debbie Jones[d]	Rape	Direct victim	WF	19	TX	1985	BM	WID, OM	2008	Y	Yes, but not prosecuted
Regina Lane	Rape	Subsequent victim of true perpetrator	WF	19	NC	1985	BM	WID, OM	2004	Y	Yes
Karen M.	Rape	Direct victim	WF	20	OK	1980	BM	WID, FMFE	1996	Y	Yes, but not prosecuted
Michele Mallin	Rape	Direct victim	WF	20	TX	1985	BM	WID, FMFE	2009	Y	Yes
Sean Malloy	Murder	Victim's brother	WF	18	PA	1988	BM	WID, PFA	2006	Y	No

(continued)

TABLE 1 *Continued*

Research Participant	Crime[a]	Victim/Survivor Status	Race/ Gender	Age at Victimization	State	Year of Crime	Exoneree's Race/ Gender	Contributing Factors[b]	Year of Exoneration	DNA	Actual Perpetrator Identified?
Millie Maxwell[d]	Murder	Victim's daughter	BF	18	NC	2000	BM (5)	FC, PFA, OM	2011, 2015	Y	Yes, but not prosecuted
Peggy Sanders	Murder	Victim's mother	WF	44	OK	1982	WM (2)	FMFE, PFA, OM	1999	Y	Yes
Christy Sheppard	Murder	Victim's cousin	WF	8							
Yolanda Thomas	Murder	Victim's sister	BF	28	NC	1991	WM	FMFE, PFA, OM	2010	Y	No
Jennifer Thompson	Rape	Direct victim	WF	22	NC	1984	BM	WID	1995	Y	Yes
Krissy Zarn	Murder	Victim's daughter	WF	14 months	OK	1984	WM	FMFE, ILD	1993	N	No
Kim Griggs Wilhoit	Murder	Victim's daughter	WF	4 months							
Ida Mae Wilhoit	Murder	Victim's mother-in-law	WF	Mid–50s							
Guy Wilhoit	Murder	Victim's father-in-law	WM	Mid–50s							
Nancy Vollertsen	Murder	Victim's sister-in-law	WF	34							

a. This column captures the official charges of the wrongful conviction. The next column displays participants' victim status: the direct victim, the victim's survivor and relationship, or a subsequent direct victim of the true perpetrator.

b. Based on the National Registry of Exonerations' review of cases, the contributing factors include witness identification (WID), false or misleading forensic evidence (FMFE), official misconduct (OM), perjury or false accusation (PFA), false confession (FC), and inadequate legal defense (ILD).

c. Shaded areas represent family members in the same case.

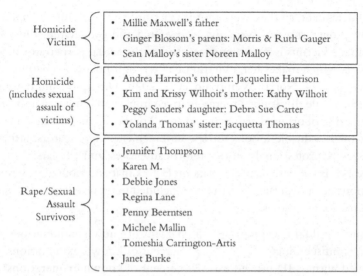

Figure 1. Overlapping Crime Categories among Participants' Cases

surrounding wrongful convictions and policy reform. Those who chose to reveal their identities often did so in order to have their experiences count for something significant—to inform the public debate on legal system reform, victim services, and overall public awareness. This research is meant to document the experiences "from within" (Wright, 2019, p. 181) their own lived realities, not to impose a framework for meaning but to construct grounded theory from their combined voices. Most of the participants in this sample expressed appreciation for their involvement in this project; Tomeshia Carrington-Artis, an African American woman who was raped by a white intruder when she was twelve years old, said, "Thank you for doing something for the victims, there's nothing ever been done like this before, to hear it from the victim's standpoint."

The twenty-one participants in this research are associated with fifteen different criminal cases: eight rape survivors and thirteen murder victims' family members in seven homicide cases. Some of the participants are members of the same family. Three of the participants are men, eighteen are women. Their ages at the time of the original crime ranged from four months old to their mid-fifties, with ages at the time of participation in this research ranging from the early thirties to eighties. The exonerations occurred in Illinois, New Jersey, North Carolina, Oklahoma, Pennsylvania, Texas, Virginia, and Wisconsin. Five of the participants are African American, and sixteen are white. Some participants were victims in crimes that became extremely high profile, while others drew less public attention. In two of the homicide cases, the murder victims were also family members to the wrongly convicted original defendant, so they were murder victims' family members supporting their loved one who was wrongly incarcerated and exonerated. One of the original rape victims is a subsequent victim of the actual perpetrator in a different case, which makes her a victim of a "wrongful liberty" (Baumgartner, Grigg, et al., 2014; Norris, Weintraub, et al., 2020; Thompson and Baumgartner, 2018). While this is not a representative sample and is not generalizable to the population of original crime victims in all of the documented exoneration cases, it offers valuable lessons for law enforcement, investigators, attorneys, victim service professionals, justice reform advocates, and scholars.

The NRE regularly captures data on factors that contributed to wrongful convictions in each of the cases that are included in their data set. Nationally, the figures are as follows:

- perjury and false accusations   58 percent of known exonerations
- official misconduct   54 percent of known exonerations
- flawed witness ID procedure   29 percent of known exonerations[5]
- false/misleading forensics   24 percent of known exonerations
- false confessions   12 percent of known exonerations

The sample in this study includes cases that have the following contributing factors: flawed witness identification procedure (9/15 [60 percent]), false or misleading forensic evidence (7/15 [46 percent]), official misconduct (6/15 [40 percent]), perjury or false accusation (6/15 [40 percent]), and false confessions (3/15 [20 percent]).

The semistructured in-depth interviews generally captured the experiences in chronological order, if the participants were comfortable with that. They were welcome to take a break and end the conversation at any time, and the length of time spent in each interview ranged from two to five hours. The participants often commented on this methodology and expressed themselves candidly. Some participated simply to be heard. Karen M., a white women in a cross-racial case, is a rape survivor from Oklahoma; she said, "I just haven't lived and I have hidden all my life. I've hidden from life and I've missed out and maybe I don't know if it's partially punishing myself for what he [the exoneree] missed out on but mainly it's just the guilt. . . . That's why I'm trying to start making contact with people [like] Jennifer and you too. You're the first two people I actually met in person besides [the exoneree]." The chance to make a difference and to be part of the landscape of concern also prompted some victims to participate in this project. Janet Burke, also a white woman and rape survivor from Virginia, said, "The ability to make a difference, that's kinda what brought me back. I don't know where I would be if I didn't have that opportunity because it's hard." Participating in this research offered a chance to share their own voices. When Andrea Harrison, an African American woman, was a small child her mother was murdered; the original defendant was exonerated when she was a young adult. A news article had been written about her mother's murder. I contacted the reporter to inquire about approaching Andrea and her father, Dwayne Jones. Andrea said, "When the [reporter] reached out to me I was surprised somebody wants to hear what I have to say."

The interviews were audio-recorded and then transcribed verbatim to produce text documents suitable for coding using MAXQDA software. Because the semistructured interviews generally captured their experiences chronologically, the data were coded to capture the victims' experiences within a timeline of common events (such as the original crime, the investigation, the exoneration, etc.). Bhattacharya (2017) suggests that inductive analysis can aid in creating analytical categories to organize the data. In this research, the analytical units that became apparent were two main categories of victims: rape survivors and homicide victims' family members. These two broad categories of experiences structure the findings in several chapters. While these are not mutually exclusive categories (four of the seven homicide cases also included sexual violence in the original crime), the realities of these crimes and later exonerations generate distinct experiences of trauma, impact, and recovery for each of the two main categories.

The coding scheme included organizing the participants' experiences beginning with the original crime, then the original trial, and later the exoneration process. Next, coding data for emergent themes (Charmaz, 2014) identified recurring lived experiences of these participants. Coding revealed intersectional layers of experiences regarding gender and race. As a feminist scholar (Cook, 2016; Cook, forthcoming), I coded to include nuances based on gender and race since a leading concern within wrongful conviction research and policy is racial bias (Gross, 2017). Intersectionality guides this analysis (Collins, 2019) and produces insights regarding gendered and racialized experiences of these participants, particularly in constructing the grounded theory of tertiary trauma. An intersectional lens explores representation of murdered Black women, interracial rape cases, and victims' experiences with these broader social structures. The most common open theme relates to the impact that the exoneration and original crimes had on the families of these participants. Their lives were shattered, and their families were profoundly changed. Additionally, the wrongful convictions were traumatic life events that occurred in slow motion. The ordeal continues well beyond court proceedings because in the wake of an exoneration there is a person who must process, make sense of, and heal from the compounded

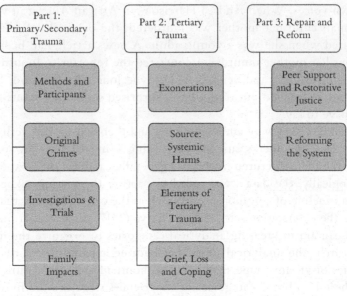

Figure 2. Book Structure Based on Coding Scheme

trauma. The coded themes are displayed in Figure 2 and provide structure for this book.

GROUNDED THEORY OF TERTIARY TRAUMA

Qualitative research in the form of in-depth interviews and collaboration with research participants generates rich and nuanced data that, when coded and compiled, construct meaning and understanding that did not previously exist. "Stated simply, grounded theory methods consist of systematic, yet flexible, guidelines for collecting and analyzing qualitative data to construct theories from the data themselves" (Charmaz, 2014, p. 1). Constructing grounded theory involves noticing patterns in the data, which represent recurring experiences among the participants, and going deep into those recurring experiences to expose a more complex understanding of the phenomenon being studied. The current research produced new grounded theory of tertiary trauma, based on inductive and abductive analyses of the in-depth interview data. Criminologists have studied the "second assault" (Martin and Powell, 1994) that occurs when rape victims report to the police and their cases go through the legal system. Since many of the participants in this research are rape survivors, their experiences with the legal system are complex. Compounding that experience of second assault is the third wave of harms they endure during and after the exonerations in their cases. All of the participants in this research experienced the primary trauma of the original crime, the secondary trauma of the original legal process, and then tertiary trauma connected to the wrongful conviction and exoneration process. Sources of tertiary trauma identified here include many stages of the legal system that may be helpful or more often harmful. Elements of tertiary trauma examined include frustration and confusion, betrayal and deception, misplaced guilt, shame, and powerlessness. Intersectional analysis reveals that institutional racism and sexism are conjoined in these cases, such that the grounded theory of tertiary trauma connects legacies of systemic racism with gendered mistreatment. Tertiary trauma is present irrespective of the original victims' views about the exoneration itself. Original victims who support and understand the exoneration are traumatized by the wrongful convictions, especially if and when the original trial depended on their eyewitness identification and testimony, or if they are then left with a cold case in the homicide of their family members. They view the exoneration as necessary to correct a terrible wrong for the innocent original defendant and yet experience a slurry of questions and emotions to manage. Original victims who are unsure of the exoneration may continue to believe that the original conviction was fair and are also traumatized in that they feel intense frustration and rage as a consequence, contributing to a sense of institutional betrayal (Smith and Freyd, 2013). And original victims whose family members were murdered and whose other family members were wrongfully convicted of those murders, who supported the exoneration and release of their loved one, are traumatized by the wrongful conviction and its aftermath (Westervelt and Cook, 2012) and also experience deep frustration, confusion, and betrayal. Thus, the tertiary trauma of wrongful convictions results in their worlds being completely shattered again; when taken as part of a decades-long ordeal, many say it is worse than the original crime.

The lived experiences were collected through in-depth interviews, an inductive and interpretive approach. Through transcribing and coding those data, commonalities that provide thick descriptions were identified (Charmaz, 2014, p. 23). Constructing this grounded theory included an abductive approach, which marries data with known research findings "in ways that may revise, re-form, or reintegrate this prior knowledge to become consistent with the surprising observation" (Charmaz, 2014, p. 203). Thus, the approach shapes this grounded theory of tertiary trauma by exposing how original victims recall their experiences in the legal system. It reveals another series of traumas that redefines their relationship to the system and to their own sense of self. And, the approach exposes brand-new contours of grief, loss, and coping in its wake.

Exposing the impact of wrongful convictions and exonerations on crime victims extends the grounded theory of tertiary trauma into research on grief and loss—a rich and complex field that mostly focuses on the process of resolving grief when the grief relates to a distinct event (Rheingold and Williams, 2015). While there is good research in the field of "ambiguous loss" (Boss, 1999), I have not found research examining how grief is impacted when it is so monumentally interrupted as in wrongful conviction and exoneration processes. For the participants in this research, resolving grief over time is rarely finished, seldom producing a sense of resolution or meaning (Kessler, 2019). During the exoneration and its aftermath, the grief process is interrupted and participants must discard whatever resolution or meaning their grief process produced to that point. Effective grieving depends on accurate information about what happened that contributed to the loss they endured; when the original victims learn during the postconviction process that their previous understanding is wrong or based on incomplete and inaccurate information, their grief process explodes, shattering whatever progress they may have made toward resolution. They are left with having to restart the grieving process based on the new information (a reality that many never anticipated), and the process may be compounded by an internalized, and misplaced, sense of personal shame and blame (particularly if they gave witness testimony) and a sense of betrayal from the legal system (particularly if the outcome is now a cold case).

The exploration of coping strategies outlined by Westervelt and Cook (2012) is refined using grounded theory methodology as "situational coping." In the strategies of withdrawal as outlined in prior research, we documented how exonerated death row survivors sometimes reduce their contact with people in order to avoid dealing with the painful stigma of their wrongful convictions. For many victims, a corollary stigma is associated with the crimes they and their families endured. They too use withdrawal and avoidance strategies depending on the situations they faced. In the strategies of incorporation, we documented how some exonerated death row survivors develop a "survivor mission" as a platform for policy reform. Original crime survivors also report that they wish their experiences to be informative to the broader public debates about reform and services to victims, though sharing their experiences can be a painful gambit. The survivor missions of these original victims involve public advocacy—and that sometimes inflicts additional harms including personal attacks and death threats from strangers.

The data presented here emerge from the lived experiences of these research participants that they shared during our in-depth interviews. Direct quotes were lightly edited for readability. I occasionally add contextualized factors from other sources, such as memoirs, to add nuance and expand understanding of their experiences. The findings combine elements of these in-depth interviews, including the common themes among them, with criminological and sociological research to connect experiences with social contexts.

CAVEATS

Readers should be aware that my central purpose is to reveal the lived experiences of these original victims and homicide survivors, not to disentangle myriad legal issues. As a sociologist, I am not rehashing the legal issues of each case, nor verifying or challenging the evidence used in each case. Sociologically, this research documents and explores the experiences of these participants. The priority is to center these research participants and their recollections in the discussion about wrongful convictions and exonerations. Because memories can differ among people experiencing the same ordeal, their unique recollections may or may not jive exactly with those of others who are connected to the same case, with the legal documentation, or with the exact legal processes they endured. Giving voice to their experiences through their unique recollections fills a gap in research and policy on wrongful convictions, which tends to be populated by system officials, journalists, lawyers, and others. Some readers might find this approach lacking in details that are important to them. But using the original victims' combined experiences to make meaning of these ordeals and translating those lessons into meaningful recommendations for policy reform are most important.

Because this research is meant to engage the community of scholars, lawyers, and policy makers to raise awareness and deepen understanding, some might find my connection to Healing Justice as a source of bias. Access to this population of people harmed by wrongful convictions is a delicate matter; Jennifer Thompson (founder of Healing Justice) is both a participant in this research and in many cases an access point for my connections to several who agreed to be part of this research. The analysis offered herein is my own; it would not have been possible without Jennifer Thompson and Healing Justice, but I am solely responsible for the analysis and interpretation of the data and for the contents of this book.

After the case summaries that follow, I limit using the exonerated persons' names, and I avoid naming other potentially high-profile people (famous lawyers, etc.) in the chapters. Much of this field is dominated by valid concern for the exonerated, and some people have gained very high-profile status, so much so that if I were to use their names systematically in these chapters, it would risk overshadowing the voices and recollections of the original victims. Therefore, I focus on presenting the voices of crime victims and survivors.

Introducing the Participants

Penny Beerntsen (crime against her: rape; contributing factor: flawed eyewitness identification procedures; exoneration: DNA)

When Penny was thirty-six years old, married, and mother of two children, she and her husband and son decided to enjoy an afternoon at a local state park in Manitowoc County, Wisconsin, on July 29, 1985.[6] An avid runner, she went for a jog on the beach, during which time she was attacked, beaten, and sexually assaulted by Gregory Allen. After reporting her attack to the police and submitting to the rape kit evidence-collection process, Penny participated in the investigation to find the man who attacked her. Through flawed investigative procedures, the actual perpetrator was not identified and Steven Avery was prosecuted and convicted of assaulting Penny in 1985. After DNA testing identified Allen as the perpetrator, Avery was released from prison in 2003.

Ginger Blossom (crime against her family: homicide of her parents, Morris and Ruth Gauger; contributing factors: false confession, perjury / false accusation, official misconduct; exoneration: pardon based on innocence)

On April 8, 1993, when Ginger was working as a ski instructor out of state, she received a phone call that her parents were found murdered in their home in northern Illinois. Her twin brother, Gary Gauger, had recently moved back to the family farm and quickly became the lead suspect in the homicide of their parents. Gary endured a flawed interrogation that resulted in his false confession and was also impacted by perjury / false accusations and official misconduct. He was wrongly convicted and sentenced to death in 1993. Ginger returned to Illinois to tend to the family farm and assist in Gary's case to prove his innocence. Gary was exonerated in 1996, and the actual perpetrators were convicted of murdering Morris and Ruth Gauger in 1997 and 2000, respectively. Gary Gauger participated in research for Westervelt and Cook (2012).

Janet Burke (crime against her: rape; contributing factor: flawed eyewitness identification procedures; exoneration: DNA)

On January 3, 1984, twenty-year-old Janet Burke was starting her usual workday at the child care center in a church when Leon Davis broke into the business before the children began to arrive. He held her at knifepoint, raped her, and then fled the scene. She called the police, who responded, and she submitted to the rape kit examination. Through flawed identification procedures used at the time, Thomas Haynesworth was wrongly convicted of raping Janet and five other women in 1984. After DNA testing confirmed that Leon Davis was the actual perpetrator, Haynesworth was exonerated in 2011.

Tomeshia Carrington-Artis (crime against her: rape, child sexual abuse; contributing factors: flawed eyewitness identification procedures, false or misleading forensic evidence; exoneration: DNA)

On September 4, 1987, when Tomeshia was twelve years old, William Neal broke into her bedroom through a screened window while she was sleeping. He sexually molested her, and she—along with her mother—reported the assault to the police. She submitted to the rape kit investigation. Due to the flawed and protracted investigation, Dwayne Dail was wrongly convicted in 1989. DNA testing led to his exoneration in 2007. North Carolina governor Michael Easley granted a pardon of innocence to Dail.

Andrea Harrison and Dwayne Jones (crime against their family: murder of her mother / his partner; contributing factors: false or misleading forensic evidence and perjury or false accusation; exoneration: DNA)

In August 1987, when Andrea was three and a half years old and her father Dwayne Jones was working, her mother Jacqueline Harrison was brutally raped and murdered, and her body was left outdoors in a ditch. Forensic evidence was collected and preserved. In 1989, Larry Peterson was convicted of the homicide and sexual assault, despite maintaining his innocence. After DNA testing, Peterson was exonerated in 2006. The actual perpetrator has not been identified.

Debbie Jones (pseudonym) (crime against her: rape, burglary, and unlawful entry; contributing factors: flawed eyewitness identification procedures and official misconduct; exoneration: DNA)

Debbie Jones was nineteen years old on May 7, 1985, when she returned to her apartment to find Kenneth Woodson had broken in. He raped her at knifepoint. When she was able to escape the attacker, she ran around her apartment complex for help. The police arrived and took her to the hospital for a forensic examination. Through a flawed identification procedure, Thomas McGowan was wrongly convicted in 1985. In 2008, DNA testing indicated that her assailant was Woodson, and McGowan was released from prison. Despite the actual perpetrator having been identified, he cannot be prosecuted due to the statute of limitations. Debbie prefers to conceal her identity and chose her pseudonym.

Regina Lane (crime against her: sexual assault and abduction; contributing factors: flawed eyewitness identification procedures, perjury or false accusation, official misconduct; exoneration: DNA)

On August 10, 1984, Willard Brown abducted and murdered Deborah Sykes in Winston-Salem, North Carolina. The investigation resulted in the arrest of Darryl Hunt, who was wrongly convicted and later exonerated based on DNA evidence. In February 1985, Brown abducted and raped Regina Lane, while Hunt was in jail awaiting trial in the Sykes homicide.

Lane was nineteen years old and engaged to be married. She managed to escape Brown and called the police. She noticed similarities with the reports of how Deborah Sykes had been abducted and murdered. When she shared these similarities, the investigators dismissed her tip because they had Hunt in jail awaiting trial. In 2004, Hunt was exonerated based on DNA evidence, and Brown was convicted of murdering Sykes. He has not been charged with crimes against Regina Lane.

Karen M. (crime against her: sexual assault; contributing factors: flawed eyewitness identification procedures, false or misleading forensic evidence; exoneration: DNA)

On March 20, 1982, Karen was a twenty-year-old college student living in her first apartment; she was asleep in her home in the middle of the night when Gilbert Harris broke in. He raped her, robbed her, and eventually left the apartment. She called the police and fully cooperated with the investigation. Due to flawed identification procedures used at the time, Thomas Webb was identified as the intruder; he was wrongly convicted in 1983. Later, DNA testing excluded Webb and eventually identified Harris as the actual perpetrator. Webb was exonerated in 1996, and Harris was charged in 2014, but later the charges were dropped due to the statute of limitations, and he was released.

Michele Mallin (crime against her: rape; contributing factors: flawed eyewitness identification procedures, false or misleading forensic evidence; exoneration: DNA)

On March 24, 1985, twenty-year-old college student Michele was parking her car on campus. Jerry Wayne Johnson approached her and requested assistance that she was not able to provide. He forced himself into her car, drove her to a remote location, and sexually assaulted her. He drove her back to the original parking lot and left. She immediately reported the crime to the police and cooperated with the investigation. After a flawed identification procedure, Timothy Cole was identified as the attacker. In 1986, Cole was wrongly convicted and died while incarcerated in 1999. In 1995, Johnson confessed to the crime, but he was ignored. Johnson persisted, and in 2008 Cole was posthumously exonerated when the DNA excluded him. Legal charges were filed against Johnson, who pled guilty.

Sean Malloy (crime against him: murder of his sister Noreen Malloy; contributing factors: flawed eyewitness-identification procedures, perjury or false accusation; exoneration: DNA)

Sean's sister, Noreen Malloy, twenty-two years old, was working the night shift and closing the fast-food restaurant where she worked on August 17, 1988. Someone approached her wearing a nylon mask and robbed her at gunpoint, pistol-whipped her, and shot her in the back as she tried to flee. The police were called to the scene, and Drew Whitley was arrested. After an investigation, Whitley was convicted in 1989. He continued to press for better forensic testing, and ultimately DNA on hairs from the nylon mask excluded Whitley, and he was released in 2006. This is now a cold case, and no suspects have been identified.

Millie Maxwell (pseudonym) (crime against her family: murder of her father and breaking and entering; contributing factors: false confession, perjury or false accusation, official misconduct; exoneration: DNA)

On September 18, 2000, Millie's father was killed when several intruders broke into his home in order to rob him. Because Millie prefers to conceal her identity, additional details of the crime are also concealed. The original conviction in this case occurred in 2001, with multiple defendants. In 2003 the actual perpetrators confessed, and the case was reinvestigated, but the actual perpetrators were never prosecuted. The DNA-based exonerations occurred in 2011 and in 2015.

Christy Sheppard and Peggy "Peppy" Sanders (crime against them: murder and rape of Peggy's daughter; contributing factors: false or misleading forensic evidence, perjury or false accusation, official misconduct; exoneration: DNA)

Peggy's daughter, Debra Sue Carter, was murdered by Glen Gore in her apartment in Ada, Oklahoma, in December 1982. Christy Sheppard is Peggy's niece and Debra's cousin; she was eight years old at the time Debbie was killed. This crime has been subject of much media exposure, including best-selling author John Grisham's 2006 book *The Innocent Man*. After a flawed investigation and prosecution, Ron Williamson and Dennis Fritz were wrongly convicted in 1988 of killing Debbie. Williamson was sentenced to death, Fritz to life in prison; they were exonerated in 1999. Gore is currently incarcerated in Oklahoma. In 2021, Christy Sheppard launched a podcast, *Defending the Lion*, wherein she shares her family's detailed and complex experiences with this situation. The podcast can be found on many platforms.

Yolanda Thomas (crime against her family: murder of her sister; contributing factors: false or misleading forensic evidence, perjury or false accusation, official misconduct; exoneration: DNA)

Yolanda's older sister, Jacquetta Thomas, was found murdered in September 1991. During the police investigation the state crime lab technician testified that blood was found on a vehicle owned by Greg Taylor that was stuck in the mud not far from where Jacquetta's body was found. The substance was not blood. Taylor was wrongly convicted in 1993 and exonerated in 2010 due to DNA testing. No one has been identified as the actual perpetrator. This is now a cold case.

Jennifer Thompson (crime against her: rape; contributing factors: flawed eyewitness-identification procedures; exoneration: DNA)

In July 1984, Jennifer Thompson was home in her apartment when Bobby Poole broke in and raped her at knife-point. She was able to escape the apartment, ran to a neighbor, and called the police. She cooperated with the investigation fully, and a rape kit was completed. Bobby Poole went on to rape another woman that same night; she also cooperated with the investigation. During a flawed identification procedure that was standard at the time, Ronald Cotton was identified as the intruder-rapist. He was wrongly convicted in 1985 and spent eleven years in prison before being exonerated in 1995. Their story has been widely shared and is available in much more depth in their book *Picking Cotton: Our Memoir of Injustice and Redemption.*

Wilhoit Family: Nancy Wilhoit Vollertsen, Ida Mae Wilhoit, Guy Wilhoit, Kim Griggs Wilhoit, Krissy Wilhoit Zarn (crime against their family: murder of Kathy Wilhoit; contributing factors: false or misleading forensic evidence, inadequate legal defense; exoneration: ineffective assistance of counsel)

Kathy Wilhoit had recently separated from her husband, Greg Wilhoit, and moved into an apartment with their two daughters, Krissy and Kim, who were aged fourteen and four months old. On June 1, 1985, Kathy was found murdered in her apartment, when a neighbor heard the children crying and contacted the authorities. Upon investigation, the authorities informed the Wilhoit family of Kathy's death, and the children were cared for by their father Greg with the support of the Wilhoit family. Later, Greg Wilhoit was charged with murdering Kathy. He was wrongly convicted and sentenced to death in 1987. The girls grew up in a foster family, without their biological parents. The extended Wilhoit family remained very involved in their lives. Greg was exonerated and released from prison in 1993 and participated in research by Westervelt and Cook (2012). Greg Wilhoit passed away in 2014. Kathy Wilhoit's daughters (Krissy and Kim), their grandparents (Guy and Ida Mae), and their aunt (Nancy) participated in the current research. The murder of Kathy Wilhoit remains an unsolved crime.

The exonerations generated an avalanche of recollections for these participants, especially of the painful details they had tried to compartmentalize. They began searching for answers to the questions that emerged during the exonerations about how this could have happened. Recalling the agony of their lives being shattered by violence, and their families struggling to manage the losses structure the experiences is the subject of this book. Framed within the context of scholarly research on primary and secondary trauma, this deep dive into the lived experiences documents the ordeals of violent crimes, the impacts on them and their families, and their frightening journeys through the courts. The findings are presented largely in chronological order. Chapter 2 explores the original victims' experiences with the violent crimes they and their families endured and their experiences with immediate responses by the police. And chapter 3 examines the original investigations and court trials. Chapter 4 explores the impact on them and their families. These retrospective accounts sometimes include details that became known during the postconviction processes but were obscured, hidden, or unknown during the original processes.

CHAPTER 2

Shattered Lives

In 1987, Andrea Harrison was soon to turn four years old.[1] She was a smart and observant child, who was doted on by her mother, Jacqueline Harrison, who was twenty-five years old. She was a confident child, with a strong family and a loving father, Dwayne Jones. She was comfortable in her larger extended family with her older sister, her grandmothers, and many other adults. One day in the late summer, her mother was going somewhere else while the rest of the family gathered for dinner. After dinner she was tucked into bed and fell asleep. When she woke up, something was different but she wasn't sure what; she saw her mother's face on the television screen but did not understand why. Her grandmother turned off the television quickly, and then the phone kept ringing. People were talking on the phone in strange ways, not the usual happy conversations Andrea was used to hearing. She kept staying with her grandmother and eventually learned that her mother had died. She was not sure what this meant. Her fourth birthday did not include her mother. Still, she wanted her mother to come home, which would never happen again.

Exonerations inevitably lead original victims to revisit the original crimes they and their families experienced, the investigations, and the original trials. The retrospective examination of these primary and secondary trauma is now filtered through the lens that something terrible went wrong in their cases. Miscarriages of justice inflicted more harm on them and on others who had no part in their victimization; and yet they were entangled in an adversarial legal process from opposing sides of the situation, meeting and merging in police stations and courts and connected in media coverage. This chapter presents detailed recollections of the crimes, their initial calls to the police, some early signs of tunnel vision, and their experiences with eyewitness identification procedures that were flawed.

The exonerations reopened their original wounds. They recalled how horrible the violence was for them to experience and recounted the loss, the grief, and the legal process that followed. Until the exonerations, many aspects of their experiences were typical of what we know based on empirical research; therefore, their recollections are woven together with research findings that situate these experiences in the broader scholarly discussions about homicide and sexual violence. Particular attention is given to research on homicide, sexual assault, and wrongful convictions. On the one hand, homicide is among the most likely crimes to be reported to the police and to result in an arrest and prosecution. On the other hand, sexual assault is among the least likely crimes to be reported to the police and least likely to result in arrest and prosecution (Johnson, 2021). Coding these data required exploration of these two categories of victims who participated: homicide victims' family members and rape / sexual assault survivors. This chapter presents aspects of the crime and reporting to the police, structured by the types of crimes (homicide and rape) within each section. It begins by exploring how murder victims' families recall their experiences and then turns to rape / sexual assault survivors recalling their experiences, while weaving research insights throughout the chapter. This chapter presents retrospective post-exoneration memories of pre-exoneration experiences; participants reflect on the excruciating agony they experienced reliving the original crime consequent to the exonerations.

These victims lost control of their bodily sovereignty, their lives, their cases, their families, and the outcomes of those prosecutions. A conceptual theme in criminological theory includes how the state steps in to investigate, arrest, prosecute, and punish after a crime has been reported. Christie (1977) argued that the state "steals" the situation away from people involved in the situation. The state claims a stake in prosecuting crimes and imposing formal punishment, irrespective of those who are directly impacted by the situation (Christie, 1977). The criminal case proceeds as "the state versus the accused," and therefore when the crime is impounded by the state, so too is the victim's body, family, and life, as evidence. Ordinarily, the crime victim serves as a witness (whenever possible) to assist the state in the prosecution of the accused but is not formally central to the prosecution of criminal charges. Some victims are glad to release the crime to the state for investigation and prosecution, while others fight against the state taking over their cases and may end up feeling ignored and irrelevant to the state. In this research, many of the participants articulated their experiences with this reality. Yolanda Thomas expressed this view: "What I learned about the justice system is: 'thank you for committing this crime against the state of North Carolina. It's not the family's issue, it is a state issue.' No, it's a family issue and if you're not including us on anything that's going on it's not just a state issue. But I took it for what it was and [the district attorney] said you can rest assured that we have the individuals in custody and we will get a conviction. Rest assured."

The adversarial legal system claims to offer support and resolution to victims of crime in its efforts to promote public safety. For victims in these cases, the system, even when the police and investigation treated them with respect and courtesy, ultimately let them down, leaving some feeling betrayed and others feeling inappropriately guilty of an injustice against an innocent person. Thus, institutional betrayal (Smith and Freyd, 2013, 2014) compounds the trauma of the original crime. Each of the participants in this research has been through harrowing ordeals of violent crimes: homicides of family members and rape / sexual assaults. While most of these crimes occurred about twenty to forty years ago, the pain remains vivid in the participants' memories. With each of these traumatic life events, the research participants' lives have been shattered in myriad ways—their coping skills put to the test, and their resiliency surfaced. It is important to note that in four of the homicide cases where women were killed, there are also elements of sexual assault present. For the surviving family members of those homicide victims, imagining the horror of their loved ones' deaths when it included sexual violence as well as lethal violence compounded their grief process.

Homicide "confronts families with the sudden and violent loss of their loved one, an experience most find isolating, disorienting, and debilitating" (Englebrecht et al., 2016, p. 356). Unlike families who lose loved ones due to noncriminal events (aging, illness, etc.), bereavement as a consequence of violent crime often results in "complicated mourning" (Rando, 1993), where the violent death is seen as preventable, which then generates the inevitable agony of retrospective guilt and regrets. The extent to which homicide victims attempted to fight off the lethal violence they faced, creates a lingering agony for their survivors. Murder victims' family members struggle returning to a normal life due to their bereavement; they may experience posttraumatic stress, complicated grief, social isolation, guilt, and despair for years after the loss of their family member (Englebrecht et al., 2016). "Violent death has been classified as an established risk factor for [complicated grief]" (Bottomley et al., 2017, p. 5). Homicides are "our most thoroughly investigated crimes," as approximately two-thirds of homicides result in an arrest (Braga and Dusseault, 2018, p. 284). According to Braga and Dusseault, the "suspect's identity is known or easily determined at the time the crime is reported to the police" (2018, p. 286). Usually, homicides are not committed by strangers: perpetrators tend to be someone the victim(s) knew in a social relationship (Miethe and Regoeczi, 2004). The crime victimizations experienced by the participants in this research are described in two groups: homicide victims' family members and rape / sexual assault survivors.

THE HOMICIDES

One homicide case included two victims, Morris and Ruth Gauger, whose son Gary Gauger was wrongly convicted of capital murder (Westervelt and Cook, 2012). Five of the eight homicide victims were murdered in their own homes, two murder victims' remains were found outdoors, and one victim was murdered at work during an armed robbery. Four of the eight homicides included evidence of sexual violence against women victims.

Most of the murder victims' family members recall exactly where they were when they learned that their loved one had been killed. It is burned into their memory as an explicitly painful moment. Generally, it happens in the course of just a normal day: at school, at work, overseas with the military. Ginger Blossom was forty-one when her parents, Morris and Ruth Gauger, were murdered on the family farm in northern Illinois. She received a message to call home, while working as a ski instructor in Taos, New Mexico:

> It was Friday afternoon and we didn't have cell phones, it was over twenty years ago. We had gotten a message from someone at the ski shop to call home. That's when I found out that my parents have been murdered. It was just totally surreal that first night. I think I went into shock. I remember being at the ski shop trying to make reservations to come back and suddenly I can't feel my feet when I walk. So, I think I was in shock but you still kind of function. I did get plane reservations and we got out the next morning. . . . [I was] in shock because the inconceivable had happened that my parents were murdered and then the other shocking thing is that [my twin brother] Gary was implicated.

Yolanda Thomas was in the army in Germany at the time she learned of her sister's death:

> So you get the call and you know somethings wrong because it's in the middle of the night in Germany. I hear my mom's friend on the phone and I immediately thought was it had to do something with my mom and she says they found [my sister]. . . . I was like, "what-what are you talking about they found her?" I said "found her where?" She says they found her body. I think, so was she in a car accident and they just couldn't find her. I wanted it to be [that] instead of it being drug related, I wanted it into be a bad car accident or anything, anything else. When I finally said "tell me what happened," and they finally said they found her body, she had been murdered. There's no words.

Indeed, words cannot adequately convey the continuing ordeal for a family of a murder victim. The Malloy family also received a phone call in the

middle of the night that Noreen Malloy had been killed in an armed robbery while she was at work. Sean Malloy, Noreen's brother, was about to
start his senior year of high school and instead was facing this devastating
loss in his family. The grief process continues for the remainder of the
family members' lives and often involves survivors reliving details of the homicide that are particularly grisly (Aldrich and Kallivayalil, 2016; Bottomley
et al., 2017).

Four participants in this research were children when their loved ones
were murdered and have fewer memories. Greg and Kathy Wilhoit had
recently separated, and Kathy had moved into an apartment with their
daughters. Kim Wilhoit and Krissy Wilhoit were four and fourteen months
old, respectively. Their grandmother, Ida Mae Wilhoit, recalled when their
mother, Kathy Wilhoit, was found murdered:

> The lady in another apartment close to Kathy called the police. They
> were going to go shopping, and the [neighbor] knocked and she didn't
> get any answer. But then she heard the babies crying and it was warm
> and the windows were open. That's how they could see them. The
> children were in there, that [neighbor] called the police and they found
> [Kathy] on the living room floor. . . . Greg jumped in his car and he
> came here, running in bare feet. "Where are my babies? Where are my
> babies?" And we had to tell him that they had taken them to the police
> where they take children like that. I mean he was really upset and then
> friends started coming.

Later, Greg Wilhoit was charged with Kathy's murder, wrongly convicted,
and sentenced to death in Oklahoma.

Christy Sheppard was eight years old when her cousin, Debra Sue Carter, was killed. In elementary school at that time, Christy remembers, "I
was supposed to have a dentist appointment that day and my mom was
going to pick me up. I remember walking out of the school and my [step-
dad] was there to pick me up. And I instantly remember like getting that
lump, getting that sick feeling, like where's my mama, you're not supposed
to be here. Then my mom came home and I remember she told me that
Debbie had been killed. I started crying and I must've been really kind of
hysterical or whatever because she said you need to settle down. That's
that." Some of the horrifying details of four homicides included in this
research are the sexual violations of the homicide victims as part of those
crimes. These include Kathy Wilhoit, Debra Sue Carter, Jacqueline Harrison, and Jacquetta Thomas. Kathy Wilhoit and Debra Carter were killed in
their own apartments, both having been sexually assaulted. The bodies of
Jacqueline Harrison and Jacquetta Thomas were both found outdoors and
showed signs of sexual assault. The details of these assaults are gruesome,

and their survivors who participated in this research express continuing rage at the salacious news coverage of their murders. Andrea Harrison and Dwayne Jones describe how Jacqueline Harrison was portrayed in the media as having been a "promiscuous party girl"; Yolanda Thomas describes how Jacquetta Thomas was portrayed as a "prostitute" who was involved with drug dealers. Both Black women were fodder for the cultural trope of the "jezebel" (Collins, 1990; Walley-Jean, 2009), which harmed their surviving family members immeasurably. These traumatic elements compound the harm for homicide victims' family members when they inevitably imagine those last moments of life and the suffering of their loved ones.

The Sexual Assaults

Bard and Sangrey explain that, for rape / sexual assault victims, "short of being killed, there is no greater insult to the self" (1986, p. 21). The damage inflicted during the attack impacts survivors for the rest of their lives (Macmillan, 2001), and the survivors are left to put the pieces of their bodies, their lives, and their families back together, if even possible. "The sudden, arbitrary, unpredictable violation of self leaves victims feeling so shattered that they cannot continue to function the way they did before the crime. Things fall apart, and victims are unable to pull themselves back together right away" (Bard and Sangrey, 1986, p. 33).

Sexual assaults are seldom reported to the police, are usually perpetrated by someone whom the victim knows rather than a stranger, and most often occur in the context of an ordinary social event (Lonsway and Archambault, 2012). Once reported to the police, most cases do not result in arrest, prosecution, or conviction. For all of the rape / sexual assault survivors who participated in this research, their cases made it through the "funnel of attrition" that accompanies crimes of sexual violence. Attrition occurs as follows: "Of 100 forcible rapes that are committed, approximately 5 to 20 will be reported, 0.4 to 5.4 will be prosecuted, and 0.2 to 5.2 will result in a conviction. Only 0.2 to 2.9 will yield a felony conviction. Then an estimated 0.2 to 2.8 will result in incarceration of the perpetrator, with 0.1 to 1.9 in prison and 0.1 to 0.9 in jail" (Lonsway and Archambault, 2012, p. 157). The decision to prosecute occurs after the assault is reported to the police, who agree that the attack merits additional investigation and may generate an arrest. The definition of forcible rape, "which, until 2012, was defined [by the Uniform Crime Reports] as 'carnal knowledge of a female, forcibly and against her will'" (Lonsway and Archambault, 2012, p. 149), shapes the early stages of potential attrition. Later stages of attrition occur at the discretion of system officials who evaluate the evidence, the relationship of victim to the alleged assailant, and the willingness and cooperation of the victim during the investigation. For a rape / sexual assault case to continue, despite this attrition, depends on the credibility of the victim and character-istics of the offender. To explore this, I turn to two concepts: ideal victims (Christie, 1986) and deserving victims (Richardson and May, 1999).

Christie (1986, p. 18) asks, "What characterizes—at the social level—the ideal victim?" He argues that such an ideal victim would be without blemish in her motives or reputation, without blame, respectable, and rela-tively weak.[2] The offender, in contrast, is "big and bad" and "has no per-sonal relationship to her" (p. 19). This ideal victim, then, has the strength to report the crime to the police and paradoxically is compliant with proce-dures that might satisfy "other important interests." In Christie's frame-work, "ideal victims need—and create—ideal offenders" (p. 25). Therefore, "the ideal offender differs from the victim. He is, morally speaking, black against the white victim. He is a dangerous man coming from far away. He is a human being close to not being one" (p. 26). This typology reinforces cultural narratives of good and evil, bolsters long-standing stereotypes of rapacious Black men (George and Martinez, 2002), and influences the inves-tigation and prosecution of such cases (Bazelon, 2018, p. 36).

When victims are seen as somehow, and at least in part, responsible for their own victimization, their status may shift from "ideal victims" to "deserving victims" (Richardson and May, 1999). Accordingly, "we under-stand and explain violence differently in relation to who the victim is" (Richardson and May, 1999, p. 309). Victims may be blamed for their own victimization if they are engaged in risky activities. "Women are more likely than are men to be blamed for making themselves vulnerable to vio-lence by being in the 'wrong' place at the 'wrong' time" (Richardson and May, 1999, p. 313). Situating these dualisms within the context of patriar-chy, feminist scholar Susan Caringella (2009) points out that when women's bodies are seen as the property of men, sexual assault becomes a "hostile sexual takeover" (p. 64). Thus, women are responsible for fending off a cul-tural backdrop that requires evidence that she fought her attacker, that she did not secretly desire the sexual contact, and that she was not "asking for it." When prosecuting such cases, the best evidence to prove "nonconsent" includes an attacker who is a stranger and used a weapon, a woman who was engaged in ordinary and respectable activity and fought back, and a victim who cooperates with the investigation, rendering her a "capable" victim (Johnson, 2021).

Racialized patterns of sexual violence factor into both reporting to the police and victim blaming (George and Martinez, 2002; Johnson, 2021; LaFree, 1982). The vast majority of rapes reported to the police are perpe-trated by intraracial acquaintances or family member. Black women are slightly more likely than white women to experience rape (Tjaden and Thoennes, 2000), though less likely to report the attack to the police (George and Martinez, 2002). Less than 23 percent of reported rapes are Black perpetrators with white victims (LaFree, 1982). White victims of interracial rapes are blamed more than victims of intraracial rapes (George and Martinez, 2002). Culturally, the racial stereotypes of the rapacious Black male have generated a "paranoia [about] racist exaggerations about black men" (LaFree, 1982, p. 312) that blame white women more than those victimized by white men (George and Martinez, 2002). Interracial sexual assault, then, serves to amplify victim blaming for white women, adding another layer of harm and demonstrating the intersecting impacts of systemic racism and sexism as coexisting social dynamics.

The rape / sexual assault participants in this research, in general, match the "ideal victim" typology: they were assaulted by strangers who broke into their homes/workplaces and/or attacked them with a weapon (a gun or a knife), which may explain why their cases continued despite the attrition. Some of the murdered women whose survivors are part of this research, on the other hand, were portrayed by authorities and in the media as having contributed to their own victimization by being engaged in disreputable activities. Johnson (2021) refers to these groups of rape / sexual assault victims as "capable" of providing assistance to the investigation and "incapacitated" by the violence such that they cannot provide assistance to the investigation. Rape and sexual assault victims frequently are blamed for their own victimization (Brownmiller, 1975; George and Martinez, 2002). Despite being "ideal victims," the participants in this research faced victim-blaming messages and legal tactics that resulted in their experiencing "secondary victimization" (Campbell et al., 1999). Of the eight rape / sexual assault cases documented in this research, seven involved cross-racial eyewitness identification, which is vulnerable to error (Cutler and Penrod, 1995).

All of the rape / sexual assault survivors in this research have clear recollection of the attack they survived and were "capable" of assisting police (Johnson, 2021). They were attacked by strangers, immediately called the police, and cooperated with the criminal investigation. The age range at the time of the assaults is from twelve to thirty-six years old. Their experiences present an opportunity to learn about their resilience in the moment and reflect on their capacity to think clearly in the midst of terrifying experiences. Their primary concern was to protect themselves and others from additional harm. Several participants described a relentless interior voice: coaching and guiding how to respond to the present threat, scanning their surroundings for anything to use as a tool, locating any resources available. To negotiate their survival, they begged for release, used logical argument that their loved ones would be looking for them, hoped for possible barriers to shield them, and used pillows to protect their naked bodies. Examples of their experiences include the assault of a child, assault in a public place, and assaults by intruders in their homes. First, consider the sexual assault of a child: Tomeshia Carrington-Artis was twelve years old and asleep when a man broke into her bedroom through a screened window. Tomeshia is African American, and her assailant is white. She recalls:

> It was just an ordinary day as a twelve-year-old child. That particular day my mom had switched my room around and, usually, she'll lock my window and she'll put a stick in the window but she forgot to that night. They were thinking that it was a peeping Tom. He thought he was going to my mom's room. About two or three o'clock in the morning I heard something at my window. So I jumped up and tried to run out, I did not scream, I just froze, I mean I just went silent. I jumped up and tried to run and he caught me when I got to the door. He grabbed me by my throat and pulled a knife on me and told me if I scream he would kill me. He talked to me like I was a grown woman, like I was his wife. He carried on conversations. Whatever he said I agreed. He kept telling me how beautiful I was. How I would thank him for turning me into a woman. For his birthday, he wanted a virgin and I was his birthday gift. [I was trying] not to be loud for my mom to come in and he stab her, and I had a little brother. [Q: And he had a knife to your throat?] Mhm. I was twelve, I was trying to not only save myself, but to save my mom and my little brother.

Second is an assault in a public place: Penny Beerntsen was a thirty-six-year-old white, married mother of two children who was attacked while jogging in a state park on a summer afternoon. The white man who assaulted her was literally a stranger who jumped out of the bushes, the classic "stranger danger" scenario:

> So when I was about half a mile from my starting point, there was a man standing with a leather jacket slung over his shoulder. And as I ran by he was maybe twenty feet away, he hollered something it's a great day. And I turned and glanced at him and said yes it's a great day for a run. Didn't think anything of it, continued running. And as I was jogging a man came out from behind a half fallen tree and had a leather jacket on and I recognized him as being the same man who had said it's a great day. And he started toward me and it's like oh my gosh I know what he wants. So I made the mistake heading out into the water, I thought I was going to swim away or run in the water. As I was running in the water I realize how much it was slowing me down so I headed back to the shoreline and he caught up with me. He grabbed me in a chokehold, put one arm over me and said, "We're going to go for a little walk in the sand dunes." . . . Once he pushed me up over the first sand

dune we were no longer visible to anyone on the beach. I remember digging my heels in the sand and he was actually physically pushing me. He was pushing me towards the wooded area, he loosened his grip with his left hand and tried to undo the top of my swimsuit. And when I felt him trying to loosen his grip I tried to get away and he tightened his grip and said "do what I tell you I have a knife." He got me into the wooded area, turned me so we were face-to-face and he unzipped his pants and exposed himself and started asking me to do sexual things and I was refusing. And I was talking to him about my kids. I said, "Please I have got two young kids, I've got to raise my kids, my husband's going to be looking for me—I have been gone too long, just let me go, I won't tell anybody." . . . But the more I talked the more angry he became.

The third type of assault is home / personal property or workplace break-ins. Six of the participants in this research who survived sexual assaults were between nineteen and twenty-two years old at the time of the assault; all of them are white women raped by Black men. The crimes involved home or workplace breaking and entering with sexual assault. These women were determined to observe the physical characteristics of the men who attacked them so that, if they survived, they would be able to report those details to the police. Like for Jennifer Thompson, the terror inevitably left these women fearing for their lives: "At 3 a.m. on July 29th, an intruder broke into my apartment, put a knife to my throat and raped me. As I struggled to understand what was happening to me, the reality was that this could be the last day of my life, that this man would be the last person my eyes would see and that violence would be the last touch my body would feel. Would the death be quick? Would it be slow?" (Thompson, 2012, p. 1531). During the research interview, she recalls her determination to remember key details of his appearance:

For me being afraid for my life heightened my brain's capacity to figure out a plan. My family always said that I was stubborn and bullheaded and I think that that actual trait of mine kicked in in overdrive that night. Part of me, that stubborn willful person that I am, was a part of me that kicked in and said "I won't die. I'm not going to die like this." I remember thinking alright he's been drinking. I could smell it. Maybe he's off balance, maybe he's using drugs, of course that can heighten his crazy psychopathic nature but it also might give me the upper hand to be more intelligent and being able to maybe outsmart him to talk about of something which was exactly what I ended up. So I think knowing that there was a relatively good chance I was going to die made me want to fight mentally. My brain totally flipped. It flipped two ways.

One is I'm not down on my back and two, I'm going to know what you look like. So as opposed to shutting down, I actually became very fierce.

Karen M. was also living in an off-campus apartment while attending college. She had been out with her boyfriend and returned home by herself.

I came back and I went to bed. I had a little fluffy, cute shaggy dog and he was my life. I went to bed, and then I heard this thunk, and I didn't know what it was. I stood up, I walked around my bedroom to this little short hallway and I could see into my living room. I saw a figure in my living room. I backed up into my bathroom, he came in. I grabbed my curling iron and he wrapped the cord and I knew my curling iron wasn't going to do it. He grabbed my neck and pushed me back to my bathroom onto the floor and he suffocated me and held a knife to my throat. You know it's funny I don't even have to think. I remember it so vividly and I remember thinking I can't breathe I can't breathe because he was suffocating me. He had the knife to my throat and he's cussing me. He pulls my hair and he pulled me back into my bed and then he took my clothes off. He hit me. He stuffed his penis in my mouth. I remember thinking can I build up can I do it can I bite his penis off can I bite him? I think he knew that and he said, "Don't you think it you fucking bitch," I knew he read my mind. And he raped me. I remember hearing my dog. I was so scared [my dog] would be killed. I didn't even care so much about me. I wanted my dog to live. After, I remember grabbing my pillows trying to cover my body. I was naked and he grabbed the pillows and threw it and he said, "Do you have guns?" and "When is your old man coming back?" So I just played along and I said, "Soon, you need to go, you need to leave." And I was just trying to think how am I going to live I don't want him to kill me. Then he asked me what he could steal. I don't have anything for him is steal. I didn't have a gun. I didn't have anything. I was a college student. I remember he dragged me into my living room—and this is not a big apartment—and I remember him going through my purse—he dumped my purse out. I remember thinking, God what can I do, what can I do, and then I hear my dog going crazy. . . . I remember [him] saying, "Come let me out, come open the front door for me." I remember being so humiliated that I had opened the door and let him out my door, my front door. And he said, "If you call anyone I will kill you. I will find you, I will come back and I will kill you." And I remember that anger, the humiliation of having to open my front door from the inside—that it was locked—for [him] to just walk out and turn around and threaten my life. And that was that.

Similar to Karen's concern for her beloved dog, concern for other potential victims factored into their survival strategies during the attacks. Janet Burke's experience illuminates a workplace assault as well as her determination to protect the children in the day care center:

> Working at a child care program, there was no one else there and I walked into my office and actually had a [message] that [my director] had a child care emergency of her own and she wasn't going to be able to be there at six thirty that morning. I was starting to kind of prepare things, when I heard a noise. I wasn't quite sure what I had heard. I looked towards the door and that's when I noticed there was someone coming towards me. He had a knife. He held it to my throat and pushed me into the child care classrooms at knife point. The only thing I really could think about in that moment was the children would be arriving and just petrified what they would find. I didn't want the children to see anything. I pleaded with him to leave because the parents would be arriving. Finally he stood up, and the doorbell rang. It was a mother and her child were the first to arrive, had seen the glass breakage and was not coming into the building.

Debbie Jones, Michele Mallin, and Regina Lane also shared harrowing experiences of being assaulted by a man with a weapon, either abducted or held captive for the purposes of sexual assault, and fighting hard to survive. Immediately upon escaping the attackers, these women reported to the police and the investigations ensued.

Reporting the Crimes

Immediately after each of these crimes occurred, the victims and their family members depended on the police to investigate their cases. They expected that officers would treat them with dignity and provide appropriate guidance on how to assist in the investigation to ensure that the perpetrator would be prosecuted. For some those expectations were satisfied, and for others they were not. None of these participants anticipated a wrongful conviction could happen in their cases. Homicide victims' survivors are explored first, then rape / sexual assault survivors.

The homicide investigations included legal system failures. When Noreen Malloy was murdered, her family anticipated an investigation would identify the perpetrator. Instead, Sean Malloy recalls that the investigation conducted at the time was cursory and inadequate, the file itself was thin, and very little evidence was collected. For Yolanda Thomas, the original investigation of her sister's murder resulted in an arrest that did not make sense to her; the fact that her sister was murdered was devastating, and the arrest of someone on what she thought was questionable evidence left her with continuing doubts about the accuracy of that conviction.

For Peggy Sanders and Christy Sheppard, the original investigation into the rape and murder of Debra Sue Carter was flawed from the start. Homicide victims' survivors describe physical evidence that was contaminated. Peggy Sanders recalls that the crime scene was contaminated: "Well, this is the first that time this had happened in Ada [Oklahoma] and they didn't know how to do it. They went up to her apartment, they got a fingerprint that was one of the detectives and dismissed it because it was his. And a bunch of people just come in and they couldn't get fingerprints or anything like that off of anything because everybody was there. The whole town come running up through her apartment, everybody but me and they wouldn't even let me go near it." For the Wilhoit family and Ginger Blossom, whose relatives' murder resulted in the wrongful arrest, prosecution, capital conviction, and death sentence of another family member, the original investigation was inadequate to inspire confidence that the truth would emerge. Nancy Wilhoit Vollertsen recalls that their family received very little information from the police prior to the arrest of her brother, Greg. When asked if they had regular updates from the police, Nancy said, "I'll be really honest with you. What we found out was only if mom and dad called . . . they basically didn't give us any information at all. They just kept saying that they were looking into it and they were following some leads. Then ten months later Greg walked out his front door and the police arrested him in his front yard."

Ginger Blossom felt the police turn against her as soon as her twin brother, Gary Gauger, was arrested for the murder of their parents: "They weren't interested in talking to me because I wasn't on their side. They had no interest in me." Ginger suggested other people who might be worth investigating and asked the police to consider these other possible theories. But they turned her away. "But again they weren't interested in getting to the truth they were just interested in getting a conviction." Ultimately, Ginger reached out to a family friend. "He's a local attorney, and was long-time friend of my parents, motorcycle rider, great guy. He could guide us through what was going on, but he was also neutral. So that was good."

As an example of retrospective understanding, many participants' experiences reveal a sense of institutional betrayal (Smith and Freyd, 2014), and they recall how the state "stole" their trauma (Christie, 1977), overlooked their needs, and failed to communicate developments in their cases. Their experiences were divergent based on the type of victimization they endured: homicide victims' family members and rape / sexual assault survivors' experiences had different contours. There were also similarities, particularly related to flaws in the investigation process, lack of information from investigators, and what they later perceived to be investigators' tunnel vision. Rape / sexual assault survivors described their experiences during investigations, such as receiving support, the forensic rape examinations ("rape kits"), lineup procedures, crime scene investigations, often-inadequate contact from the police in homicide investigations that stretched for years before prosecution, and investigative tunnel vision.

Immediate help-seeking behavior by rape / sexual assault survivors included pleading with strangers and contacting family members to help them. With no phone, and being in a remote area, Regina Lane had few options available to her when seeking assistance. She broke free of Willard Brown, after being abducted and assaulted by him, and she ran to the nearest place she could find:

> When I ran to the house and that awesome gentleman let me in. I was afraid even at the door because here I was a broken bleeding person, naked, beating on this person's door and I didn't know who was going to answer. I didn't know if it was a good person or another bad person. I didn't know where the person was that had been attacking me and it was very scary and I [was] knocking on the door beating on the door and begging for someone to open that door because someone was trying to kill me. I just didn't know whether the door will be opened or not.

The door was opened and a kind man took her in, wrapped her in a blanket, and called the police.

After the assailant left the day care center where Janet Burke worked she called her parents, who immediately took her to the hospital and called the police. She recalls, "And my parents actually came and picked me up and took me to hospital which was another whole ordeal." This ordeal involved an emotional slurry of reactions between Janet and her father reacting to the horrifying attack. Janet and her parents were all very upset by the attack, and their emotions were on edge:

> The world just turned upside down and as we were driving to [the hospital]. I was crying hysterically. My father turned around from the front seat and said, "Just stop crying, just stop crying." It impacted me so much because I thought it was so harsh in the moment but he had no earthly idea how to deal with any of it. He didn't know what to do. He didn't know what to say. That impacted me because it was like what do you mean stop crying? I don't know if that's even possible for me to stop crying. It was just an awful moment and that must've been for him.

The traumatic impacts of reporting a rape are clearly documented (Caringella, 2009; Martin and Powell, 1994). Campbell and Raja (1999, p. 267) report that 89 percent of mental health professionals see the rape exam itself is traumatic for rape victims and that 58 percent agree that their professional colleagues "engage in harmful counseling practices . . . [and] 80% of the sample agreed that contact with community professionals can leave rape victims feeling guilty, reluctant to seek further help, bad about themselves, distrustful of others, and depressed." Campbell and Raja define secondary victimization as "a prolonged and compounded consequence of certain crimes; it results from negative, judgmental attitudes (and behaviors) directed towards the victim, [which results] in a lack of support, perhaps even condemnation and/or alienation of the victim" (p. 262). This secondary trauma varies among rape victims: white women tend to fare better than women of color who are victims of sexual assault. The perceived impact of services on women of color is more damaging than for white women victims. Campbell and Raja point out that mental health professionals who serve predominantly white women earn higher incomes and are "more likely to report that contact with social systems can have a positive effect on rape survivors" (p. 270).

DISCUSSION

The recollections of the original crimes and the early investigations reveal that signs of wrongful convictions were present from the beginning of each case. These original victims are now more aware that reporting to the police does not ensure an accurate outcome for their case. As traumatic events, these cases also demonstrate that even though the original violence is over, the trauma continues. It ebbs, flows, and overlaps with later stressful conditions that often trigger trauma responses to resurface. The primary trauma of the original crime creates damage that, in itself, lasts a lifetime. The secondary trauma of reporting to police creates damage that lingers for many years. Evidence of secondary trauma is present when the state takes over the case, and the original victims have little control of how the state proceeds with the case. Secondary trauma also ripples through the families of those whose experiences are reported here.

CHAPTER 3

Shattered Investigations and Trials

AFTER ESCAPING HER ATTACKER, Debbie Jones was determined to aid the police in their effort to apprehend and arrest him. In the hospital for the rape kit examination, she cooperated with the process and, despite being so traumatized by the attack, was resolved to help them collect and preserve evidence. There was physical evidence, including biological samples. She answered their questions; she provided a description of the man who assaulted her: she is white and he was Black. She participated in the procedures they used for eyewitness identification; she was confident that she identified the right man. The police arrested a man, and she attended the hearings and answered all the questions asked of her. At one of the early hearings, the man who was arrested was so angry that he threatened to kill Debbie; this confirmed for her that he was the same dangerous man who broke into her apartment and raped her. She wanted justice to be done so no one else would be hurt by this man. After he was convicted, she tried to move on with her life and put the attack behind her.

None of the participants in this research expected or anticipated that their lives would be consumed by the impacts of violent crimes, investigations, and trials that demanded so much of them. Nor did they anticipate an exoneration process that some welcomed and others deeply feared. They very much wanted their lives to be ordinary, not marred by violence. In the wake of the violent crimes, they turned to the police and the legal system to help achieve redress, by pursuing the person who harmed them and their loved ones and by securing the promise of accountability from the perpetrator. Secondary victimization (Campbell et al., 2001; Campbell and Raja, 1999; Martin and Powell, 1994) occurs irrespective of how they were treated by legal system officials; the investigation and trial processes added to their agony by placing expectations and demands on them with often inadequate support or information about the process. This chapter examines two aspects of their experiences: during investigations and leading up to trials and during the original trials that produced the wrongful convictions. Woven through all of these experiences are secondary traumas associated with ongoing investigations and trials. The secondary traumas include being ignored by officials during forensic rape examinations, being caught in the middle of police jurisdictions with differing information about the suspect, acknowledging the weakness of the prosecution's case, and experiencing traumas associated with how their broader communities responded to their ordeals. Each section of the chapter presents the voices from the homicide victims' survivors first and then the sexual assault / rape survivors.

When police receive a report that a crime has been committed, they arrive at the scene, interview the people who are present (as much as possible), and make decisions about how to proceed with the investigation. One of the main goals of the investigation is to identify and arrest the perpetrator of the crime and then prepare for prosecution. Collecting and testing forensic evidence, other physical evidence, victim statements, and witness statements are part of this preparation process. For the purposes of this examination, I organize these factors into two areas: preparing to prosecute and going to trial. The preparations include physical and forensic evidence gathering (rape kits, homicide evidence collection), witness identification procedures, and tunnel vision emerging. The trials that produced wrongful conviction include contaminated evidence and flawed procedures. Furthermore, because these violent crimes also became public events, the communities' responses also harmed these victims. The chapter reports on how crime victims and survivors describe their experiences with the investigation and trials. This is not a guide for how investigations are typically conducted, nor is it a retrospective critique of these particular investigations.

PREPARING TO PROSECUTE

Preparations for prosecutions are complex and painful to the victim; they often report feeling confused and unsure of the purpose of each question or procedure. Despite this emotional distress, victims "were satisfied with their encounter *if they were confident in the police*" (Posick and Policastro, 2013, p. 9, emphasis added). When police receive a report that someone has been murdered or raped, they enter situations that are often chaotic, frantic, and confusing. Therein, police officers are expected to provide answers, solutions, and information to those who have been harmed. Victims expect information directly from the legal authorities handling their case: police, investigators, and/or prosecutors. They want to aid in the investigation to the extent that they can and be kept apprised of new developments as they occur, and the case can unfold slowly or quickly. These victims found themselves at the mercy of legal system officials.

Peggy Sanders and Christy Sheppard learned of developments through local news media because the police did not maintain regular contact with them. The police did not arrest anyone until five years after the murder of Debra Sue Carter. During this excruciatingly slow process, the investigators pursued a theory that two perpetrators were involved in the crime, and to prove it required additional testing of Debbie's body, namely her palm print. To obtain a print of her palm, they exhumed her body and took it to the crime lab for testing. Peggy shared her experiences:

> [The district attorney] brings me these papers. He said "sign them" and I said "well what is it?" And he says "we need to exhume Debbie." And I said "nope you're not going to do that!" He said "Why?" And I said "cause have you ever read what's on her tomb what it said, she's sleeping in peace and you're not going to do that." He said "well do you want this case solved or not?" I said well yeah and he said "well you need to sign it." And I said tell me what's going on and he said "well there was a handprint and we need to find out if it's Debbie's. If it's not the [two suspects'] and if it's not Debbie's, there's somebody else involved." But I said "I will sign it on one condition: I get to go with you when you take her to the city." He said "no you can't do that." And I said why, and he said "well you just can't." Nobody ever gets another chance, but I'm going to get one more chance to see her and just to kiss her and love her and touch her hand and pat her one more time. And they said no I couldn't go. Well I signed it anyway because I did want them to find out if that belonged to Debbie. . . . Then I went to work one morning at eight o'clock and a coworker asked "Peggy, what are they doing out there digging up Debbie's grave?" I run out there to [her grave], but she's already gone. Nobody knows this but I just sat there in that grave and kicked the inside of it. I just sat there. I was so mad because she's gone and they didn't tell me. Just like everything else and I sat there and think they don't tell me anything and I'm the mother! You're supposed to tell me everything going on but they don't. They don't tell me and down in empty grave is bugs and spiders. That's pitiful. So, I get up and I sat there in my car and I just cry. I don't know what else to do, you know?

This excruciating event demonstrates how the state takes over the case and offers little information to the victims, who look to legal system officials for answers. Peggy signed her permission for the exhumation under extreme duress and with the misguided belief that she would be able to see her deceased daughter's body. When that did not occur, her mental health was shattered and the grief of her loss was compounded by the unfortunate (and as it turned out unnecessary) secondary trauma of the exhumation of her daughter's body.

All of the homicide victims' survivors hoped for support, comprehensive and accurate evidence, and compassion while awaiting trial. In six

investigations, crime victims' survivors learned that officials willfully mis-
interpreted evidence that would have revealed important information in
their cases. When Millie Maxwell's father was killed during a home invasion, collecting physical evidence included going beyond the home where
her father was murdered. The search for evidence in other locations (in the
woods nearby, at the corner store, etc.) missed items that were not located
by the police or were tampered with (perhaps by the police). For example,
when the assailants broke into the home they wore bandanas, which the
police were unable to find. Millie says, "It was the mail lady who found the
bandanas up the road, I guess where they had threw them off the next day."
Security footage from the local corner store could have provided information regarding the perpetrators, but instead during the critical time frame
for investigating her father's murder, the security footage had been recorded
over with a television program. She believes the investigators tampered
with the video tape: "I think it was them because by it being at a convenience store which records the property area all day long, roughly twenty-
four hours a day I'm not understanding why, at that particular moment,
why that piece of information was recorded over. That might have been
your piece of information that shows that it was already this [other] group
that you're now coming back with. I think it was recorded over to hide
some piece of information."

Ginger Blossom, whose twin brother was accused of killing their parents, attempted to provide information regarding her parents' murders:

> I remember making a list of possible suspects and all that, people that
> my parents may have had problems with. I remember there was one guy
> in biker colors, I don't know what motorcycle gang he was but it was
> the summer before my parents were killed and my mom said look at this
> guy and remember his face. He's going around like he is casing the
> place. The police didn't want any details. They didn't want to know
> who it was. [Q: So you gave them a potential lead and they ignored it?]
> Yes, a bunch of potential leads.

Ginger also discussed finding in the barn clothes that were used by police
to indicate that her brother had "discarded his bloody clothes" after they
claimed he committed the crimes. She explained to the police,

> We found bloodied clothes out in the chicken coop. My dad would
> wear clothes until they were like shredded sleeves and stuff so my mom
> would take them and hide them and when he didn't notice that they
> were gone, she would get rid of them. Well they were out in the unused
> chicken house. It was my mom trying to get rid of my dad's really rag-
> gedy old clothes but she had to see if he noticed that they were gone or

not. I told the police this! They didn't want to hear it. [Q: So, your concerns were ignored?] Yes. But again they weren't interested in getting to the truth they were just interested in getting a conviction.

The Wilhoit family was not informed about developments in the murder case, so when Greg was arrested and charged with capital murder, it shocked the family. This arrest completely changed the Wilhoit family's relationship to the courts—they went from being murder victims' family members to suspected murderer's family. Nancy Wilhoit Vollertsen recalled, "Whoever killed Kathy pulled the telephone out of the socket, out of the wall, there was a bloodied thumbprint on the phone that was never identified. It wasn't Greg's and it wasn't Kathy's. They never identified [whose it was]." Secondary trauma emerges when officials overlook and/or contaminate evidence or information, when they fail to understand a victim/survivor's position, when information about the investigation is withheld, or when the victims are treated as adversaries of the investigation into their own family members' deaths.

How secondary trauma spans the entire justice-seeking process is less well documented for homicide victims' family members than for most rape victims (Campbell et al., 2001). "When rape victims' needs are not addressed by the very organizations they turn to for assistance, the effects can be quite devastating" (Campbell et al., 2001, p. 1240). In measuring help-seeking experiences with rape / sexual assault survivors, Campbell et al. (2001) found that survivors sought assistance from community agencies, police, medical care providers, faith communities, mental health agencies, and rape crisis centers. Survivors of rape / sexual assault by strangers compared to survivors of acquaintance rape were more likely to seek help from the justice system. After the typical attrition of cases following a report to the police, 75 percent of cases resulted in no prosecution, and cases with white women victims were more frequently prosecuted than those of women of color. In the end, they report that "contact with the legal system was experienced as hurtful for at least half of the survivors in this study (52%)" (p. 1250). The contours of secondary trauma in the sexual assault / rape cases are different, with victims more personally involved throughout the process. Initially, these victims were grateful for the compassionate care they received from the authorities during the investigations. All of the victims endured the forensic rape examination and later participated in eyewitness identification procedures conducted by the investigators. Secondary trauma includes recognizing that tunnel vision, which is intertwined with eyewitness-identification procedures, developed early in the case. Every rape / sexual assault survivor participating in this research described the rape kit examination as invasive, painful, and traumatic. Jennifer Thompson experienced her body becoming a crime scene and offered this recollection:

> That's where all the evidence was. While it is necessary and has to be done, it's still violating, particularly considering the doctor who was administrating the first one was such a jerk. So it was traumatizing, it's disgusting. I mean he kind of sloppily did it and it was done in a very just noncompassionate way. There was no regard to what I just endured. There was no sympathy. You felt like you were the fetal pig or the frog that has to be dissected. It was just part of his job, I was just another victim. I'm twenty-two years old and I had never heard of things like rape kits. There's nobody there explaining it to you, nobody holding your hand saying here's the process we're going to go through.

Tomeshia Carrington-Artis, who was twelve years old, recalled the rape kit experience as matter-of-fact as she coped with the immediate shock of her victimization:

> The police came and when they sent the police they sent two male cops [who said] "she needed a female cop." And they went straight to the hospital through the back and it was just doctors and nurses, injecting me with this and giving me this to take, doing a rape kit and all that. And when we finally left the hospital and got home they had the crime scene tape up by the apartment and they wouldn't let us go back in the bedroom. It was I guess they had a specialist in there to do the sheets and get the sheets and vacuum the floor, the mattress. They took my clothes at the hospital. And the chair that he climbed through the window was still left at the window.

Ultimately, not able to return to her home, similar to several of the rape / sexual assault victims, Tomeshia went to live with other relatives during this upheaval in her home and family. For victims who were assaulted in their homes or their workplaces, returning to those locations was not feasible. They needed distance and time away from those places in order to deal with their injuries and trauma.

EYEWITNESS PROCEDURES

All of the investigations for the rape / sexual assault survivors involved an eyewitness-identification process. For some, this process included helping to create a composite sketch that led to a photo array lineup and ultimately an in-person lineup. Debbie Jones expresses the views of all of the rape victims in this research when she says, "I wanted to be sure. I didn't want the wrong person to go to jail and I never questioned it was the wrong person because I *knew* that was him." During the witness identification process, at the time, they were certain it was accurate and not contaminated. None of these rape victims/survivors intentionally misidentified the men who were wrongly convicted. Referring to this as "mistaken eyewitness identification" implies that the fault resides with the witness rather than with the flawed process for identification. This later generates a misplaced sense of guilt and shame on the witnesses who did their best to aid in the investigation. Eyewitness-identification procedures are intertwined with tunnel vision, which these participants reflect on retrospectively throughout their experiences.

Eyewitness identification is a contributing factor in 28 percent (792/2,812) of known exonerations overall, 67 percent (229/343) of known exonerations in sexual assault cases, and 26 percent (300/1,134) of known homicide cases, as documented by the National Registry of Exonerations.[1] Norris et al. (2018, pp. 23–53) summarize estimator and system variables associated with eyewitness identification. Estimator variables are factors beyond the control of the legal system (circumstances of the original crime, racial identities of the people involved in the event, and presence of a weapon). System variables are factors that are within the control of the criminal justice system (lineup procedures, behavior of officers, and discretion applied during the investigation). In the crimes represented here, the estimator variables in the sexual assault cases included mostly cross-racial identification and the weapon-focus effect. "Witnesses may be more likely to make an error when the culprit is someone of a different race than them" (Norris et al., 2018, p. 27). The weapon-focus effect, according to Norris et al. (2018, p. 26), "suggests that in crimes involving weapons, witnesses may have difficulty remembering characteristics of the perpetrator because their focus is on the weapon" in an effort to survive. System variables that impact the original crimes represented in this research include the nature of the lineup processes, the collection of evidence, and the discretion of the investigators. While the victims cooperated with and were involved in helping the police investigate the crimes, they were not in critical decision-making roles.

These victims did not decide how to conduct the lineups or whom the fillers would be, nor did they determine whom the police would identify as their prime suspects. Clark (2011) argues that eyewitness-identification *procedures*, not the witnesses themselves, generate error. A significant source of error is the system, not "mistakes" made by the original victims or witnesses. As such, "False identification incorrectly confirms the suspicions of the police. A false identification is an important first step toward a false conviction" (p. 1113). Jennifer Thompson recalls being praised by the police after identifying Ronald Cotton in the lineup: "Good Job Jennifer, that's who we thought it was!" (Thompson, 2012, p. 1531). Zalman suggests that system pressures to arrest a suspect drives the investigation toward this conclusion, where the victim's identification of the accused attacker is the "most important factor in solving cases" (2014, p. 154). Two facts are worth considering. First, unless the actual perpetrator is included in the lineup, there is no way for the victim to make a correct identification. Flawed procedures include inadvertently cueing the witness to identify the suspect who best matches investigators' hunches. Second, victims depend on the system to get it right, have faith in the system when an arrest is made, and yet take sole responsibility when the erroneous identification is revealed. Therefore, the error belongs to the system, not to the witness, and certainly not to the original victim who cooperates with the investigation. Popular vernacular that "mistaken witness identification" means only that the *witness/victim* got it wrong obfuscates the procedural flaws and unnecessarily burdens these participants with a crushing sense of sole responsibility for the wrongful convictions the system generated, exacerbating their trauma. Thompson (2012, p. 1532) reveals what this sole responsibility feels like "I had let down everyone—the police department, the district attorney's office, the community, the other women who became victims of Bobby Poole (the man identified by DNA as my actual rapist), but especially Ronald Cotton and his family."

The identification process of Ronald Cotton is well documented in Jennifer's book (Thompson-Cannino et al., 2009) and in a highly regarded PBS *Frontline* documentary, "What Jennifer Saw."[2] She was trying to do everything right: she talked to her assailant throughout the attack, kept trying to turn the lights on so she could see him more clearly, and studied his face to recall his features; ultimately, when a moment to escape occurred, she fled. Jennifer called the police immediately and provided an urgent description of her attacker. The sketch that resulted from her description looked like her attacker, so she was satisfied. She looked through the photos that the police provided her and saw a photo that also looked like the sketch and thus her attacker. During the lineup, she studied the features of all the men present; she was determined to get it right. This flawed procedure buttressed confidence in the identification and fueled the prosecution forward (Johnson, 2021).

Janet Burke was also determined to get her identification right: "I don't know why I picked [the exoneree] out of that lineup. I mean I would have sworn all my life that was who had done it. When I saw him in court I still knew it was him. I *knew* it was him." Memory can be contaminated during the standard procedures used by police during investigations (Clark, 2011). Seeing it as a consequence of what victims may have done "wrong" inflicts additional trauma on victims.

Investigations continued for months and years, and while most experienced victim-blaming responses from within or outside of the system, they were determined to continue cooperating. Blaming victims occurs when they are believed to have contributed to their own victimization and is a common element of secondary trauma that is particularly gendered. Women are more likely to be blamed for the gendered violence they experience, and the blame itself reveals sexist social conditions (Caringella, 2009). In this research victim blaming is entangled with the eyewitness-identification procedures experienced by the rape / sexual assault survivors, who all participated in the witness identification process. They assisted the police by working on photo and in-person lineups. They provided retrospective understanding of the process that was used decades earlier, which has now been criticized as contaminating the memory of the witness. Like other rape / sexual assault victims, Penny Beerntsen endured the process of providing a description, developing a sketch, and looking through a photo array and then a physical lineup:

> [The investigator] had just gone to training on doing composites, but I was the first victim that he had interviewed and then subsequently generated a sketch. It wasn't done with any overlays it was done with my description, what was the shape of the head and then he would draw it and show it to me and I would make corrections. So he completes the sketch, and there was one feature that it seemed that he couldn't translate my words into. It wasn't quite right on the sketch and I don't know if that was the nose. But I felt like it was a close enough approximation. So immediately after the sketch was completed I said to the sheriff, "Do you have a suspect in mind?," and he said yes and he then put down nine photos in three rows of three on my bedside table. So it was a simultaneous photo array and obviously the photos were pulled before the composite had been done. I looked carefully at each one and I selected Steven Avery's photo. The next morning I received confirmation that the person's photo who I had selected was the suspect they had in mind and that he had been arrested.

Other rape / sexual assault survivors who provided witness evidence through lineup procedures reflected on the flaws they now see in the process. Michele Mallin was parking her car while a student at Texas Tech University when she was approached by a man who requested her assistance. He abducted and raped her, and later returned her to the parking lot near her dormitory. She called the police and participated in the eyewitness-identification procedures commonly used at the time. Her recollection now includes an understanding of the science of memory and cross-racial identification process:

> Of course we went through all the investigation. They showed me the paper lineup with the six people. That's when I first saw [the exoneree],

and his picture was a Polaroid picture. I didn't know this back then I didn't even notice it, but I found out in 2008 that that's what it was. They were trying to lead me to pick out that picture I guess. But all the other pictures were black-and-white mugshots where in background was the measurement thing. They were altogether guys faced to the right or the left whichever way they were facing, but his picture was a Polaroid color picture facing forward and he was smiling. It was my friend who is our chief of police, told me that they are not allowed to do that, [because] it's like leading the witness to pick that person. He said if you had a victim that says the rapist has a gold tooth they all have to have gold teeth. You can't just put one person in there with a gold tooth. And then the next day they had me come up to the police station and do a lineup or whatever and that's when I picked [him] again right away. And then I guess it was about a year and half later then they had the trial and he was convicted and sentenced to twenty-five years in prison.

As an example of cross-racial eyewitness identification, fueled by tunnel vision toward one suspect, Michele Mallin shows that she cooperated to make sure her identification was accurate, but she was not responsible for that tunnel vision.

Tunnel Vision

In reflecting on their original victimization and investigations, several victims identified early signs of tunnel vision contributing to wrongful convictions. Tunnel vision encroaches when investigators have identified a suspect; the investigation then becomes focused on obtaining evidence of that suspect's guilt. Tunnel vision within the criminal justice system "leads investigators, prosecutors, judges, and defense lawyers alike to focus on a particular conclusion and then filter all evidence in a case through the lens provided by that conclusion" (Findley, 2012, p. 304). This elevates information that supports the conclusion to being highly significant and diminishes contrary information as being insignificant to the case, according to Findley. When Ginger Blossom recalled that her attempts to inform police of alternative suspects in the murder of her parents were ignored, she saw this as an example of tunnel vision. Millie Maxwell, whose father was killed during a home invasion, whose investigation resulted in flawed forensics and tainted evidence, said, "They swept it under the rug because we no longer need that [information] because we're already going to make them think with our tunnel vision that this is what happened."

Penny Beerntsen experienced the early onset tunnel vision. When she was assaulted, Penny saw her attacker wearing a leather jacket and made a concerted effort to remember as many details about the jacket as she could to aid the police: "So a couple of days before trial miraculously two deputies remember seeing [the wrongly accused man] wear a leather jacket that [they said] matched the description I gave." Another lineup procedure was organized for the leather jacket. Penny was not able to identify the jacket that investigators had in mind. She wonders, "So my question is at what point was this tunnel vision? At what point was it another missed opportunity?"

An example of how powerful tunnel vision can be comes from Regina Lane, the subsequent rape victim of a "wrongful liberty" and wrongful conviction case. On the morning of February 2, 1985, Regina Lane was abducted by Willard Brown on her way to work in Winston-Salem, North Carolina. He took her to a remote area in the woods and assaulted her, and she was ultimately able to flee to safety. It was eerily similar to the manner in which Deborah Sykes was abducted, raped, and murdered on August 10, 1984. When the police responded to the call that Regina Lane had been attacked, after she had undergone the forensic rape examination and provided a description of the man who attacked her, she pointed out similarities between her and Deborah Sykes's attacks (Rabil, 2012). But Darryl Hunt had been arrested and was in jail awaiting trial when Regina was attacked. During the identification process,

> Regina Lane identified [Brown] from an in-person lineup as her rapist in a fourth incident on February 2, 1985, which started just two blocks from where the Sykes murder happened. However, the police dissuaded Ms. Lane from pressing charges because it would have called into question the case against the man they had already charged with the Sykes murder—Darryl Hunt. For over nineteen years, Brown was able to keep his secret, saying, at his plea hearing on December 16, 2004: "It's part of the game, it's all been a game. The devil started it, and I played it. I just took something I can't give back." (Rabil, 2012, p. 1540)[3]

Regina Lane expressed frustration when the police did not follow up on her belief that her attacker was the same man who killed Deborah Sykes: "[The detective] doubted me and I didn't doubt myself because I told him the truth. There's nothing else I could've told him. It's insulting." When she requested that the investigation include police dogs to sniff the car and locations where her attacker held her captive, the police refused: "I just felt unimportant unfortunately." When asked what difference it would have made if the police had granted her request or made the connections to Sykes's murder, Regina replied, "It would have really opened the eyes of the police department and probably the people who were working other cases. It would've made a difference to the public to know that it was truly a bad person on the street, doing horrible things to women. I feel like I could have made a difference for people at that time, helping them to understand what I had lived through because I don't think anybody really knew what I have lived through except for the first people that were there with me."

In retrospect, it would have made an important difference to the family of Sykes, and to Darryl Hunt, to have the actual perpetrator apprehended. Adding to Regina's trauma, the investigators also asked her if she had voluntarily gone with Willard Brown rather than having been abducted. When rape / sexual assault survivors are disbelieved, they suffer increased pain and trauma. Regina offers this recollection of her experience:

> I didn't know this person that took me in my car and I did not know anything about him and like I said I didn't want to be with him. I went with the gun pointed at my body and I had no desire to do anything but what I had set my mind to do that day. [Q: When the detective was asking you these questions, how did it feel for you?] Well I sat in the back of the car and I teared up. I don't know if they could see it from the rear view mirror but he later apologized. I figured it was just been standard questioning practice but it still stays. It's still in your thought process because he doubted me.

Unrelated to the identification procedures used, Penny Beerntsen also described tunnel vision as a jurisdictional conflict among investigators. Two law enforcement agencies were involved in the investigation of her attack: the sheriff's office and the police department. The sheriff's office had settled on the original defendant as the suspect in her case and, through a series of identification procedures, arrested him shortly afterward. But the local police department disagreed and continued working on the case and ultimately suspected the actual perpetrator at this early stage. Penny was caught in the middle of these two agencies:

> I get a phone call, within a couple of weeks of the assault from the Manitowoc Police Department, saying we know that Steven Avery is in custody for assaulting you but we have another suspect in mind who looks similar to [him] and we want to ask you some questions. I don't remember being given a name but they said, "Did you ever notice a car parked either outside your house or along your jogging route? Because the suspect we have a mind generally stalks his victims before he chooses to attack them." And I hadn't noticed that. Then they asked, [because] I taught fitness classes at the Y, "Have you ever noticed anyone standing in the door of the gymnasium watching you teach fitness classes?" And I hadn't noticed that either. But I was alarmed. So I hang up and I call the sheriff. I say to him, "What's this about another suspect? I just got a

call from the police department they're talking about someone who looks like Steven Avery and likes to stalk his victims?" That's when the sheriff said, "Do not talk to the Manitowoc Police Department they do not have jurisdiction. It will only confuse you we will look into it." Now again, when the attorney general investigated the case post-exoneration she found that the deputy who called me also went to the sheriff. The police deputy said to the sheriff this sounds more like Gregory Allen's MO. He likes to stalk his victims. He had attempted to assault a woman approximately a year before I was assaulted on the same beach. His nickname was "the sand man" because he liked to come up out of the sand dunes and grab his victims. And the victim in this case was not able to identify him. I think the case was dropped. But it was the same district attorney who had filed the charges which were then later dropped. So I actually made a follow-up phone call to the sheriff and said, "Did you check out this other suspect?" And I was told yes we did he could not have possibly been your assailant because he was with his probation officer at the time you were assaulted so he has an airtight alibi. So years later the attorney general uncovered the fact that not only was he not with his probation officer, he was not on probation.

Public Awareness

These criminal investigations were not private. Because criminal investigations are taken over by the state, there is a vested interest in protecting public safety. When communities were alerted to these crimes, some of which were very high profile, the original victims and their families experienced additional traumas. As more people learned about the homicides and sexual assaults, the public curiosity generated some painful experiences for victims. Rumors circulated and activists became involved (without the victims' consent). Obscene and threatening phone calls were part of their secondary victimization experiences.

For example, anonymous phone calls occurred in Ada, Oklahoma, after Debra Sue Carter was murdered. Her cousin, Christy Sheppard recalled her family receiving threatening phone calls from someone: "And we don't know who called and there were phonebooks, anybody could have called us. It's a small town and everybody knew who my mom was. I don't know who called, but it's all the little parts that make it worse." Ultimately, experiences such as these might result in original victims self-isolating in order to avoid interactions or reduce contact in the broader community.

A local activist inserted herself into one case, without the consent of the victim or her family. Janet Burke was raped as a young woman while working in a church day care center; it was one in a series of sexual assaults in her city. The activist generated more public attention than there otherwise would have been:

> At that point, there was a random person in the community. I don't know that she had any personal connection to any of the rapes but she had started this campaign to find this person. There had been a sketch, and from what I can remember about her is that she was a concerned parent that was worried for her own children's safety. And the ironic part is that she actually got an award after [the wrongly convicted man] was captured because of what she had done for the community. It was just kind of a crazy time period during that process, they took him into custody, [then] I started getting threatening phone calls at the center. "You better not testify, you don't have the right person. If you want to see the right person come to such a such a such a such." So the police were involved in all of this of course.

These corollary harms from communities compounded the trauma for these victims. While some were well-meaning interactions, others were foreboding and frightening.

TRIALS

Once the investigations concluded, the focus shifted to the trial. The trials often inflicted additional harm in both the homicide and rape / sexual assault cases. Victims of crime anticipate receiving answers and being able to generate an understanding that assists them to process and grieve their losses. And there is another painful cost. Secondary trauma includes the experience of cooperating with an investigation and testifying in court (Campbell and Raja, 1999; Caringella, 2009; Martin and Powell, 1994). Secondary trauma also includes listening to graphic testimony about the harms they have endured—murder victims' family members who listen to the graphic autopsy testimony from the medical examiner, for example—and testifying against the accused rapist before being subjected to traumatizing cross-examination by defense attorneys. For the original crime victims in this research who were adults at the time of the original trial, their experiences offer insights into this lived reality. All of the rape / sexual assault survivors who participated in this research testified against the original defendant at trial, and none had doubts about the accuracy of their testimony. All but one of the murder victims' family members who were adults at the time of the original trial attended court to listen and either support or oppose the process; but, unlike the rape survivors, some of the homicide victims' family members had lingering doubts about the guilt of the accused.

Attending the trial of someone accused of killing a family member is an extremely emotional ordeal. It generates fear, confusion, and frustration and often produces little resolution. Some murder victims' survivors who participated in this research also acknowledged how weak the criminal cases were that resulted in the conviction of the original defendants. For Peggy Sanders, the arrest of the original defendants came years after her daughter, Debra Sue Carter, was murdered. She was relieved:

> [The arrest] tickled me to death. I thought finally they found who did it. And when we went to court, the third day [one of the original defendants] was in there, I can't remember what was said or what was done, but he picked this table up and flipped it. When he did that I could see him flipping Debbie all over that apartment. But this [other guy], I couldn't figure him out but he was crazy and he kept hollering, "I didn't kill Debbie Carter, I didn't kill her." And I thought he's crazy, look at what all he did to Debbie and Debbie didn't know him.

Sean Malloy, whose sister Noreen was killed in a robbery while at work, attended the trial and said it was "miserable." The Malloy family observed a "weak" investigation that generated flimsy evidence and then attended the trial that resulted in a conviction that felt hollow. Sean recalls the trial this way:

> [The defense attorney] was a scumbag lawyer, and he sat in his high backseat and they're doing this thing and [the original defendant] is right here and we're behind [him] in the gallery so every time they would cross-examine he would turn around and say, "Ha ha we got them we got them." Oh my God the lawyer I wanted to beat his ass. Literally, we had victims [support] people with us and [the advocate] knew. She stuck right by me the whole time. My mom's [on one side of me] and she's here and [she's] like come on, come with me and she pulls me out. I was more PO'd about his antics than I was at the testimony. But the whole trial was just like surreal. Kind of dry, but it was pretty much unanimous. They thought he was guilty. [Q: And so for many years you had faith in that conviction?] Um yeah, it was kind of weak. Even my dad said so. But, what are we going to do, Dad? What are we gonna do?

Sean recalls that they did not attend the sentencing hearing: "I remember going through the trial thinking that I would have this catharsis afterwards but nothing, just another day. I remember people were going down to the sentencing. My dad didn't go. I didn't go either. Because I had enough with it."

For Millie Maxwell, who was eighteen when her father was murdered during a home invasion, the ordeal of the trial was "overwhelming" and the case itself was extremely complex. On top of the stress and complexity of the trial, Millie recalls her impressions of the prosecutor: "So I don't know if the district attorney at that time, who I don't think was an honest person in the justice system, had something against these [original defendants] that he just insisted on making it seem like it was them because they insist that they were pressured into taking these guilty pleas." Pressuring a defendant into a guilty plea (ultimately on a crime they did not commit) left Millie without comfort or a sense of resolution:

> I think most of the family felt like we were hurting and grieving and then we wondered, "Who takes a guilty plea if you didn't have some involvement with this?" So it wasn't so much that we were pointing the finger at them. This is what the justice system told us, this is who we have with this evidence "proving" that these are the ones who did it. . . . That's what made it hard once they did came back to court and got off on this. Because these are people, some we come up in the neighborhood with or went to school with and they're out all this time you don't know how person feels.

For Dwayne Jones, whose partner, Jacqueline Harrison, was killed, attending the trial was grueling because of the graphic photos and because she was described at court as "promiscuous":

> First of all, it was packed. A whole lot of people knew more than they said. Those people were there, I can tell you that. Those people were there. People from our community, media from all over the place were there. New York, Philadelphia, Delaware, everybody was there. It was long; it was trying. It was some of the worst days of my life. It wasn't a good thing. The trial was not good at all. They kept painting her, the [graphic pictures]. . . . I couldn't, some days I would only be in court for fifteen minutes and they were doing these pictures for hours. They were just saying that all the stuff that was going on with her could've been a result of what happened to her, but it couldn't have been right.

For the murder victims' survivors, hearing victim-blaming messages during the trial adds to the trauma of the original loss. Losing a life partner and then having her maligned in public court proceedings, with journalists present, ultimately robs survivors of the right to see their loved one as a whole person; she becomes reduced to a salacious story, her body a platform for curiosities and grotesque theories of self-inflicted suffering. The trial steals from the survivors their right to see, know, and grieve the goodness and the love they shared.

For the murder victims' families who also faced capital murder trials of other family members, who they knew to be wrongly accused, the ordeal of the trial itself is unbearable. Ginger Blossom, whose parents were murdered and whose twin brother was wrongly convicted of killing them, the sentencing phase of the capital trial was "so bad":

> The jury was so quick to convict him, and you can have either the judge do the sentencing or you can have the jury do the sentencing. Because they were so quick to get a conviction, it was only a couple of hours, I thought well we don't want to go with the jury let's go with the judge. At least then, in theory, he should be able to weigh premeditation and all these other factors then I thought he would be more lenient and no he wasn't. It's like being hit in the face with a sledgehammer when they sentenced him to death. This is where I'm going to start crying again, my cousins were there, and they were crying and it was bad.

At the sentencing hearing, the prosecutor tried to prevent Ginger from giving her victim-impact statement: "Yeah [the prosecutor] wasn't gonna let me read my victim-impact statement at Gary's sentencing because it wasn't what they wanted. I read it anyway." In her statement she made the point that "you guys have really screwed up and you have the wrong person, and this is wrong and that's the impact on my life."

For Ida Mae and Guy Wilhoit, who attended the trial of their son Greg when he was charged with murdering his wife Kathy, the frustration they felt with the defense attorney was matched only by the horror of Greg being sentenced to death. About the defense attorney, Ida Mae says, "And that drunk one, he didn't know what to do. I mean when they came back and said he was guilty. I was always thankful that we had no TV or anybody [from the news]. We were the only two people in the place for the whole thing. Nobody but just the two of us." Greg's defense attorney was drunk through most of the trial, and though they wanted to address that, the judge was "one of his drinking buddies," so that made it difficult to address. And to compound their frustration, the jury in Osage County was empaneled with the following process:

GUY: The judge said, "Is there anyone here"—I'll probably say this the wrong way—"is there anyone here who will not send a man to his death based on circumstantial evidence?" And there was not one of the fifty [prospective jurors].

IDA MAE: They all would.

GUY: They all said we could send a man to death purely on circumstantial evidence. Now can you imagine? What are the odds of that? It just blows my mind.

Some of the murder victims' family members were unable to attend the trial. Andrea Harrison and Krissy and Kim Wilhoit were very small children at the time of the original convictions and therefore did not attend the trial.

Nancy Wilhoit Vollertsen and Yolanda Thomas were both overseas on military service during the murder trials. Yolanda remembers hearing the news of the conviction this way: "He was convicted on [my sister's] birthday [a year later]. We did not get a phone call, not a piece of mail. Lord knows, I'm in the military. You can find me. Nothing. [Q: Did your parents get any news?] No ma'am. NO. NO. Nobody. My mom said that after Jacquetta died she got one phone call from someone in North Carolina from the media."

The original trial in the rape / sexual assault cases was mainly a time of vindication, or so the victims felt at the time. By surviving the assault, providing evidence to the police, cooperating with the investigations, and giving eyewitness identification against the original defendants, they often approached the trials as a time when they might receive some relief and begin to put this ordeal behind them. Seven of the rape / sexual assault survivors provided testimony at the original trials; Regina Lane was not afforded the opportunity because her case was not prosecuted.

Tomeshia Carrington-Artis, twelve at the time she was raped, was fourteen years old when she testified against the original defendant: "On the stand I said it was him that raped me." She trusted the police and their investigation: "I didn't doubt it because the police told me it was him because of his hair matched what was found on me so any doubts I had, I didn't have them long because the police told me that they had the right guy. And I've never known anybody that went to prison that was not guilty."

Preparing for that moment, in itself, is a grueling experience for these victims. In Penny Beerntsen's case, the law enforcement community provided important support to her through the process: "The DA took me into the courtroom [prior to the trial]. I mean he had met with me obviously and gone over my testimony and because we had had two preliminary hearings. But he was [kind], and we had these preliminary conversations in his office, often with the sheriff present." Being heard and being able to share the painful details with the investigators and prosecutors in advance of the trial was important for these victims to face the ordeal of testifying at trial. Anticipating what the trial and cross-examination would be like helped the rape / sexual assault survivors to deliver their testimony effectively. Penny continues,

> So anyway in this prep that the DA did with me he said, "I'm gonna be the devil's advocate, I'm gonna pretend I'm the defense attorney." So he actually had me sit in the witness chair. I think it was a Sunday night, it was dark. It was like quiet in the courtroom. He said things like whoever asking you the question whether it's me or the defense attorney look at the person asking the question and when you answer the question look at the jury. Make eye contact with the jury. So it was that kind of

thing. Stuff like don't wear brown in court because people don't respond well to the color brown. The one thing he asked me at one point, "How sure are you that you identified the correct person?" And I think I said something between 90 and 95 percent, and he said when I ask you that on the stand you damn well better say you're 100 percent certain.

Most of the rape / sexual assault survivors, the courts decided, could not attend the full trial since they were giving testimony—this is not uncommon (Wemmers, 2009). So while these survivors were able to describe in court what happened to them and testified that the original defendants were their attackers, they did not observe other witnesses' testimony. Michele Mallin recalls being comfortable with this: "The only time I was in the courtroom was when they swore me in and we had to all be sworn in, all the witnesses, and I was there for my testimony and I didn't see or hear I didn't see anything else because I wasn't allowed to be in the courtroom." And when she provided eyewitness identification that the original defendant was the person who attacked her, she says, "I remember I thought I was pretty positive. I may have second-guessed it for second, but after that I knew I was right. I felt confident that I was right."

During the cross-examination by the defense attorneys, these rape / sexual assault survivors experienced intense questioning about their prior sexual behavior and their memories of the attacks. Debbie Jones recalls, "The [district attorney] warned me that the [defense] might try to make me look bad and they really questioned me about [my boyfriend] and had I been with him and all that and I remember thinking are you kidding me? So what I had a boyfriend? So what I'm nineteen and I'm having sex? What does it matter? That doesn't entitle someone to rape me and put their body part inside me. No. That does not give them the right to come into my apartment and violate me."

Seven of the eight rape / sexual assault survivors provided cross-racial eyewitness identification. Tomeshia Carrington-Artis is African American and was assaulted by a white man when she was twelve years old; six participants are white women who were assaulted by African American men, and one is a white woman who was assaulted by a white man.

Karen M. is white and was raped in her home by an African American intruder. The flawed cross-racial eyewitness-identification procedures caused her irreparable harm once she learned that the original defendant was not her attacker: "I'm white and when I see pictures of both of them [the exonerated original defendant, the actual attacker] I see similarities but I never compared African American men. I just wish this has never happened. I wish I'd never reported it. It has just ruined my life and more importantly ruined [the exoneree's life] and yet now . . . I look at [him] now and I talk to him and honestly I think he has a more productive, healthy life than I do, really I do and I'm like in all of that he really does and I'm thankful for that."

It is important to point out that all of these crimes occurred between 1980 and 1985, when eyewitness-identification procedures were comparatively underdeveloped. The rape victims here provided critical assistance to the investigations of the crimes they endured, cooperated fully with the eyewitness-identification processes used at the time, and did not fabricate accusations against the original defendants. The fact remains that one of the visible characteristics of the assailants is their racial identity. In addition to having unsophisticated knowledge of the higher probability of error in cross-racial eyewitness identification in the 1980s, there was little acknowledgment that racial bias that may have impacted the investigators. Sadly, American history is contaminated by centuries of African American men being portrayed as "rapists"; moral panics have ensured that when white women are raped by African American men, the law enforcement community engages quickly with the investigation (Johnson, 2021). Recall that stranger rapes are more likely than the more commonly experienced acquaintance rapes to be investigated by law enforcement. Six of the rape / sexual assault survivors in this research had no way of knowing that the crimes against them would unfold in a crucible of racially charged social forces that increased community concern and contributed additional fuel to an already incendiary social predicament. As such, they became unwilling fodder who, as "ideal victims," galvanized the historical tropes so painfully familiar (Johnson, 2021; Petersen and Ward, 2015). Sexism and racism are intersecting historical dynamics that impacted these cases, through no fault of the women who were victimized. Therefore, secondary trauma experienced by these rape / sexual assault survivors is a consequence of the flawed procedures used during investigations, as well as the conjoined oppressive systems of sexism and racism.

CONCLUSION

This chapter examined how crime victims and survivors experienced the original investigations and trials. Given the benefit of hindsight and the new information that came from the exonerations, their recollections remain detailed about the traumatic experiences while also adding new critical insights about where and how the errors occurred. Several participants described their views on tunnel vision, particularly as it shaped the eyewitness-identification processes in which they gave evidence. Secondary trauma is present in all of their experiences, some of which includes deeply personal invasions of their bodies (which became crimes scenes in the rape cases) or deeply painful portrayals of their deceased family members that were grotesquely sexist and racist.

CHAPTER 4

Shattered Families

IN MAY 1985, Kathy Wilhoit moved into her new apartment with her two daughters. She and Greg were struggling to make a go of marriage. Perhaps a little time apart would help? The girls were so young: Krissy was a toddler (fourteen months old), and Kim was born prematurely and was four months old. Kathy had plans to run errands with her neighbor on June 1. When the neighbor arrived to hear the babies crying, she called for help. Once they learned that Kathy was dead and the girls were unharmed, the police began investigating. Eventually, they arrested Greg Wilhoit, Kathy's husband and Krissy and Kim's father. The extended Wilhoit family was close; Greg's parents, Guy and Ida Mae, helped with the girls as much as possible, but once Greg was arrested they had to figure out something else. They found a foster family for the girls in their church, thankfully. They were able to remain close with Krissy and Kim during their childhoods, while also fighting what they knew was a wrongful conviction and death sentence. Nancy Wilhoit Vollertsen also pitched in to help with the girls and the entire family. It took all that they had financially. All their emotional and social resources were spent on this nightmare. Kathy was dead; Greg was accused of capital murder, convicted, and sentenced to death. When he was exonerated, Krissy and Kim were finally able to know their biological father; and their family worked to recover from the traumas of this situation.

In reflecting on their experiences with the original crime, these participants often described how their families handled the ordeals. This chapter explores the effects of violent crimes on the families of the victims' survivors, particularly in light of the wrongful convictions and exonerations that later occurred. When asked to reflect on their family's involvement in the exoneration process, most participants shared more deeply about the original crime and its effects. These crimes are pivotal events in their lives and within their families. There is a *before* and *after* timeline where crime itself serves as a fulcrum. How families reacted to the original crime often was mirrored by their response to the exoneration. These responses can range from supportive and compassionate to abusive and victim blaming. They reveal a family's resiliency and may expose their debilitation. For some, the original framing of a strong emotional bond and devoted family was proved in the aftermath; for others, the experience was marred by abuse within the family that became worse in the aftermath. Their experiences reveal often-invisible traumas associated with collateral harms and ambiguous loss (Boss, 1999), which is characterized by gradations of presence or absence of a loved one or of a condition. "The greater the ambiguity surrounding one's loss, the more difficult it is to master it and the greater one's depression, anxiety, and family conflict" (Boss, 1999, p. 7). Furthermore, impacts on families can be profound: "Ambiguous loss blurs the tidy [family] boundaries . . . causing people to question their most intimate relationships" (Boss, 1999, p. 64). The participants described their experiences of collateral harms that reframed their families. Homicide victims' family members reported a profound reframing of the family's identity, dynamic, and focus; sexual assault survivors reported a reframing of their understanding of family support during a time of crisis.

The invisible rupture of one's previous understanding of their family comes as a surprise and may generate a sense of loss they cannot name until many years later. It arrives by chance, at the invitation of the victims searching for support from the people who are relationally closest to them. The "family gamble" (Boss, 1999), to wager on family support, may produce unanticipated results: will the trauma be shared with compassion, or will it be met with victim-blaming, judgment, and possibly gendered and/or racial bias? Ultimately, what is lost or gained in this gamble is a continuation of compassionate family relationships where the trauma is shared, or a revelation that inflicts more harm and compounds the trauma.

Family life provides a mooring for people to anchor their lives. Humans are born or adopted into families, are nurtured and taught life skills, and find belonging. We develop a sense of identity from our families. They become our foundation and our framework: the place from which we launch our lives and the place to which we return for holidays, celebrations, reunions, and milestones such as weddings, funerals, graduations, baptisms, and mitzvahs. Family members tend to be companions we depend on for celebrating life's joys and enduring life's challenges. In the United States we perpetuate a cultural idealism that family is a place of refuge, a place for wholesome growth and guidance. In reality, families are more complex and can be "worlds of pain" (Rubin, 1976) where poverty, conflict, abuse, addiction, and betrayal exist. Family challenges can be opportunities to support each other and may reveal some painful realities about emotional bonds. The tragedies endured by these participants occurred in their families in whatever the situation they may have been facing at the time. They may have been happy and healthy, or recovering from alcoholism;

nurturing and loving, or marred by abuse; engaged and interdependent, or controlling and manipulative; and on and on. Participants described how their families responded to unimaginable loss and injury at the time their lives were shattered by violence. The impacts reveal, reinforce, and/or reframe how their families functioned.

The immediate impact of their violent victimization on these participants and their families was profound and enduring. The homicide victims' families were forever altered by the violent deaths of their loved ones. The faith the rape / sexual assault survivors once had in their families might have been a source of profound comfort and safety or a source of unexpected judgment, rejection, isolation, and pain. I turn to the homicide victims' families first.

HOMICIDE VICTIMS' FAMILY MEMBERS

The void left in the family with the death of a loved one affects every aspect of the family's life, across multiple generations. When the homicide victim is a mother, the children are uniquely impacted irrespective of their age, as is true for Krissy and Kim Wilhoit, for Andrea Harrison, and for Ginger Blossom. When the victim is a father, the whole family loses one of the foundations of their life and identity and their emotional center; this is true for Millie Maxwell and Ginger Blossom. When the victim is a sister, her siblings lose an aunt for their children, they lose a best friend and confidante, they lose someone who knows their story in ways few other people do; this is true for Yolanda Thomas and Sean Malloy. When the victim is one's own child, the loss is staggering in that the child is brutally removed, taking with them the past, the effort invested in rearing the child, the future that was anticipated for them, including whatever family they might have grown for themselves; this is true for Peggy Sanders. No matter what type of family relationship, the pain endures a lifetime and the grief shapes how the surviving family members live their lives—it profoundly reframes their emotional terrain. Christy Sheppard stated succinctly, "Our family was never the same."

For two of the homicide victims' families, the Wilhoit and Gauger families, their loss and grief was complicated by the wrongful capital convictions of surviving family members.[1] The tragedy in the Wilhoit family reveals how supportive and resilient family bonds can be when they faced the unimaginable destruction of a murdered family member and then the implication of another family member in that crime. This lengthy example offers multigenerational perspectives and nuances. When Kathy Wilhoit's body was discovered, her daughters were very small children. The Wilhoit family described themselves as "very close," and as Nancy Wilhoit Vollertsen stated, "Even before all this happened I had really enjoyed being close to family. Then after Kathy was killed, we were having a reasonably normal family life. Until June 1, 1985, and then everything changed. We were very grief stricken, obviously. Kathy had not been in our family a long time, but we had really come to care for her and Greg loved her." One immediate concern was caring for the girls: Krissy and Kim. Their father, Greg Wilhoit, was their surviving parent who depended on the extended family in raising the girls. Nancy described this: "Kim and Krissy were so young. Greg had these babies and he was emotionally a wreck. He was a wreck . . . and I was getting ready to move to Germany [on Army orders]. And Greg, at least for the first couple months, really was just not capable of taking care of them. So we've got to figure out how to take care of the girls and try to figure out how to keep Greg afloat and keep him from just completely going off the deep end." As the police investigation was unfolding, the family did their best to mourn their loss and rebuild normalcy for themselves and the girls. Nancy continues, "By then [when he was arrested] he did actually have his act together somewhat so it wasn't quite as dire a situation. He had a day care for the girls, he had his two babies and he would come home and fix them dinner. He was doing it and he was really trying. So, [when he was arrested] truly it came out of the blue."

For Guy and Ida Mae Wilhoit, the immediate impact of Kathy's murder meant "we pretty much kept [the girls] during that time, you know, we had the funeral and then Greg had to get back to work. And very quickly we had to make decisions." Kathy's family of origin lived in a different state, and her parents were not available to participate in caring for the girls.

After settling into this new routine, the family was then shocked by the police arresting Greg for Kathy's murder. Ida Mae recalled that "he literally walked out the front door to go to work and they arrested him and charged him with first-degree murder." There was no warning in advance to expect this; there was no inclination that this would ultimately occur. The Wilhoit family was shattered even more severely when Greg was charged with capital murder. For Krissy and Kim, this compounded the loss of their mother, with the removal of their father and the attention of the extended family diverted to defending Greg during his yearslong legal ordeal. Krissy and Kim explain their experience of being raised by foster parents:

KIM: Grandma [Ida Mae] has said that they never let us get adopted because they were selfish and wanted us as well. They were just scared I think, that they would never see us again.
KRISSY: Our [foster parents], yeah, they could have just taken us. I don't think they would have.
KIM: They wouldn't have done that, no.
KRISSY: I think we were fortunate.

Their foster parents ensured that Krissy and Kim maintained regular contact with the extended Wilhoit family. They celebrated birthdays and holidays together throughout their childhood, and often the girls accompanied the Wilhoits on family vacations. They grew up referring to Greg as "Daddy Greg" and had a fictional understanding that he was "in the Navy," which is why he could not be at home with them. The Wilhoits rallied to support and care for each other in the immediate aftermath of Kathy's death. The family's resilience in handling the impact of Kathy's murder and later Greg's wrongful capital conviction reflects a core value system of sharing responsibility and devotion to each other, despite the exceedingly stressful ordeal.

When Morris and Ruth Gauger were murdered at their farm, their son Gary found his father's body in the motorcycle repair shop and immediately called the police. Later that morning, the police discovered his mother's body; she was also murdered. The police investigated, and after questioning Gary, they ultimately charged him with capital murder (Westervelt and Cook, 2012). For Ginger Blossom, the loss of her parents was devastating. After returning to her childhood home, the family immediately had to prepare for the dual funeral and confront the criminal charges against Gary. Ginger never believed that Gary had murdered their parents and continued to support him through his trial, his death sentence, his exoneration, and his return home. The murder of her parents profoundly reframed her life and livelihood when she left everything behind to tend to the family situation: "My life as professional ski instructor [ended], and then all of a sudden I am unemployed. However, I had started with my rug shop business maybe a couple of years before all this happened and my mom would run it when I was gone. So at least I had some income from that, and that's when I really had to start ramping up and getting serious about the business because that was my only income. So there was a lot going on." Ginger also had to navigate the impact of her family's identity and reputation upon returning to Illinois. Her example reveals that identity can be both a source of pain and a source of comfort:

> After I got married, I used [my maiden name] Ginger Gauger because I was out in Taos, New Mexico, and if I used [my married name] Ginger Blossom everyone would think this is [typical], because Taos is the last bastion of the hippie communities. So when I came back I used Ginger Blossom. I remember writing out a check to buy plants at the local nursery and the lady gasps and she said, "Oh my God you're the daughter of those people who were murdered, ohhhh. . . ." But, I just shrug and get on with life. And [sometimes] it's kind of comforting, you go to the bank and everybody knows you and you go to the hardware store and everybody knows you. Yeah it is comforting. [And after

reopening the import business] at first it was coming to the farm with a stigma of this is where "those people" were murdered—that always drove me nuts. Well no, those are my parents. People who know the story are very kind and supportive. And now [the shop is] a destination.

Ginger also reports that while she and Gary remain close, living next door to each other, another brother remains distant from the family and her nieces and nephews, and their children are estranged: "Unfortunately Gary has no relationship with his kids because all they heard was what was filtered through [their mother] which is that Gary killed their grandparents." The homicide of her parents and Gary's wrongful conviction have taken a very heavy toll on the family that may never be repaired. Still, her affection for her twin brother remains important to Ginger: "I'll see him [every] day. We will meet out in the field and we will chitchat. Every time I hear [him driving the] tractor I still get happy."

Demonstrating resiliency and reframing family so that a deceased mother remains present in her child's life is Dwayne Jones, Andrea Harrison's father. Dwayne reports that losing Jacqueline Harrison to murder left a void that cannot be filled: "She was a great mother. She was one of the best mothers you ever would've known. Andrea remembers: she was with her every single day." Shortly after Jacqueline was murdered, Dwayne's extended family moved away and evaporated around him; he felt alone and lost. He also felt ignored by the authorities investigating the homicide: "We were overlooked. We were nothing. And it was sad, you can be reduced so quick to nothing. Your world falls apart very quickly. There were days when you feel like a peanut in a nut factory and that was not good."

For Andrea Harrison, losing her mother at three years old meant that grief framed her whole life: "Next year will make thirty years since my mother was murdered. And it's still a cold case, and this year I'll be thirty-three and my sister just turned thirty-six. Our whole lives, for me and my sister, it is a lingering thing." Andrea remains grateful that her immediate family stayed connected, and though she was raised by her maternal grandmother, she remains in close contact with her father Dwayne. The loss continues to have reverberations in her life:

There wasn't a cut off with our relationship [with my dad] which I'm glad about because to not have your mom is a big detriment but if I didn't have my daddy either. . . . Granted, my grandmother was a good woman but to not have your parents is already hard enough. It's not like my mother had some disease or she had cancer and just passed away like something that's inevitable. She was taken from me. Somebody stole her from me. And if I didn't have my dad then I would just be like I am an orphan. You know, when your parents are just removed from your life there's PTSD from that. Abandonment is a big thing for me. Even with relationships with friends or significant others abandonment is a thing.

While their family structure and time together were reshaped due to her mother's death, Andrea and Dwayne retain a close relationship. They often celebrate achievements and big occasions with each other and their extended family.

An extended example that articulates the before-and-after nature of these families reframing their lives involves Peggy Sanders and Christy Sheppard's family. When Debra Sue Carter was murdered in her first apartment as a young woman, her mother Peggy Sanders was emotionally destroyed. Debbie was excited to be in her first apartment and was a devoted daughter and sister. Her young cousin, Christy, was eight years old at the time she died, and Christy has an especially close bond with Peggy. As an adult woman, Christy observes how this reframed her family: "It was devastating and I think that's why I pick and search for the missing pieces to all this because when that happened *it changed everything.* It changed the way we lived our lives and the way that we interacted with one another. It's interesting to see how that event, that day those few minutes changed family structure, changed the dynamics of who we were. That is the craziest thing." In the immediate aftermath of the homicide, the family was operating on autopilot, going through the motions of what needed to be done, but not really processing what was happening to them as a family. Some of the first signs of Peggy's (whose family nickname is "Peppy") eventual emotional breakdown were in the first few days after Debbie died. Christy recalls, "Yep, [my mother] had to deal with Peppy. She had to bathe her. She had to wash her hair because Peppy refused to go to the funeral. And so my mom knew it would be very emotional."

The murder scene in Debbie's apartment was ghastly: Debbie had been brutally raped and murdered, blood was everywhere, and the bedding was saturated with bodily fluids. After the police had collected evidence, Debbie's apartment was released from police custody. Christy's mother (Peggy's sister) stepped in to deal with it. "It was a month after Debbie died, they released the apartment to be cleaned out, which again fell on my mom because that's what she does. She's the cleaner, the caretaker of the business end."

The murder investigation stagnated for several years, and with no arrest or information conveyed to Peggy, the family was left to wonder what the authorities were doing to solve the crime. Several years later, when the investigators told Peggy that they required Debbie's body to be exhumed and Peggy broke down again, her relationship with her sister, Christy's mother, became so frayed that full repair seemed nearly impossible. After pulling Peggy out of the empty grave where Debbie had been buried,

> [my mom] got Peggy calmed down and that was the first night she spent in the psychiatric hospital. That was Peggy's breaking point which is another real bitter spot with me about all that. That all they created in this extra trauma [ordering the exhumation], wasn't real [the test wasn't actually necessary]. Well it was very real to us . . . and that was kind of my mom's breaking point. My mom told her, "I can't do this with you every day, I can't. I have a child to raise, I have a job, I can't relive this and do this every day with you, I cannot." They've never been the same.

Peggy was so broken by the loss of her daughter that when asked to talk about the impact on her whole family, she had a hard time focusing on any other person besides Debbie. She was able to say, "I have three daughters; [two live here], and one lives in heaven." Accepting that Debbie is gone is a process that has eluded Peggy. Reinforcing their bond as a family, Christy is now an adult woman and has become the advocate for Peggy and the spokesperson for their family as it relates to this tragic crime. In fact, Christy Sheppard has become a nationally prominent activist in the fields of wrongful convictions and death penalty abolition.

Another devastating situation was the murder of Jaquetta Thomas, whose half-sister, Yolanda Thomas, recalls, "Her dad was devastated yeah . . . to see a man like that, to go through, yeah it's, you know, he was a mess. No, I've never since or before ever seen a man break like that but she was his only child." Yolanda and Jacquetta were born to the same mother but had different fathers. The debilitating grief of a parent for a murdered child is indescribable. Yolanda reveals that the debilitation impacted her mother and other family members too. When a bereaved person is completely grief-stricken, the family loses emotional and social access to them and no longer benefits from their contributions to the family. They are so broken by the loss that they cannot remain available to each other as they might have been before the homicide.

Compounding the effects of homicide on families is the financial burdens associated with the burial. Without insurance, families may not have the resources to support a dignified burial in accordance with their religious views. Yolanda Thomas commented that on the rare occasion when her mother asked for assistance it was for help with the funeral costs. However, her mother was additionally harmed by a victim-blaming policy.

> The only thing the people at the funeral home had said to her was, because my sister had been murdered and my mom didn't have insurance so there was no life insurance or anything. The burial was going to cost us. The funeral home had mentioned when someone's murdered

you can call this [phone] number and they can help you, they can help you with the kids and all that. So she did reach out and I'm going to paraphrase. My sister "contributed to her own death, so there was no money available" for her or her kids. My mother said, "Someone murdered my daughter but she contributed to her own death because she had drugs in her system. So now we can't get any help." Yeah pretty much.

Furthermore, the intergenerational harms are evident. Yolanda has remained as close as possible to Jacquetta's children and reveals that they all continue to struggle with the cascading traumatic impact of their mother's death, and having children of their own by now, Jacquetta's grandchildren are also impacted by the family trauma.

Another example of how a family may be debilitated by the violent death of a loved one is the Malloy family. Noreen Malloy was working at a fast-food restaurant when she was killed while closing the business at the end of her shift. Sean Malloy, her brother, showed that the Malloys' experience reinforces their family's strength and dedication as well as the long-term devastation of their loss: "[After Noreen died, my mom] died in 1998 of lung cancer. We always said she died of a broken heart. She was never the same. She was quiet, sweet, anybody that has ever met my mom . . . [knew she was] just very loving, very nurturing."

The Malloys are a big Irish Catholic family—rambunctious, hilarious, practical jokers. There were six children, five sons and one daughter, Noreen, who was murdered. Sean reports that the brothers were all devastated by this tragic loss and all coped with it in different ways. The camaraderie and fun were gone, replaced with a devastated family, heartbroken parents, and a sense of loss that endures today. When Noreen died, Sean was entering his senior year of high school, and her death left him feeling like he was barely functioning during his final year of school: "Oh yeah my senior year was terrible. I don't even remember picking up a book. You're supposed to love your senior year."

The loss of Noreen continues to frame his life as an adult man. Now married and raising his own daughter, Sean feels like his daughter has lost out on having Noreen as an aunt and role model in her life, which also breaks his heart. And to further the harms, his daughter has lost out on having her grandmother, who died "of a broken heart" before Sean's daughter was born. For Sean, the loss is rooted in the impact on his whole family: "I've explained the whole thing to my daughter. She feels gipped. My wife feels cheated out of a mother-in-law and a sister-in-law. And [my daughter] says, 'Tell me stories dad.' So I have to tell stories. And some of it's painful."

These lingering impacts do not end for any of the participants or in homicide cases overall. The invisible and ambiguous losses experienced by families going through these ordeals included a lost sense of family cohesion. Some families gained a deeper sense of resiliency and commitment to each other, as is evident within the Wilhoit family. Grief and loss are explored in more detail in chapter 8. The effects on families profoundly reframe identity, relationships, and emotional connections.

RAPE / SEXUAL ASSAULT VICTIMS

The eight sexual assault survivors in this research report that their families were deeply impacted by the crimes they endured. As with the homicide victims' families, there is no way to be prepared for a severe trauma. It harms the entire family. Each family has its unique emotional dynamics, and it is within these established dynamics that they all confront the violence of rape and sexual assault that occurred. Some families were very supportive, while other families were marred by abuse prior to the crimes against these participants. These violent crimes resulted in the families revealing, reframing, and/or reinforcing their existing dynamics. The families could be either present or absent. Presence includes both physically present to these participants as well as emotionally present to aid in recovery. Absence includes being both physically and emotionally distant from the victims of these violent crimes. Emotional distance may occur in physical proximity and can be rendered visible in the situations where victims were blamed by family members for their victimization and where sexism and racism impact how their families responded to their needs.

Regina Lane's supportive family immediately came to her side when she was in the hospital for the forensic rape examination, reinforcing her framework of love and compassion within her family: "It was very comforting. My parents stayed with me through the whole process of giving the police report and telling everything that happened to me. The one thing I love about my parents, they're beautiful people. Our family is very special. So it makes all the difference when you have that kind of love and encouragement around you."

Janet Burke's supportive and attentive parents drove her to the hospital from the day care center, affirming their devotion and exposing their despair. Her father struggled during that car ride, however, dealing with his own emotional response to the trauma Janet had just experienced: "Your parents try to protect you your whole life and then you know they send you off to work in a church and this happens. The world just turned upside down." Janet acknowledged how challenging it must have been for her mother to discuss topics regarding sexual assault, since conversations related to sex did not normally occur: "[She's an] incredible mom, but [she] grew up in an era where you didn't talk about sex. You just didn't talk about those things you know and she was very supportive and incredible to be there with me." Janet also expressed deep appreciation that as the police investigation was unfolding her parents were able to track that in order to protect her from having to deal with it as much as she otherwise might have had to.

Penny Beerntsen was married with two children at the time of the assault; her husband has remained supportive throughout the years and was an especially important source of support for her in the immediate aftermath of the attack. When trauma survivors face the ordinary interactions of everyday life, there may be "overreactions" to those events due to the fear of losing control or a heightened perception of risk that can generate a sense of hypervigilance of one's surroundings (Herman, 1997). Penny's husband provided a foil for her in those moments, reinforcing his commitment to her well-being, especially through this ordeal.

> There were days when I would feel strong and in control, and there were other days where something simple would intimidate me. This is kind of a crazy example, but I remember [my husband] and I were traveling somewhere with the kids and we were out to dinner. I went up to the dessert buffet, me and my love of sweets. I had my eye on a chocolate dessert and I cut in line in front of someone and I didn't realize I did, I went to the head of the line instead of the back of the line. The guy I cut in front of really got in my face and [my husband] said, "Just go sit down." He walked away and sat down. Well I grab my chocolate and I go sit down, and I light into [him], "Why didn't you say something why didn't you stand up for me?" He said because it would've only escalated the situation. He was totally right. But then there was another incident where, I don't even remember what it was, someone had said something and he stood up for me and intervened and I ringed him for that saying, "Don't you think I can talk for myself?" I was sending him very mixed messages based on how much in control I was feeling in my own life.

The challenges to their marriage presented by the assault were complex and nuanced. Penny's husband remains a calm and supportive presence in her life: "It definitely has an impact and you understand why there's a high percentage of relationships that end after. I know that from being an advocate for assault victims that many partners don't know how to cope and I don't mean this as a judgment but people are in different places and it's just very difficult. But he never viewed me as damaged goods."

The mothers of both Tomeshia Carrington-Artis and Michele Mallin were their primary resource for support and guidance in the immediate aftermath of being raped. Michele called her mother, who told her to go to the police, go to the hospital, and be sure to have medical tests done to ensure she was not pregnant or infected with a sexually transmitted disease.

Her mother was an important support system through the entire process. Tomeshia, who was merely twelve years old at the time she was assaulted, depended almost entirely on her mother, though she also stayed with extended family members for a few months to recover. This reframed their relationship in that her mother became "very protective" of her and "turned into a detective" to try to find the man who attacked Tomeshia, in large part due to the racial issues involved. "Because she didn't want it to be unsolved because I was a young Black girl, and it was a white man that did it. So she did not want them to just let it go. . . . Somebody was going to pay for what they did. So she turned into a detective herself."

For other participants, their families were less present in supporting them through the crisis. And in some painful situations, family members reinforced victim-blaming messages to these participants. Jennifer Thompson's experience is an example. She attempted to find support from her family, and they were emotionally unavailable to her.

> I called my mom and dad and I didn't get the response that I hoped for; nobody came. [Q: What did that feel like for you?] Well, I felt like what happened to me was just no big deal. I knew it was a big deal, but people were reacting to me as if I skinned my knee. So I felt pretty dismissed, abandoned, ignored, invalidated, all those things. The very act that just happened to me was leaving me without power, and without being in control, and without a voice. Then when people respond to you in ways that are less than compassionate, once again you feel powerless, without control, without a voice.

Reinforcing the sexism and racism of American culture, and Jennifer being a white woman, she was hurt by her mother's reaction to her assault: "I remember when I told my parents that I'm at the police station and I've just been raped and the first question was, 'Was it a Black man? Was he Black? Do you think he saw you in your leotards?' Those kind of questions that imply it's my fault, and it's worse because it was a Black man. So at some point she said, 'Are you okay?' And knowing me I would've said, 'I guess I'm okay. I'm not dead.' No one ever came. My mom never came to [me]."

Before Debbie Jones was raped, her family of origin was extremely abusive, and as a young woman she was living on her own for the first time when the intruder attacked her. While she returned to her mother's home, it was marred by past abuse that included her mother insisting she move out of her childhood home. Debbie recalls, "My sister and I had just moved into that townhouse because we both had been living with my mom who was having some of her own issues. She said that we had to move out and we were too old to live at home. So I really sometimes blamed my mom for that because if my mom hadn't pushed us to move out. . . ." Immediately after the attack, Debbie returned to her mother's house where she faced additional abuse.

> She told me to clean my room and I did, and I was nineteen and had just been raped, so I was not in the best frame of mind. But she said I had not cleaned it well enough, so she came in there and was punching me. She was punching me in the face over and over and over. I would never hit my mom because I knew she would kill me and so I am just trying to survive. We hear a knock at the door and my sister got it. And [my boyfriend] came barreling in and says, "What's going on?" And of course, she was embarrassed, [because] child abuse happens in private and he comes in. So she says, "What are you doing here?!" And he says, "What's going on in here?" And she proceeds to tell him what a piece of shit I am and I didn't clean my room. He said, "[Ma'am], Debbie loves you." She said, "That's too bad I don't love her now, I never loved her and I never will love her. Get her out of my house!" I remember bawling, and I am so broken. Where am I supposed to go and what am I supposed to do? I was barely even working because I was still healing from the rape and [my boyfriend] just said, "Get whatever you can and we're leaving."

In Debbie's experience, reframing her family situation included the relationship with her then-boyfriend transitioning into marriage and children. Within that situation, given his support during the immediate aftermath of the rape, Debbie felt safe and comforted.

CONCLUSION

This chapter has demonstrated that violent victimization impacted families in profound ways. The before-and-after realities for families were apparent to many of the participants. The primary and secondary traumas included their bodies, their lives, and their families being shattered. They sought relief and justice from the legal system. The criminal investigations and trials held out a promise that the perpetrators would be identified and incarcerated. They endured lengthy preparations for trial. The original defendants were convicted of those crimes, and many of these participants believed those convictions were just. Others, whose family members were wrongly convicted and sentenced to death, continued to fight against the legal system, not wanting the death of their family members to be compounded by the execution of other family members.

PART TWO

Tertiary Trauma

PART 2 TRANSITIONS from primary and secondary traumas to tertiary traumas associated with the wrongful convictions and exonerations. Chapter 5 documents these participants' experiences with the postconviction process and exonerations in their cases. And overall, this section offers a grounded theory of tertiary trauma constructed from the lived experiences of victims/survivors of original crimes in wrongful conviction and exonerations. Grounded theory is "a rigorous method of conducting research in which researchers construct conceptual frameworks or theories through building inductive theoretical analysis from data and subsequently checking their theoretical interpretations" (Charmaz, 2014, p. 343). By constructing a theory of tertiary trauma, the analysis presented explores sources of tertiary trauma (chapter 6), elements of tertiary trauma (chapter 7), and impacts of tertiary trauma (chapter 8). Constructing grounded theory requires analysts to collect relevant data, transcribe and code those data to reveal common aspects of lived experiences, and organize the data into meaningful lessons that promote understanding complexities (Bhattacharya, 2017).

Chapter 6, "Shattered System," analyzes how these participants experience their interactions with the legal system, from police to the postconviction process. The adversarial nature of the legal system produces winners and losers. Careers of legal system officials are made on the basis of their wins and in the context of a "tough-on-crime" legal climate that fuels racially disparate outcomes, ostensibly on behalf of victims. It does not serve victims' needs for healing in the aftermath of crime and in fact is "traumagenic" (Yoder, 2020, p. xiii). Participants in this research described both compassionate and careless experiences with police. They were included and excluded by officials. They learned about developments in their cases from media and from advocates. Their deceased loved ones were dehumanized and/or forgotten, while their own individual injuries were overlooked and minimized as concern for the exonerated original defendants rose to the surface. The tertiary trauma included discovering the identity of the actual perpetrators. When the actual perpetrator was identified, additional victims of the actual perpetrators may also have been discovered, which unleashed a wave of agony and misplaced guilt, particularly for those who provided eyewitness identification. While some of these participants were comforted by the treatment they received from specific officials in their cases, others were not. Irrespective of this, none of these participants wanted miscarriages of justice in their cases. In the end, however, the exoneration may also produce answers they need to process their anguish and confusion in their cases.

Chapter 7, "Elements of Tertiary Trauma," analyzes the contours of trauma in these participants' experiences. The contours include frustration and confusion, betrayal and deception, misplaced guilt, shame, and power-lessness. Finally, when viewed through a lens of dehumanizing sexism and racism that are present in these cases, the tertiary trauma connects to his-torical legacies of racialized harms and gendered mistreatment. In the end, this tertiary trauma alters the sense of identity of these participants and their relationship to the legal system: from crime victims to being perceived as "responsible for an injustice" (as Penny Beerntsen said), or forgotten and ignored in the aftermath of the exoneration. In the Wilhoit and Gauger families, the identity shifts included first being murder victims' family members, then being disenfranchised family members of a convicted sibling condemned to death, then being forgotten exonerees' family members with-out explanation or apology.

Chapter 8, "Shattered Grief, Loss, and Coping," explores how these participants confront the inevitable emotional toll associated with their grief and how they cope with these conditions. It presents grief as a braided fabric that includes strands of anger, depression, denial, acceptance, and bar-gaining, rather than stages as described by earlier grief scholars (Kubler-Ross, 1969). These interwoven strands ultimately shape an integration of new information into their emotional tapestry. Chapter 8 also revises the theory of coping originally offered by Westervelt and Cook (2012) that includes strategies of incorporation and avoidance and now is viewed as situational coping. Coping strategies are adapted situationally and can shift with the many circumstances these participants describe. A major consider-ation includes how connecting to the exonerated person, as a turning point, demonstrates the conjoined nature of these tertiary traumas.

CHAPTER 5

Shattered Justice

JANET BURKE'S LIFE had moved on. She was happily married and raising her teenaged children. There were moments when the traumas of being raped resurfaced in her life; she tried to cope with those moments as best she could. She was doing okay, for the most part. One day her mother called to let her know that the police wanted to talk to her about the case. When the police arrived, Janet was anxious and listened as they explained that the man who has been incarcerated for seventeen years had DNA testing done, which proved he was not guilty. The man who raped her was someone else, someone she never heard of before. They also informed her that the news would probably be in the newspapers and she needed to prepare herself and her family for the possibility of media coverage. She had tried to put the horror behind her, to let it all go, and to not think about it all the time. Janet had never told her children about her ordeal; why would she? She did not want to deal with this again. It was a "mistaken eyewitness identification" issue, that she identified the wrong man. She felt solely responsible for the error.

Exonerations typically resulted in these participants retrospectively examining the original crime, its impact in their lives, as well as the original investigations and trials and how these miscarriages of justice could have happened. Crime victims involved in this research do not always include the exact points in the postconviction processes where these events occurred. Thematic findings are presented within a broad understanding of the postconviction and exoneration process. Exonerations erupted in their lives when they learned of postconviction claims of innocence or after assisting their family members who were wrongly convicted. The postconviction events included more DNA testing, discovering the identity of the actual perpetrators, postconviction hearings and more lawyers, victims' support, and media coverage. Sprinkled throughout this chapter are hints, clues, and foreshadows to themes examined in more depth in later chapters: misplaced guilt, shame, self-blame, betrayal, trauma, confusion, frustration, grief, loss, and the quest for healing and reform.

Decades had elapsed since the victims were involved in the original trials. They worked toward healing from those unbearable traumas, their bereavements, and the original verdicts not knowing they were destined to unravel. They had been moving forward with and establishing their lives, growing up, building families. The children had continued in school, though their families felt crippled by these ordeals. The young adults had moved into adulthood, trying to find a new normal, and families of murder victims grieved their losses and continued living. They experienced many of the usual aspects of life and living: marriages, births, holidays, employment opportunities, educational aspirations, divorces, deaths, and cross-country moves. They paid their bills, bought houses, went to college, remained active in their communities as best they could, and continued trying to be strong even when they felt completely deflated by trauma triggers.

The postconviction process to pursue a claim of innocence is long, serpentine, and dependent (most often) on new evidence of innocence that was not available at the time of the original trial (Gross, 2014). Claims of innocence usually linger past the typical appeals process when the defendant has expired their legal challenges to the processes contributing to the criminal conviction. Most usual postconviction appeals occur with little awareness of the original crime victims, and seldom with their involvement. Insofar as the claims of innocence are being considered by the courts, the "defendant has no right to reconsideration; he has to convince the courts that there is a high probability of error. He has to do that without . . . access to an attorney . . . , and in a legal culture in which reconsidering trial verdicts is heavily disfavored" (Gross, 2014, p. 236). The cases represented in this study experienced postconviction procedures that included the standard appeals and then claims of innocence. The development of DNA testing in 1989, with Gary Dotson the first convicted criminal to be exonerated via DNA (Norris, 2017), generated a great deal of interest among incarcerated populations and resulted in a spike in the number of exonerations, particularly with sexual assault and homicide cases where biological evidence is more likely to be available. When forensic samples are degraded, DNA testing requires the collection of fresh biological samples whenever possible. This can include asking the original victims to provide more bodily fluids for testing. Furthermore, there may be some media coverage about the claims of innocence unfolding in court, and the original victims would surely have an interest in keeping apprised of those developments. Learning that this process is happening can be extremely traumatic for the original victims and survivors.

NOTIFICATIONS OF POSTCONVICTION CLAIMS OF INNOCENCE

The participants who were strangers to the original defendant learned about their claims of innocence in various ways. Some notifications reflected a compassionate trauma-informed approach. Presented here, for example, are Janet Burke and Regina Lane, both rape survivors, who received information from a team of police officers who called ahead and met them in person.[1] On the other hand, some notifications reflect less trauma-informed care. For example, the notification for Christy Sheppard and Peggy Sanders, family members of a homicide victim, was not personal. They saw in the local newspaper print edition that the original defendants were likely to be released within a few days.

As a young woman in 1984, Janet Burke was working at a child care center in a church early one morning when a man broke in, found her there, raped her at knifepoint, and then fled when he heard others arriving with their children. The original defendant maintained his innocence, and DNA evidence exonerated him in 2011. Two local police officers (a man and a woman) contacted her before the DNA results were reported in the media; they met her at her home and provided her with the information and with answers to her many questions as best they could. Janet recalls,

> They sat down and started talking about DNA evidence. They said the DNA evidence is showing that Thomas Haynesworth was not my attacker. And then, "We're pretty conclusive that Leon Davis was your attacker. He is in prison for other attacks." I was in this cloud it was almost like I was sitting there but I was like hovering somewhere listening. And they told me, "You've got to tell your close friends and your family because we don't know what this is going to do in the media." My friends now have no earthly idea that I was raped. My kids don't know. I never told my daughter and my son. I've got to open up all this again to my family. So they left. I didn't hear from them again until the DNA was conclusive that Leon Davis was the person and Thomas was not.

Even with an effort at compassionate in-person notification, Janet's trauma response was triggered when she felt like she was "hovering" outside of her own body. This sensation of disorientation is common within traumatic events.

Regina Lane was abducted and raped a few months after Deborah Sykes had been abducted, raped, and murdered in Winston-Salem, North Carolina. When she reported the attack to the police, she submitted to the forensic rape examination and provided evidence to the police. During the investigation she suggested to the police that it might have been the same perpetrator as the person who killed Sykes. However, the police had arrested Darryl Hunt for the Sykes murder and he was in jail awaiting trial, so they dismissed this connection, leaving Willard Brown undetected and free. As a subsequent victim of the actual perpetrator, Regina learned about the DNA results exonerating Darryl Hunt in 2004 from police officers. The police had no obligation to inform her of the outcome in the Sykes murder case, but they appeared concerned about publicity. She recalls,

> Well the receptionist at work told me, "I have two men here that need to talk to you and I've told them that you're busy, you're working and she said they're just very insistent." They told me that the person I picked out of the lineup was the DNA match for Deborah Sykes's rapist and murderer. I was stunned. I thought, "All these years and you're going to tell me this today? Why couldn't you tell me this years ago?" They said that I would probably be contacted by the press and asked me if I would not talk about the case because they were doing their investigations. They let me know that Darryl was going to be released from prison. . . . It was just very shocking.

Regina maintained a close relationship with Deborah Sykes's mother, who continued to believe that Darryl Hunt was involved in the murder of her daughter, despite the evidence pointing to Willard Brown. Regina said, "That was heartbreaking, and I can't blame her for feeling that way." With consideration for Regina, the police provided her with privacy and information, permitted her to have a supportive colleague with her, and gave her time to ask questions.

In contrast, when Christy Sheppard and Peggy Sanders learned that Ron Williamson and Dennis Fritz were to be released, the news came as a shock since they had not been kept informed of the innocence claims during the postconviction process. Debra Sue Carter had been murdered and raped in her apartment in Ada, Oklahoma, in December 1982. Her mother, Peggy Sanders, was devastated, and her young cousin, Christy, was eight years old when she died. Peggy and Christy enjoy a very close bond, and Christy has become a vocal advocate for Peggy throughout this ordeal. They learned about the exoneration in the local newspaper.

> I was in graduate school then, and Peppy called me. She was upset. There's stuff in the paper about Ron Williamson getting a new trial. And so I got the paper. And I was reading this story about what this judge said and all of that poor Ron shit just came crashing in. I had had enough. I stormed into the *Ada News* with the paper in my hand and I said, "Can you tell me where [the reporter's] office is?" I marched right upstairs and he's sitting in his office and I have that paper in my hand, and I threw it at him. And he was just shocked. I said, "I want to know what in the hell that is. So you know my people are upset and I've had damn near twenty years of too much. I've had it with this bull crap in the paper!" and "I want to know what the hell this is." And he goes to stammering around and I said, "Do you know year after year, article

after article, all you do is write about that poor son-of-a-bitch and I've had it!" I said, "You don't ever talk to our family." I mean I just went off and then I just turned around and left. Then I called Peppy and said, "I just threw myself a fit in the newspaper office."

Dissociation, shock, and outrage are understandable reactions for victims/survivors when they hear that the person they thought had harmed them was in fact claiming innocence. Learning about the claims can be jarring and disorienting and may trigger old traumas, complicate existing traumas, and inflict new traumas, especially when officials do not follow compassionate, trauma-informed care and deliver the news through trained victim advocates (see chapter 10). Such practices may be evident in Janet's and Regina's experiences where they had advance notice, time to ask questions, and additional support people present. However, more support is needed if the investigation requires additional DNA testing and biological samples collected from the victims.

DNA Testing

In the fifteen exonerations represented in this research, thirteen involved DNA evidence that exculpated the original defendants. For the homicide victims' family members, DNA evidence is one piece of a bigger puzzle that may have pointed to guilt. For the rape survivors, the process of DNA testing involved traumatic invasions of their bodies—the old rape kit swabs that were necessary, of course, but may still have required the victims to give more DNA samples, through buccal (cheek) swabs or other techniques. Janet Burke's experience included DNA evidence that exonerated the wrongfully convicted man. Accepting the DNA exoneration was extremely difficult for those victims who provided eyewitness identification of the original defendants. They described the news as shocking, disorienting, and exceedingly confusing.

Debbie Jones was nineteen years old and returning to her apartment in 1985. Robbing her apartment was an intruder, who then raped her at knifepoint. She cooperated with the forensic rape examination and with eyewitness-identification procedures; she was certain that she had identified the right man, especially since at the first court hearing the original defendant threatened to kill her, which confirmed for her that he was in fact her assailant. In 2008, she learned about the claims of innocence proceeding from the same investigator who responded to her call immediately after she was raped. His victim-centered approach was evident. He took care to be thoughtful and helpful to Debbie when he reconnected with her during the postconviction process. He informed her about the need for her to contribute a DNA sample that would be collected by scraping cells from her cheeks.

He said, "It's just a formality, they always say [he's] not guilty and of course he's guilty. We're going to test his DNA. We need to do more buccal swabs. Do you know where to find [your husband]?" . . . I said, "We are divorced and he lives [out of state]," and [the investigator] said, "We need a buccal swab on him and you and on [the defendant]." And "fortunately we still have your shirts and panties." They still have all of my DNA so they were going send that to a lab . . . and I am at work and I get up and I walk into my boss's office and look at him and started bawling crying, and nobody [at work] knew about this.

By referring to it as "just a formality," however, the investigator downplayed the possibility of the original defendant being exonerated and created a possibly false expectation that the claims of innocence would be dismissed. Months later, while at work, Debbie was informed that the DNA did not match the original defendant.

My mom was there with [the investigators], and I knew it wasn't good. They sat me down and said, "We have the results." They had a piece of paper and they said, "It wasn't [the original defendant]." And I think I smiled and I looked at them and I said, "That's not funny." And they said, "We know it's not funny, this is going to be hard for you to process." [The investigator] started tearing up and he said, "Debbie, I cannot believe it myself, but it wasn't him." I started getting mad at him, and said, "It was him! You heard him threaten to kill me!" He said, "I know, Debbie, I know, but he didn't rape you." And [it's like] you get dropped on your ass and get the wind knocked out of you, it hurts so bad in that moment you think you will die because you can't breathe can't even try to breathe, you just know you are going to die. That's what happened to me, I got the breath knocked out of me and stayed at that level of pain for a long time. I can't even quantify how long, months. Months if not a solid year of that level of pain. . . . I could not reconcile until they found [the actual perpetrator]. I could not reconcile. I hated everybody, it was an unanswered question for approximately three to four months.

While having a compassionate and advance notification is critical, presenting it as "just a formality" may create an expectation that an exoneration is not imminent, such that when it occurs the shock and trauma may be compounded. The fact is that an exoneration may be imminent, and the original victims deserve to know and have time to process and ask questions as it unfolds.

When being informed of an exoneration, crime victims may be warned by officials that the original defendant presents a danger to them. In contrast to Debbie Jones's notification, Karen M.'s experience was much briefer and occurred after the exoneration. She was unaware of the postconviction process: "I got a phone call. It was [the detective] that told me he has been exonerated. 'He was not the man that raped you and you need to stay home, do not come to the courthouse,' and that was it." Her reaction to the news that the wrongly convicted man was exonerated was to flee:

When I found out [he] was exonerated I just collapsed to my knees and I just screamed and I cried. Then I just started running. I ran and I ran. I went to a church and banged on this huge wooden door and it was locked. I kept banging on this church door and they thought I was trying to break in. Finally some lady secretary came and unlocked the church door. I'll never forget it. I explained that I needed to talk to a minister. . . . And when I realized they thought I was crazy trying to break in and it made me feel so bad. Then a minister took me into the sanctuary and I'll never forget sitting by myself in an empty sanctuary with this minister. I told him and I figured he would look at me like a piece of crap, and I was looking for mercy.

DNA evidence factored into five of the seven homicide cases, where murdered family members were unrelated to the accused person. In 1987, Jacqueline Harrison was sexually assaulted and murdered in rural southern New Jersey; her body, partially clothed with contusions and puncture wounds, including a stick protruding from her mouth, was discarded in a ditch. Her daughter, Andrea Harrison, was nearly four years old, and Dwayne Jones, her domestic partner and Andrea's father, was at work. The original defendant pursued a postconviction process that included DNA evidence. Andrea and Dwayne learned about the DNA results excluding the original defendant while attending a court hearing as part of the exoneration process. By now an adult, Andrea said, "I wanted to understand for myself," so she paid careful attention to the details in the hearing. She learned that "they did not properly store DNA samples, knowing that some of the evidence was lost or missing we don't know what happened to it. I don't know. These seven hairs are the only ones we had left. What about the other stuff, [they] just tossed it in a box? [They] literally toss it somewhere? [They] didn't store it properly?" For her, the questions and frustrations encompassed more than the DNA evidence and results: a constellation of other evidence that factored into the original conviction.

Because his DNA didn't match what they had saved, heck yeah, he is done, he is off then good for him. However, in my mind if you were the person that even was just there you know you should be in trouble too. And the only reason I think that stays on my mind is because the level of detail with what has been said by those other people in the car with him. He said this: he tossed her up in the air and watched her fall to the ground and she looked like a butterfly—who says that? [Two witnesses] just happen to both say he threw her up in the air and she floated like a butterfly? That sticks out to me.

So for Andrea and Dwayne to have faith in the DNA exoneration, they must grapple with other evidence that contributed to the conviction of the original defendant. The DNA may have excluded the original defendant as a contributor of some biological evidence, but it did not undermine the testimony evidence. The DNA results dislodged the confidence they had in the original conviction, and they had to confront the remaining nonbiological evidence that pointed to guilt.

For Christy Sheppard and Peggy Sanders, Debra Sue Carter's family, the exoneration was relatively early in the evolution of DNA evidence testing and they had one frame of reference for understanding it. Christy recalls, "They were going to test this DNA business on these jeans. The only DNA stuff I'd ever watched was on the O. J. [Simpson] trial. It came out in the paper that they were going to be released, that the DNA that had been tested did not match."[2]

Without support to make sense of the DNA results, original victims are left to their own resources to carve out a new path forward in their own healing, if they can. The revelation that the DNA is not a match to the originally convicted defendant shatters years of emotional grief and loss that they have processed. Especially for the victims who participated in police lineup processes, and whose witness testimony factored into the wrongful conviction of the original suspect, the irrefutable DNA evidence that an innocent person was incarcerated for decades detonates an emotional bomb: misplaced guilt and shame.

For example, Penny Beerntsen was sexually assaulted on a summer day while at a park with her husband and son in Wisconsin. During the investigation, Penny cooperated with the witness identification process and remained involved in the prosecution of Steven Avery, the original defendant. When DNA evidence exculpated him, she was shocked: "I want the earth to swallow me. I want a meteor to come down from heaven and just squish me. It's like this man who is the father of five children has spent eighteen years in prison for something he didn't do. And his wife, who is living in poverty, has raised five kids on her own. And his parents and his siblings have lost his companionship. And it doesn't matter that he had a record beforehand. He should not have been convicted." The conclusive evidence of the DNA results helped these participants to accept the exoneration and come to terms with the criminal justice system's fallibility in their cases, but the misplaced guilt, shame, and self-blame remained with them.

ACTUAL PERPETRATORS IDENTIFIED

The exoneration inevitably leads to questions about who actually committed the crimes. They knew they were victims of unspeakable violence; they knew *someone* had done this to them or their loved ones, and if not the person who was originally convicted, then who? And how did this happen? As mentioned before, Janet Burke learned the identity of the man who raped her at the same time she learned about the DNA exoneration. For some, the information was available upon learning of the exoneration; for others, the identity of the actual perpetrator was delayed for months or years or may never emerge.

Still, knowing the identity of the actual perpetrator does not result in successful prosecution or correct convictions. Karen M.'s case from 1980 is an example. She was home in her apartment, twenty years old, sleeping soundly. She was awakened by sounds coming from her living room; when she got up to investigate, she was attacked by the intruder and raped at knifepoint. She survived and cooperated with the investigation, including lineup procedures. The original defendant was convicted, and his DNA-based exoneration occurred in 1996. Ten years later, the DNA finally identified the culprit after the Combined DNA Index System (CODIS) revealed his identity. The actual perpetrator was arrested in a different state and charged with the crimes against Karen. Ultimately, those charges were dismissed in 2015 because the statute of limitations had expired in 1985, while the wrong man was in prison.

For Christy Sheppard and Peggy Sanders, the identity of the man who killed Debra Sue Carter was revealed to them during a court hearing, and this information was coupled with frightening and infuriating news. Christy describes the hearing:

> So the judge apologizes and explains how this works. And of course we're all just like mouth gaped open. He explained that there was indeed a DNA match to Glenn Gore. And he told us in open court, and [Peggy] found out with the whole damn town. And of course you're like what? Glenn? That doesn't make sense. How does he fit into all this? Wait a minute, [the district attorney] always said there was two [perpetrators]. What about all this evidence about two perpetrators, and now there's one? It just didn't make sense. So, they put us in a room and then the victim coordinator came in. She was wringing her hands. She explained that in fact Glenn Gore had escaped from prison that day. Are you kidding me? This has got to be a joke.

Knowing the identity of the actual perpetrator can provide important resolution to the victims/survivors. They now know who did this to them or their loved ones; they can stitch together a more accurate understanding of the events that altered their lives and can move forward with some deeper understanding of the legal system and its flaws. However, knowing the identity does not automatically result in the actual perpetrator being prosecuted and rightly convicted of the crimes. Like Karen M., Debbie Jones learned the DNA results conclusively identified the man who raped her, but the statute of limitations had expired. Millie Maxwell's father was murdered in 2000 during a home invasion by three young men wearing face masks. The originally convicted men were exonerated in 2011 and 2015 partly due to DNA evidence. One of the actual perpetrators confessed before the wrongly convicted men were exonerated. However, that confession has not resulted in charges against the actual perpetrators. While she knows that one confessed, the prosecutor's decision not to prosecute them has left her and her extended family without recourse or answers and feeling ignored and betrayed.

Learning the identity of the actual perpetrators provides answers to questions that victims need but raises other questions: who else was hurt by the actual perpetrators while the wrongly convicted people were incarcerated? When Penny learned the identity of the man who attacked her, she also learned that he had attacked many other women afterward: "[The actual perpetrator] was in the community for ten years and was finally convicted of a very brutal rape in 1995. That woman has been through hell and her life has been altered forever. And how many women were there between 1985 and 1995? He was suspected of, or charged with I think between eight and ten crimes that were sexual in nature and they can never make them stick and charges were dropped and finally this woman was finally able to identify him." This "wrongful liberty" (Norris et al., 2020; Thompson and Baumgartner, 2018) of the actual perpetrator weighs heavily on the original victims in this research because despite their best efforts to cooperate throughout the legal process, the wrongful conviction meant subsequent victims were harmed.

Exonerations do not always produce the identities of the actual perpetrators, and for those victims/survivors, not knowing who is responsible for the crimes against them contributes to a sense of frustration and betrayal by the legal system. The anguish and grief are palpable. For example, Andrea Harrison and Dwayne Jones do not know who killed Jacqueline Harrison, and they may never know. The aftermath of the exoneration leaves them with little information or understanding about how this happened or who did it, and the residual sense of betrayal for their family is evident.

POSTCONVICTION PROCEDURES AND LAWYERS

When claims of innocence were proceeding in the courts, regardless of whether DNA testing was part of it, lawyers and court schedules became central to their experiences. With the renewed activity in their cases, the original victims had no idea how long resolution would take or the traumatic toll it would exact on them. Postconviction court proceedings punctuated the lives of victims/survivors for years. They had no control over when the proceedings would occur or if they would be permitted to attend or who would help them to understand the often confusing jargon and tactics of lawyers. Each time a hearing was scheduled, the original victims had to brace themselves for the inevitable traumatic impact of attending. They would go into these events knowing that prosecuting attorneys, defense attorneys, and judges would be discussing and deciding issues about the victim's own life with little consultation or consideration given to them. They also had to brace themselves to see the original defendant in person. Some victims attended legal proceedings to learn more about what happened to them or their loved ones. Some went to support the exoneration of the wrongly convicted defendant. The original crime victims did not always recall or know the purpose of each proceeding that they attended, and none were in control of the process, which created confusion and frustration for the victims. Penny Beerntsen's frustration exploded when the judge decided to delay the proceeding by several more weeks:

> I don't even remember what the hearing was about but the judge says, "Something has come up unexpectedly" on his calendar and he can't finish the hearing and he says, "Well we need to postpone this and we need to postpone it in a timely manner." And I'm thinking [he] means tomorrow. So he looks at his calendar and he postpones the hearing until like six weeks. So he says court is adjourned. And I stand up in court and I've been in this court for years, and he kept slaughtering our last name, and I said, "I've been in this courtroom for years and you can't pronounce my name right? And then you think six weeks is timely? You are a [expletive]!" And I stormed out of court and I am halfway down the steps and the DA comes out and I have no memory of what I said, that's how out of control I was.

Despite little control over the timing or the pace of these procedures, the original victims recognized that it was a main source of information—they desired to learn about the case and to be present. For Andrea Harrison, attending the hearings was an opportunity to learn about what the courts knew about her mother's murder. She was a small child when her mother was killed and was not present during the original trial. At the postconviction hearings she listened, learned, and attended to honor her mother's life:

> This was my time to be there for myself, to see it for myself, understand for myself without anybody trying to feed me the narrative they thought that I should believe. And people think that I thought [the exoneree] did it because that's the narrative that the media painted for the first fifteen almost years after her murder. But that wasn't the case. I wanted to go because I wanted to understand for myself because if I could interpret and understand it and say, well yeah I think you guys probably did get the wrong guy. But looking at things as they started to present it, like my dad was saying, I saw how they did not do a great job.

An aspect of attending the hearings is that the accused would likely be present in order to confer with his attorneys at key moments. One of the procedures in Christy Sheppard's case involved a competency hearing for the wrongly convicted man, Ron Williamson. By this time, Christy was an adult woman with an advanced degree working in the field of mental health. She attended the hearing to learn more about the facts. She unexpectedly realized how fragile his mental health was at the time of the hearing:

> And there he is. He could've been my client. He's just sad, unmedicated, missing teeth, disheveled, you know? And [it's] really taking the wind out of me. I'm a mental health professional too and you're doing a competency hearing. Boy, it was just pitiful. And the questions they were asking him and he would refer to her as the deceased. And he talked about hearing through the TV, "They always ask me why I killed Debbie Carter, why I killed Debbie—I didn't kill her." . . . And that's the first time that my professional and my personal life just collided. I was so disappointed that he wasn't the monster, the bogeyman. He was just institutionalized, sad, and ill and pitiful. There's no justice in this. I called Peggy and said, "It's over Peppy, this man can't aid in his own defense. He doesn't even know what day it is, it's pitiful."

Attending and sometimes participating in hearings associated with the crimes against them were also part of the exoneration process for these participants. In 1991, Jacquetta Thomas's body was discovered in Raleigh, North Carolina. The investigation resulted in the arrest of someone who turned out to not be the perpetrator. Her sister Yolanda Thomas long doubted the accuracy of the original conviction. Postconviction, the innocence claim was heard before the North Carolina Innocence Inquiry Commission (NCIIC). After reading a brief that had been filed in the case, Yolanda attended the hearings in support for the wrongly convicted man and participated in the hearing: "I was not ready. I was not. I read [the brief] and it took me three days. I read it and I reread it and I read it again. I was done because everything in me from that little ounce of 'this man did not kill my sister' just blossomed. I couldn't contain myself. He didn't do it, no, there was no way, I was convinced he didn't do this." Yolanda was invited to give testimony during the process, behind closed doors and without media present. "I knew what I wanted to say, I knew how I wanted to say it, but how dare you say it because [it felt like] betrayal. This is the betrayal. I spoke to them maybe ten minutes. There was nobody in the room but us. Just the panel and me. I pleaded on [his] behalf. I said there's no way, there's no way this man killed my sister."

The ordeal of these hearings and the wrongful conviction left Yolanda Thomas with a sense of overwhelming grief, loss, and betrayal. Millie Maxwell's case also went before the NCIIC. She attended the hearings based on the compassionate support she received from the postconviction attorney representing the wrongly convicted men. "So I get the call from [the attorney], he asked if he could come to meet with us. He would like to talk with us and as many of the family members that would like to be present. So I think it was me, my grandmother, my mom and my brother went that day and we all met him at the lobby of [a hotel]. He started explaining what was going on. And he had mentioned he was going to want someone to come to the three-day hearing. Well out of the family, I agreed to go." Being drawn back into legal procedures that occur years after the original crime can be very disorienting. The hearings inevitably expose the participants to new information based on the evidence; they have no control but a deep interest in being informed. The proceedings do not change the realities of the crimes they experienced but do shift their understanding of how it happened and whatever meaning they make from it. Ultimately, their grief and loss continue and are compounded by new information and a realization of systemic flaws.

In 1984, Kathy Wilhoit's body was discovered in her small apartment. Her crying daughters were overheard by a neighbor, who called the police. When they entered the apartment they found Kathy dead and her daughters Krissy (fourteen months old) and Kim (four months old) in their cribs. Months later, the police arrested her husband, Greg Wilhoit, who was wrongly convicted and sentenced to death. The Wilhoit family remained strong and supportive of Greg, knowing that he was not responsible for Kathy's death. Krissy and Kim were raised in a loving foster family and remained close with the extended Wilhoit family. During the postconviction proceedings, the Wilhoits kept each other informed as best they could, however the lawyers did not keep them informed. The final evidentiary hearing in 1993 was another in a long series of legal events that lasted eight years. No one expected the judge to issue a directed verdict of innocence and release Greg

Wilhoit that day, but when his parents Guy and Ida Mae and sister Nancy attended the hearing, they were pleased that this transpired. Nancy Wilhoit Vollertsen recalls,

> They were trying to do two things with the evidentiary hearings: one, to disprove the bite marks and, two, to show ineffective counsel: Greg's attorney was a drunk. They did both of those things as it turned out. So we go in the courtroom and I can't get Greg to look at me. He's sitting at the defense table and he's looking down. Then the judge was talking and there's nobody else in the courtroom. It's just us. I don't remember exactly how he said it, he said, "In the case where the prosecution doesn't prove their case I can take it upon myself to make the verdict and the defense's motion for a directed verdict of innocence is granted. Mr. Wilhoit you're a free man." Just like that. I've never heard of a directed verdict of innocence.

And so suddenly Greg Wilhoit was released, returned to his family, with little or no support to help them adjust or prepare for the aftermath of this family trauma (Westervelt and Cook, 2012). Relieved with the outcome, no longer subjected to the fear that Greg would be put to death for a crime he did not commit, the Wilhoits nevertheless experienced a deep sense of betrayal by system for the prosecution and wrongful capital conviction. The murder of Kathy Wilhoit remains a cold case.

VICTIM SUPPORT

At the time these participants were experiencing the postconviction process, victim service professionals were not generally trained to help them through these procedures. Victim support, when offered, came from different sources; much of it was serendipitous instead of systematic. Several participants reported that there was no formal victim support offered to them through the exoneration process. Janet Burke concisely responds:

Q: So there was no support network around you? No victim advocate, no—?
JANET: Nothing.
Q: No counseling services, no—?
JANET: Nothing.
Q: No strategy for keeping you apprised of what was happening?
JANET: No. I had nothing. Nothing.

Likewise, Millie Maxwell reported that the "district attorney didn't even speak to us."

The victim support, however limited and untrained, was available to some as a continuation of support from the original trial trom police or investigators who worked on their cases. For example, Jennifer Thompson benefitted from the compassionate care of the original investigator in her case, Mike Gauldin. In 1984, Jennifer was sleeping in her home when an intruder broke in and raped her at knifepoint. She survived and ran for help, calling the police. The detective treated her with respect, was kind throughout the original investigation, and returned to support her through the exoneration in 1995. Jennifer reports that she trusted him in the original investigation and trial, and she continued to trust him through the exoneration process: "I'm not sure what I'd do without him." Similarly, when Debbie Jones learned that she needed to give another DNA sample, the one person who was there to support her was the investigator in her original case. "I asked why is [he] coming, how does he even remember me? He said, 'In the years I have moved to [a new] office and every time I would pack up, your case file has always been in my box.' He had it with him. Every place he went he carried me. He said, 'You touched me then, you are such a smart witness.' Even then doing the buccal swab he said, 'He did this, and we know he did this. You were the best witness I've ever had.'" Again, in an effort to be supportive of the victim, the police officer continued to support the conviction that was destined to unravel. Doing so may have been soothing in the moment, but in the end it caused unintentional additional harm for the victims. When these detectives returned to these cases, they did so to support the survivors and to answer questions as the process unfolded. It was not policy but serendipity and kindness that brought them back into the lives of these victims. While they were fortunate to have these detectives supporting them, their presence did not lessen the trauma of the exoneration or the realization that an innocent person was incarcerated for assaulting them and that the actual perpetrator was not held accountable.

Victim support also came from unexpected sources: the defendant's postconviction attorneys and legal team and other postconviction entities. Millie Maxwell's experience with the wrongly convicted defendant's post-conviction attorney was already mentioned. It was the first time someone with knowledge and authority explained everything to her and her family, what the evidence indicated, and what the process would be going forward. Yolanda Thomas, who harbored doubts about the original conviction in her sister's murder, was contacted by a postconviction attorney representing the wrongly convicted man. This call ultimately lead to Yolanda having continuing contact with the staff members of the NCIIC. These staff members provided essential information and support to Yolanda. They wanted Yolanda and her family to be informed before developments were published in the media: "They said I deserved a right to hear it first." During the hearings, the NCIIC staff members ensured that Yolanda had control over what portions of the evidence she would hear: some details of the homicide of her sister, she knew, would be too painful. "They would stop, signal I needed to leave, they would let me leave, they would show whatever [evidence] and then they would come and get me back in."

For Janet Burke, the postconviction attorney representing the wrongly convicted man offered her very helpful support: "[The attorney] showed up at my mom's house. My mom gave her my phone number, and we spoke and [she] wanted to meet. I spoke with her and fell in love with her because she was just incredible. She was absolutely incredible."

When the Wisconsin Innocence Project was handling the postconviction case of Steven Avery, Penny Beerntsen received no information from the district attorney. Out of frustration, she contacted the Innocence Project. "And I'm calling the DA to find out what's going on and he's not answering my phone calls. So I start calling the Innocence Project, [who] asked if I had an attorney and I say I have a friend, I don't pay her but she's just helping me navigate this. They said we really shouldn't be talking to you but if you have questions you can get them to [a third party] and she can call. So that's how we did it. I started to warm up to them a little bit." For postconviction attorneys, reaching out to victims is uncommon and very risky. The postconviction attorney's ethical obligation is to represent their client, even if doing so might upset victims in their cases. Postconviction attorneys may presume that victims see them as trying to undo the justice that they believed existed in their case, and reaching out may be ethically inappropriate. Everyone would be on edge. The attorneys have potentially exculpatory evidence that may overturn the conviction, leaving the victim with many questions. Answering those questions honestly and with evidence helps the victims to process and resolve the upheaval brought on by the exoneration. And these answers may not always be forthcoming from the prosecution, leaving them without options to seek support and information. This may compound the sense of betrayal by the system and resulting frustration many original victims experience.

MEDIA COVERAGE

These exonerations generated media exposure that the original victims and survivors did not control and could not limit and often compounded the traumas they endured. Several participants describe their views that the legal system had "stolen" or taken over their cases. To the extent that this occurs, the news media also serve as an accomplice to that theft. When a crime becomes a public event and the public becomes entitled to know most details, news outlets may capitalize on these cases by saturating local and sometimes national markets with lurid details and/or next steps in the cases. Most, but not all, of these participants talked about the media coverage their cases generated in complex ways; for Krissy Wilhoit Zarn and Kim Wilhoit, who were shielded from the sparse coverage of their mother's murder and their father's wrongful conviction, it was a less salient factor. In some cases, media coverage was harmful and compounded the traumas they experienced, and in other cases media coverage became a source of information and support.

Ginger Blossom's parents, Morris and Ruth Gauger, were murdered at their farm in rural northern Illinois in 1993. Her twin brother, Gary Gauger, discovered the grisly crime against his father and called the police, who later found his mother. Gary was later interrogated; the local news reported that he had confessed during the interrogation. The legal case against him produced a wrongful capital conviction, and he was sentenced to death. In 1996 he was exonerated and released. This homicide generated local press coverage, and Ginger, who continued to support her twin brother during his wrongful conviction, ignored the local media coverage of her parents' murder and brother's arrest because it was "always very negative." Because the crime occurred in a small town, the media coverage impacted how Ginger was treated in public places "because everybody knows you," despite her determination to not read it.

Most of the media coverage was local and reported graphic details of the crimes, which caused pain for these victims/survivors. It was particularly painful when the homicides also included sexual assaults. Jacqueline Harrison, Andrea's mother, for example, was depicted as a "promiscuous party girl." A recurring agony for Yolanda Thomas was that her sister, Jacquetta, was called a "prostitute" in media coverage. She was frustrated, pained, and concerned about the impact of this depiction on her sister's children. She appealed to the reporters directly,

> My last speaking out to the media, [I said] "If I can't get you to understand from the viewpoint of her immediate family, then let me appeal to you on behalf of *her children!* They are now adults, who don't know a whole lot about this, but are now reading about it because this thing has come back up in the news." We never shared with them how she lived her life and we know that the internet is [bigger] than and it was all those years ago. So these kids can find what they want to find. I said, "If you don't remember for any other reason, don't do that for the sake of her kids." She has three daughters. But, it did not stop.

Both Jacquetta Thomas and Jacqueline Harrison were Black women and were denied the basic human dignity of compassionate concern from the public; both were seen as having contributed to their own deaths. The racist and sexist coverage of their deaths created unnecessary suffering for their family members and stole from their families the opportunity to mourn with dignity and respect for the deceased.

In contrast, specific reporters became an avenue for information when communications from state officials ceased. Andrea Harrison and Dwayne Jones, Janet Burke, and Regina Lane all spoke about having helpful relationships with specific reporters. Andrea and Dwayne were interviewed by Kate King, in her *Wall Street Journal* article about the agony family members experience with exonerations.[3] They chose to participate in this report to create more public pressure to investigate the twenty-nine-year-old cold case, largely because they felt "betrayed" by the justice system. Andrea said, "If you have any information that could lead to helping us solve this case call [us], I want them to do that. I want it in the media all day every day." And Dwayne expressed his frustration: "The police have to say okay we dropped the ball, we're willing to let you open [the case] up. Until the police say that nothing can be done. And that's terrible, unfortunately they won't do it for us. They just won't do it."

Janet Burke depended on a reporter from the *Richmond Times-Dispatch* who was covering the exoneration, and he became an important source of information. "Frank Green was incredible. You know he would say, 'Janet I feel as much blame as you feel. I've reported on this and I should've seen it. I should have connected the dots.'" They built a rapport of trust and mutual respect that offered Janet essential support: "I was so lucky to have Frank Green reporting the truth."

Regina Lane, the subsequent victim of the actual perpetrator in the wrongful conviction case of Darryl Hunt, worked closely with *Winston-Salem Journal* reporter Phoebe Zerwick, at her mother-in-law's urging:

> I met Phoebe standing over my mother-in-law's bed in the hospital. And my mother-in-law was so mad at me and she said, "Why won't you talk to her?" and I said because it's not time yet. I can't do this because this has been such a big story in Winston-Salem. There's so many people involved in it and so much research and I didn't want to tell my story until I talked to the authority that needed to hear it. And even though it would have been so easy for me, I just felt like it needed to be done a certain way.

Despite her initial trepidation, Regina shared her experiences with Ms. Zerwick and the media exposure contributed to the public concern because of the "missed opportunity" (Rabil, 2012, p. 1553) to prevent the wrongful conviction of Darryl Hunt.

In cases that generated (inter)national high-profile coverage, such as those of Jennifer Thompson, Peggy Sanders and Christy Sheppard, and Penny Beerntsen, the media exposure introduced new issues to navigate. Jennifer Thompson's story has literally changed the world of eyewitness-identification procedures and wrongful convictions, thanks largely to her willingness to go public and media coverage that treated her with dignity. The PBS *Frontline* documentary "What Jennifer Saw" provided a deep dive into the flawed procedures of eyewitness identification, the hideous crime that Jennifer survived, and the legal quagmire she and Ronald Cotton endured.[4] Later, Jennifer and Ronald told their own story in the pioneering book *Picking Cotton* (Thompson–Cannino et al., 2009). This level of national exposure offered Jennifer a platform for her own voice, her own words, her own experience with this ordeal to be featured, rather than filtered through someone's editorial lens. This media exposure catapulted Jennifer into the national spotlight and gave her a voice to declare that, as a victim of violence, she never intended or wanted the wrong person to be convicted and incarcerated. Still, the journey to this national spotlight has been difficult in itself.

Christy Sheppard and Peggy Sanders learned about critical developments in their case by reading the local newspapers, and the frustration exploded when Christy confronted the local journalist. After the exonerations, more national attention came to Oklahoma when John Grisham (2006) published *The Innocent Man*, focusing on Ron Williamson and Dennis Fritz. The arrival of Grisham into their lives was part of a larger flurry of media attention. Christy recalls helping Peggy through this time:

> Around that time was when Court TV was here and Glenn Gore was going to trial again. John Grisham was going to write this book. Court TV called, and Peppy called me to be moral support. So they ended up interviewing me too, which I never did before. That's when it really sunk in that a lot of other people knew what happened to [Debbie] and we didn't. Strangers knew more about what happened to her than her own mother knew! I asked that lady, "So this John Grisham thing is this real?" She said, "It's happening, it's under way." So I told Peppy, "This John Grisham deal is for real and it's going to blow up just because of who he is." It turned out to be a good book. "This has a name, a brand attached to it and they're going to talk about Debbie in this you know. You need to get right with yourself. This book is not about her [alone]; it is about [Ron]." But Ron and Dennis and Debbie are forever entangled.

Penny Beerntsen's case also exploded on a global level due to the Netflix documentary *Making a Murderer*, featuring the wrongful conviction of Steven Avery and later the homicide of Teresa Halbach and Avery's homicide conviction.[5] During the exoneration process, Penny lived outside of Wisconsin and remained aware of the media coverage. "When Steve was exonerated he becomes a local celebrity. There's a lot of media attention. We're living out of state but I have friends saying every day the front page of the newspaper is another article about Steve. Some beauty salon out of

Green Bay, because he came out of prison with a long beard gave him a makeover, cut his hair and beard. So initially I'm really feeling I'm a horrible person and all the attention on Steve isn't helping that. It's making me feel like everything I dealt with is now considered irrelevant."

Having been rendered publicly irrelevant after the exoneration, Penny went on with her life, volunteering as a restorative justice practitioner in prisons, sharing her experience and dialoguing with incarcerated men. Finding purpose and meaning in that work was very rewarding. When she was invited to participate in the Netflix documentary, which was a ten-year process, she declined. Because so much of her case was now in the public domain, and because she was identified publicly, the documentarians were free to use her name, information, and images in their film.

> I watched the first episode and I felt they did an accurate job. As I watched the remaining episodes I felt there were things that were left out. And then with the huge response and Dr. Phil did two shows and he has a picture of my battered face up there and my daughter has never seen that photo so I'm very angry at the loss of the privacy. . . . So I feel like I don't have any privacy anymore. That's been shattered. I guess it was shattered when I chose to go public with my name. I felt you should be able to put your name behind your story and say this is what happened. I made a horrible mistake this is how that mistake happened, and these are things we can do to prevent that mistake.

Penny is also concerned that, given this loss of privacy and the extremely popular documentary, if she speaks or writes publicly it might generate additional pain for the Halbach family. She regrets that impact and bears it in mind. Furthermore, by referring to herself having made "a horrible mistake" when identifying the wrong man, she absorbs the misplaced guilt and self-blame for the flawed process that generated the wrongful conviction. Another layer of painful impact from media exposure includes, as Penny continues,

> online comments—it's like enough with the guilt already! Which is why I don't read anything online anymore. It about killed me. That people not understanding the process and like "she lied about his eye color" well my actual assailant has blue eyes too so it wasn't like I lied, I got it wrong. It was a mistake. But anyway . . . it's out there my name is out there, Dr. Phil had my picture up. Local media has been wonderful. No local media has called me and they haven't use my name so bless their hearts. . . . BBC is calling me and getting my phone number and Australia[n reporters are] calling.

Online comments have been extremely painful for several of these victims. Jennifer Thompson talked about reading hateful and violent comments toward her and being a target of death threats. Seven of the eight rape cases include interracial crimes, and the racial tensions present in our culture boil over in the online comments people post on these news articles. Tomeshia Carrington-Artis, who was twelve years old when she was raped, is African American, and her attacker was a white man; she was targeted with horribly racist comments from online news reports: "'You black b[itch] sent the wrong guy to prison,' and 'her family needs to be burned up' and 'she needs to go to prison, that n——need to go to prison,' stuff like that." Janet Burke, who is white and was raped by a Black man, reported, "Most of them were racial comments, and one of the comments was 'they should allow him to rape her daughter.'"

Media coverage for victims in wrongful conviction and exoneration cases compounds the traumas of the exonerations themselves. Perpetuating the cultural narrative that the victims are solely responsible for the wrongful conviction shackles these victims with misplaced guilt, shame, and self-blame for the errors that the legal system produced. The media do little to correct that fallacy. Racist and sexist attacks from online comments and in other forums add more pain to an already excruciating situation.

FINDING ACCEPTANCE AND MOVING FORWARD

These participants also described some family impacts of the exonerations, several decades after the original crimes. They came to accept that their families would continue to integrate or avoid the pain of the original losses they endured. A weariness may have set in for these families. For Peggy Sanders and Christy Sheppard, the exoneration brought intense public attention, media coverage, and additional agonies. They remained close, and Christy Sheppard remained devoted to her aunt, Peggy Sanders. "It never really ends," Christy said. But they did become more adept at navigating their lives within this high-profile attention, and Christy's devotion to her family remains strong. For the Wilhoit family, when Greg was exonerated and released from Oklahoma's death row, they faced another challenge: his reentry needs (Westervelt and Cook, 2012). Again, the Wilhoit family rallied in support of Greg, who was able to build a stronger relationship with his daughters, Kim and Krissy. Bereavements continued: Greg Wilhoit passed away in 2014, and then Guy and Ida Mae followed him in 2017 and 2018, respectively. Through it all, the Wilhoit family remains close, resilient, and devoted to each other.

Making sense of the hard realities of family members' hurtful responses to their crimes, and in the aftermath of the exonerations decades later, the rape / sexual assault survivors and their families had to navigate a tricky set of conditions: internal family dynamics and possible internalization of racism on account of the interracial violence they endured. Jennifer Thompson, whose mother did not come to care for her in the wake of her being sexually assaulted, has come to understand that her mother does not exhibit empathy. Jennifer now understands the emotional distance with loving detachment. "I love my mother. I've spent most of my life trying to seek her approval and get her to care, but that's just not going to happen. It's kept me very guarded with her and I don't give her a lot. She's not an evil person that just sits there, trying to figure out ways she could hurt me, she just doesn't have an empathy gene." Finding acceptance and moving forward within those parameters frame possible options of what can be expected within a family during tough times. When Debbie Jones learned about the exoneration in her rape case, she was raising her three sons, none of whom knew about her ordeal. The exoneration required her to tell her sons, and she was concerned that the fact she had been raped by a Black man could ignite some racism among her sons. She had to navigate that possibility: "It was horribly hard. I don't want to raise racist children. I don't like racism, it disgusts me, I don't want to be a part of it."

Ultimately, families remain a cornerstone in the lives of these participants and affect how these participants move forward. They have seen their loved ones react to their visible and invisible losses in ways that shore up support for each other and/or compound the harms among each other. The harrowing ordeals of violent crimes and exonerations in their lives transform these experiences from a horrible event that happened decades ago from which they may never heal to a trauma that resurfaces and opens old wounds, inflicts new wounds, and tests the mettle of a family. Reframing a life, and a future, is inevitable in these situations; as the original victims were catapulted into these situations without control, consent, or guidance, their families exhibited coping strategies that reflected their devotion or debilitation, their resiliency or refusal to concede support to the victims.

Experiences with exonerations varied. For those whose loved ones were wrongly convicted of the murders of other family members, the exonerations came as a welcome relief, though beyond their control. They remained closely involved in the legal process following the original conviction. For those whose crimes did not involve family members, the exoneration process was also uncontrollable and often confusing. For most of these victims/ survivors, the exoneration process ultimately revealed the identity of the actual perpetrator, who may or may not have been prosecuted. This unleashed more layers of stress, frustration, and fear. When the actual perpetrators are not identified, the victims/survivors are left without answers, without information, and with a sense that the legal system has betrayed their trust. When the actual perpetrators are identified it may provide answers, and the need for the truth never expires.

CONCLUSION

This chapter examined the experiences of original crime victims and survivors whose cases resulted in exonerations of the originally convicted defendants. The exonerations occurred years after the crimes. For some the exoneration came suddenly without advance notification; for others it came after years of doubt about the guilt of the originally convicted defendants; and for others it came after years of advocating for their wrongly convicted family members. Notifying victims alternated between no effort from the system officials to keep the victims informed to compassionate and conscientious efforts to do so. The process sometimes included the original victims having to provide additional biological samples from their body to test the DNA evidence, and for some it shocked their recollections of victimization based on their eyewitness identification. The results left most of these original victims confused, frustrated, angry, and relieved when the wrongly convicted person was their family member. A vexing problem in these situations for legal system professionals is determining when and how to involve crime victims when their cases move toward postconviction innocence claims. Drawing from these experiences, chapter 10 outlines policy recommendations for victim service professionals and legal system officials to consider as exonerations unfold in their jurisdictions.

The exonerations, though, propelled these victims into an excavation of their cases and a crisis of faith in the legal system. They searched for answers: How could this have happened? Where did the mistake occur in the process? Are they to blame for the miscarriage of justice? What happens next? The traumatic reactions that confront them include misplaced guilt, shame, self-blame, confusion, betrayal, frustration, anger, and in some situations relief that the nightmare of wrongful conviction is over and, acknowledging unexpected and new ordeals awaiting them, coping and healing.

CHAPTER 6

Shattered System

SEAN MALLOY WAS JUST starting his senior year of high school when his sister Noreen was killed in an armed robbery at her job. Losing his sister to a violent crime caused unbearable agony in his family; his parents were devastated, as were his brothers. They depended on the police and prosecutor to investigate the crime, arrest the perpetrator, and lock him up. That did not alleviate the loss, and Sean's mother died a few years later of "a broken heart." He had feared that the investigation was inadequate. Both Sean and his father thought the conviction was based on a "weak" case. Ultimately, the convicted man was exonerated after many years. This meant that the homicide of Noreen Malloy was now a cold case. It is unlikely that new evidence will emerge or that reinvestigating with the existing evidence would produce answers to their questions. Sean Malloy said his father will probably never know what happened to Noreen.

Going into the criminal legal system can provide victims an opportunity to seek redress, to find information, and to deal with their traumatic experiences. Cultural expectations for seeking redress in the legal system include being treated with compassion, being taken seriously, and being offered support. The cultural lore is that justice, however that may be defined by people seeking it, is available through the legal system. This lore produces expectations for victims and for the public when they engage in the criminal investigation process. Media portrayals of crime and justice in the late twentieth century typically reinforced law and order and punitive mentalities that saturate political and entertainment landscapes (Cook, 1998; Kohm, 2009). Thus, the legal system as a public institution provides victims "the opportunity for justice" (Walklate, 2012, p. 113) and may produce an overexpectation from people in the system. "Reporting the crime, cooperating with the police, working with the prosecutor, and taking the case to court can be positive experiences for crime victims. . . . It gives victims a way to fight back, to do something to achieve the satisfaction they need and deserve" (Bard and Sangrey, 1986, p. 110). Thus, justice system officials become crime fighters alongside the victims of crime whose cases are processed in the legal system, despite their training that "encourage[s] them to give the victim low priority" (Bard and Sangrey, 1986, p. 133) and the low priority given to "accuracy of criminal verdicts" (Simon, 2012, p. 221).

Victims' involvement in the legal process is believed to increase the accuracy of the outcome, by providing critical information for the prosecution of crimes (Kelly, 1990). Generating expectations that criminal justice proceedings involve a "search for compassion" (Walklate, 2012, p. 116) produces ancillary expectations that victims' needs will be met through the legal system by deploying the state's punitive power; and in fact, it is the only avenue to meet victims' needs (Bard and Sangrey, 1986). Therefore, the lure of justice includes the legal system being available to people who are harmed, where their pain can be taken seriously and they can seek compassionate remedy. The lure of justice also includes a determination among crime victims that once apprehended the culprit will not have an opportunity to harm others (Bard and Sangrey, 1986). Victims withstand the ordeal of the legal process in seeking the promise of safety for themselves and potential future victims.

While the lore provides the lure, the experiences of victims presented here offer some bleak realities that justice remains elusive, that the system itself is traumagenic, as additional harms occur during the process and may recur years after the original ordeal is believed to be over. The legal process produces winners and losers as the ultimate outcome (Simon, 2012). The adversarial process creates a "trial [that] is not concerned with what actually happened at the crime scene, but with what can be proven in court" (Simon, 2012, p. 210). Victims are caught in the machinery of the legal system believing the lore that cooperating will produce safety and answers. This chapter explores how these crime victims describe their experiences in the system: with police, prosecutors, defense attorneys, postconviction attorneys, innocence projects, the death penalty, the pain of wrongful liberties for actual offenders, and additional harms to more victims. It closes with their thoughts on how well the system works. Often, to make sense of the wrongful convictions and exonerations and the system that produced those catastrophes, these participants incorporated their original investigations and trials as a frame of reference or backdrop to their experiences during the exonerations. This chapter includes participants' retrospective recollections about their experiences within the legal system from the beginning of their ordeal through to exonerations.

During the 2016 Innocence Network conference in San Antonio, Texas, Darryl Burton attended a panel where Jennifer Thompson was speaking on post-exoneration issues. Burton was incarcerated for twenty-four years, wrongly convicted of homicide in Missouri. During her presentation Thompson outlined the "circles of harm" that wrongful convictions create for original crime victims and the wrongly convicted. Burton referred to these shared experiences as "parallel hell." This research confirms their paired observations. Both the original crime victims and the wrongly convicted defendants experience intense anxiety, fear, and uncertainty along the way. A compelling demonstration of this parallel experience is documented in *Picking Cotton* (Thompson-Cannino et al., 2009). The parallel journey for Jennifer Thompson includes acknowledging that while Ronald Cotton was incarcerated, she tried to pick up the pieces of her life while recovering from primary and secondary traumas. Upon learning of his exoneration, she experienced excruciating anguish and grief, confusion and turmoil. The parallel journeys unfold on the same obstacle course of adversarial legal proceedings, investigations, lineups, court dates, hearings, and so on. Several other victims/survivors experienced similar feelings; as Christy Sheppard pointed out previously, their lives were "forever entangled."

None of these original victims in this research expected to be caught in the "web of impact" (Westervelt and Cook, 2012, p. 84) that exonerees also experienced. Alan Gell, for example, shared that after receiving an apology from the surviving son of the man who was murdered in which he was wrongly condemned to death, "it felt real good because I was, all that time, [thinking] the victim's family [was] hating me and wanting me dead. I wanted somehow to let them know that I didn't do it and they got the wrong person, . . . that means you're not getting justice" (Westervelt and Cook, 2012, p. 164). The agony of the original crimes and then the legal ordeals that followed impact the victims conjointly with the wrongly convicted. Their experiences collided and converged in courts, in hearings, in the media, in the post-exoneration process, and in reconciliation or healing opportunities in the aftermath.

Debra Sue Carter's cousin, Christy Sheppard, captures this parallel impact when she recalls an experience at the Innocence Project:

I had my first trip to New York. [My husband, Peggy Sanders, and I] got on an elevator to go to the fundraiser and this nice-looking Black guy gets on the elevator, not very tall, real cute, about our age. He is all dressed up and he looks at my husband says, "Man, do you know how to tie?" He had a tie in his hand and [my husband] was like, "Man you don't want me to tie it. I don't wear a tie enough to know how to tie it." And he's like, "All right thanks." And we went our separate ways. We get down to the fundraiser and there's this big screen where they were showing a video and I looked at the screen, and it's that guy that was in the elevator. He was [an] exoneree, and they had done a documentary about him. I don't remember his name. I realized he's my age and he

was nineteen when he was convicted; and I was going to college, buying a cell phone, and buying my first house, and getting married, and
having a kid, and having another kid, and graduating from college, and
all these huge milestones. He sat in a jail cell.

And Christy's cousin who was murdered also never had these opportunities
to build her own life, which is a painful reality that her mother, Peggy
Sanders, faces every day: "All she ever talked about was she wanted to get
married and have some children. She always wanted that."

In a less public interaction, Tomeshia Carrington-Artis bumped into
the exoneree's family in an elevator at one of the legal proceedings, and it
became a moment for understanding and compassion to be expressed
between them: "When we were on the elevator [his mother] looked at me
and she said 'Tomeshia, you still look like that beautiful twelve-year-old
little girl.' And I just busted out crying and she hugged me and hugged me.
She said, 'It's not your fault, you were a child.'"

Demonstrating the conjoined harms and healing is Karen M.'s commitment to the exoneree's need for financial compensation. When asked what
would help her to feel whole again, she revealed how her harm is connected
to the exoneree's harm: "[Q: So compensation for [the exoneree] is one of
the things that you would identify that you need to feel whole?] Yeah but
mainly for him to feel whole. I want him to feel whole. I'm okay. I want
him to get that. He deserves it. He spent fourteen years in prison for a crime
he didn't commit, you know how could you make that okay? I don't know
how to start—I talked to [several officials]. I don't know where to go. [They]
won't talk to me, I don't know what to do."

By acknowledging this parallel agony, many participants see the actual
perpetrators and legal system as the main sources of the pain they all endure.
The actual perpetrators inflict the most terrifying and tragic harm, and the
legal system steps in to investigate and pursue charges. Because it is a system
run by humans, errors are inevitable: there may be a completely responsible
and ethical investigation, a rush to judgment, a problem of tunnel vision, or
a lackadaisical investigation. This generates collisions that these victims,
additional victims of the actual perpetrators, and the wrongly convicted
experience at every step in the process, from investigation to aftermath.

POLICE

To protect and serve. This cultural lore of law enforcement suggests a
promise of assistance, compassion, and support. For the murder victims'
family members, there was no action required to report the crime; for the
rape / sexual assault victims, they desperately engaged the police and participated in the investigation process. Thus, police officers began their work:

to establish some control over the situation, secure the crime scene, inter-view the immediate victims and/or witnesses, and so on. In retrospect, some victims described their experiences with police who delivered com-passionate care, information, assistance, and support throughout the entire process and were centered on the victims. Some described police officers whose behavior toward them was confusing, frustrating, and traumatic, who were less victim centered. Their experiences include feeling alienated, appreciating victim-centered treatment, and experiencing less victim-centered treatment.

Establishing control over the case can bring relief to survivors, but can be alienating at the same time. Alienation emerges when victims come to realize that their trauma is no longer only their trauma. In an adversarial system, the state becomes the institutional victim of crime (Walklate, 2012) and proceeds to exercise discretion in how to proceed with the case. As mentioned previously, after Jacquetta Thomas was murdered, her sister Yolanda Thomas said, "It's a state issue." Penny Beerntsen's sexual assault investigation resulted in a conflict between the police department and the sheriff's office, both of which were investigating different suspects; one was the actual perpetrator. As a result, she was unsure about which agency to believe.

When law enforcement takes control of the case, it may comfort and reassure victims, but they risk alienating crime victims who depend on them for protection and resolution. Police become custodians of the case, using their discretion to conduct the investigations and make decisions about evidence and suspects and about how to process many sources of information (Simon, 2012). In some of these cases, victims described their interactions with police officers who were respectful and supportive from their first contact after the original crime to the exoneration outcome. In other cases, original victims describe police officers who were unhelpful, unavailable, or unconcerned about the victims. Both types of experiences are presented here, pre-exoneration and post-exoneration.

Experiences with victim-centered police officers who responded with compassion and information about the case and who answered questions in a timely manner are plentiful in this group of crime victims and survivors. Debbie Jones, who was raped by an intruder at age nineteen, immediately called the police. She said, "He was not a bad cop. This was not bad police work; this was human error. That is all it was. It was human error, and it wasn't my error—it was the perfect storm." Jennifer Thompson's experience is emblematic. Mike Gauldin was the police officer who treated her with respect and compassion: "Oh my God, I'm not sure what I'd do without Mike Gauldin and I wonder that a lot." He answered her questions, pro-vided accurate information, reconnected with her during the exoneration process, and remained an important supporter throughout the ordeal. For Debbie Jones, Jim Hammond, the police officer who took her to the hospital after she was raped, returned when the exoneration process was unfolding. He never forgot her: during the intervening years, he kept her file on his desk. "He protected me from this horrible guy and he walked me through the process and he really cared about me and I remember that." After the exonerations in these two cases, the police officers facilitated their meeting the exonerated men. Here's how Debbie recalls it:

> [The police officer] thought he was really going to have to twist my arm to get me to do it. He said, "[The other detective] and I are going to come eat lunch with you and you think about it and we will talk about it." They picked me up and we went to lunch, and immediately I said, "I want to meet him." They just knew how bad I hated him. And they were like, "Are you sure?" "Yeah I want to meet him." [So they asked] "Well how did you get to that?" They were shocked and I said, "Because when you called me I could hear the peace in your voice and I need that peace." That's why I met [him]. I needed that peace.

This experience demonstrates the importance of trauma-informed care that police officers can use when aiding a crime victim: informing them ahead of time, asking what they need, providing it to them, and supporting the choices that they make along the way (within the framework of the law, of course). Elements of victim-centered treatment experience included compassionate gestures in the immediate wake of the assault. Karen M. recalls a woman police officer who helped her put on her robe. For Penny Beerntsen, one of the police officers called to ask her more questions about the days leading up to her assault because they had a hunch about the perpetrator and needed more information from her (their hunch turned out to be accurate, but that was not known until years later). This victim-centered police response was described primarily by white women rape victims.

Experiences with police by homicide victims' family members revealed some painful, disappointing, and frustrating trends. Their experiences ranged from receiving no or little information about the investigation to unfilled promises to reinvestigate cold cases. The experiences include the early investigations immediately after the original crime and then continue with police responses to requests for renewed efforts after the exonerations. For example, after his sister was murdered, Sean Malloy recalled, "It went on from August, we didn't find out [about the arrest] till after the New Year. And it was 'Oh we had somebody but we didn't want to tell you because we had him in jail,'" which frustrated the Malloy family. The post-exoneration promise to reinvestigate the case and find the actual perpetrators also frustrated these victims. Sean Malloy commented, "It is sickening isn't it? It's just sick. You know, my dad is going to go to his grave not knowing what happened to his daughter."

After the exoneration in her sister's homicide, Yolanda Thomas recalls the police officers' promise to reinvestigate the case, which she learned about when a news reporter called her. "That police commissioner . . . looked me in my face and couldn't explain to me why he went on TV and said he was going to start this investigation all over again, but he couldn't call me. I'm getting phone calls from [local media], and I'm at work. . . . 'Um yes did you hear the chief of police just made an announcement?' Okay 'will you tell me what he said?' Can you imagine how I felt? Yeah I'm still a little hot about that." As of this writing, no new information has emerged in this case.

The impact of an unsolved homicide lingers forever. The bereaved feel a sense of betrayal and frustration that the police have not fulfilled their promise to protect and serve them. For Andrea Harrison and Dwayne Jones, the agony of the cold case is palpable, especially when they socialize in the small town where Jacqueline Harrison was murdered. Dwayne shared this, "The fact that the police in our town weren't equipped to handle a murder like this but they had the avenues to go to the state police. They could have gone to the [state] right there down the street. And she deserves that. I think because they weren't equipped to handle this a lot of stuff they didn't do right. They should've asked for help. She deserved for them to ask for help. That's not right. And yet we live with it every day."

And for Andrea Harrison, also frustrated with the cold case, there is a persistent fear that the violence might recur: "[It's over] thirty years since my mother was murdered. And it still a cold case. For me and my sister it is a lingering thing because if [the exoneree] didn't do it [who did]? Who's to say that somebody hasn't just moved around the corner? Or they live around the corner from my dad?" For the participants whose family members were murdered and whose other family members were wrongly convicted, the disappointing experiences with police started early. Ginger Blossom recalled that after her parents were murdered and her brother was arrested, the police did not maintain contact about the investigation: "They weren't interested in talking to me because I wasn't on their side; they had no interest in me."

And for the Wilhoit family, Nancy Wilhoit Vollertsen recalls, "As far as the police calling us, no. I know mom would periodically call them, but they basically didn't give us any information at all. They just kept saying that they were looking into it and they were following some leads you know stuff they always say." Nancy also shared that her nieces wanted to know more about her mother: "My youngest niece [was] showing interest in her mother's murder and she and my mom and dad went down to the to the Tulsa County police department and talked to them and they said that they were going to reopen the case but they didn't." Kim and Krissy Wilhoit added this:

KIM: We've gone to speak with detectives numerous times throughout the years and they say they're looking into it but we really don't know.
KRISSY: We really need to put forth more [effort].
KIM: We go about once a year and bug them. We've even done some of our own research a little bit into Kathy and just trying to find people before she met Greg so we could just find out more about her.

The failed investigations represented in these victims' experiences belie the lore and lure of a criminal justice system that serves victims' needs. Furthermore, when cases remain unsolved for decades, the fear of the actual perpetrator returning to inflict more harm does not end, as Andrea Harrison expressed. These experiences reveal that some survivors encountered a police process that was compassionate, while others did not. As disappointing as these experiences are, they also provide valuable lessons for reform, covered in chapter 10.

LAWYERS

Lawyers were mentioned regularly by these participants. Lawyers are officers of the court and generally fall into two broad groups when it comes to criminal courts: prosecutors and defense attorneys. Most people who endure criminal proceedings do not spend much time with lawyers; the assembly-line legal system shuffles people through depending on what they say and when they say it. The majority of criminal charges are resolved through defendants pleading guilty, with the advice of a defense attorney who may try to procure the best deal possible from the prosecutor. Usually, crime victims or survivors have little involvement in those proceedings (Sered, 2019). For criminal cases resulting in exonerations, original crime victims had recurring contact with local district attorneys, defense attorneys, and later postconviction attorneys as well as lawyers from various innocence projects. This section explores the varying experiences victims described with attorneys. As with their interactions with the police, their experiences reveal some caring and helpful attorneys, and others who did not serve these survivors well. Several victims were surprised by the support they received from the postconviction attorneys who worked for innocence projects in their cases representing the original wrongly convicted defendants.

Local district attorneys (DAs) typically present themselves as champions for victims, seeking justice on their behalf. The victims in this research shared examples that reveal helpfulness, as well as perceived incompetence, carelessness, and selfishness. All told, the lingering harms from DAs continue to impact these victims. Initially, the local DAs were victims' lifeline to information: Tomeshia Carrington–Artis recalls that the DA offered her helpful advice on what to expect from the media coverage that sometimes was inaccurate: "[He] had told me that in the beginning that 'that's what the media does. It's a story. You know what happened.' Because there were times I really did call his office, 'Well I didn't know about [a detail the news reported.] Why didn't you tell me this?' and he was like, 'That's not true. But I tell you, I'm going to tell you the truth.' So he made me very comfortable, [he] did, and my detectives."

Millie Maxwell described helpfulness after upheaval in the DA's office. The new prosecutor is someone with whom she hopes to find answers and possibly resolution to the murder of her father. "So we're sitting and we're waiting and I think more or less the family is comfortable with [the DA] now. We're not going to try to rush it because we know it takes time. After all these years it's going to take time to figure out because this is a pretty exhausting case." She appreciates that "he listens" to her and her family.

Penny Beerntsen described incompetence and upheaval in the prosecutor's office that exacerbated her sense of frustration. "After the preliminary hearing, the district attorney forgot to file the formal violent charges, even though [the defense] attorney reminded him you've got like one day so we didn't file the information on time which means, under Wisconsin statute, the judge had to throw out the first preliminary hearing. There had to be a second preliminary hearing. So I was upset with that and then his attorney got pneumonia and was ill for quite a while so there had to be an attorney substitution which then obviously the new attorney needed time to prepare, so there was another delay."

Dwayne Jones, whose domestic partner, Jacqueline Harrison, was murdered more than thirty years ago, a case that is now cold, said the current prosecutors with jurisdiction over the case "won't talk to me." There is evidence of someone (a "Mr. X") involved in killing Jaqueline Harrison, though police will not provide information to Dwayne about this person. "I asked back when they told us about [Mr. X]. I said, 'Can you just tell me if they're Black or white?' . . . 'I can't tell you that.' That immediately cuts us right out. And I hope you write that." Prosecutorial discretion can be complex and nuanced; however, these victims desired an opportunity to be heard, to listen to those complexities, and to be informed about the process as it unfolds. Christy Sheppard shares an unsparing conclusion about the local DAs: "They were all so selfish about how this is going to affect themselves, how they don't want to look bad in handling this just right." Christy (and others) reached this point of outrage after many years of legal turmoil.

In the cases where family members were accused of killing other family members, the local prosecutor ceased being a source of information or solace. The animosity creates lingering harms that these victims must then deal with. Guy Wilhoit, whose son Greg was wrongly convicted of killing his wife, recalls, "I tell you the worst part of it for me was the trial when you listen to this prosecutor telling how bad [Greg] was. . . . Even after Greg had been released, the prosecutor keeps talking about he's guilty."

Few participants spoke about the original defense attorneys to express similar frustration. Continuing with the Wilhoit family case, Ida Mae recalled struggling to find a defense attorney for Greg, whose original lawyer who was frequently drunk. "We had [hired] attorneys and then when it came time to have the trial they didn't know what was going on. So we fired them." Guy Wilhoit summed it up: "We were terrible at picking attorneys. We were so naïve." Eventually, Nancy Wilhoit Vollertsen shared this observation about the defense attorneys:

> [They were] two of the top defense attorneys in the state. And mom and dad paid them either thirty or forty thousand dollars and they took the case. . . . Greg said they spent the next year just telling him that the prosecution had this smoking gun and these two expert witnesses. They were offering a really good deal and the DA would give him a really good deal if he would plead guilty. And to Greg's credit, he refused to do that. He said, "How could I ever look my children in the eye again if I said I killed their mother just to save my own skin? I won't do it." And he didn't. And we still have the letters my dad wrote to the Oklahoma Bar Association that said these guys are doing nothing. We've paid them we paid them about thirty thousand dollars and they have done nothing.

Surprisingly, though it is not their responsibility, some postconviction attorneys representing the incarcerated person whose claims of innocence drove these cases provided critical support and information to these participants.[1] But it did not always start out smoothly. After registering with the victims' services office to be notified of developments in the case involving her sister's death, Yolanda Thomas received an unexpected call from someone who wanted to talk to her about it. Still, Yolanda was surprised.

> She probably didn't get a chance to tell me who she was. Just the fact that she wanted to talk to me about my sisters' death, I wasn't hearing it! "No ma'am, don't call me. I don't even know why you're on my phone. I don't want to talk to you." I was very nasty to her. I was. I'll be honest. And she got her two cents in and she said, "Oh I just wanted you to know that we're looking into the possibility of the person who was convicted of killing your sister did not kill your sister." And I didn't want to hear it. I was more on, "How did you get my number? Why are

you on my phone? Why would you call me on my job?" I mean I was just angry and but I let her get her spiel out and then we were getting ready to hang up and I said, "I just want you to know I never believed he did it." And I hung up. I didn't want to talk to her anymore.

Cold calls to original victims/survivors can be jarring and traumatic. Even with the best of intentions, and in a situation like Yolanda's where she had lingering doubts about the guilt of the original defendant, they can be very upsetting.

When the innocence project attorney first contacted Janet Burke, she was very apprehensive. After making an appointment in advance, the attorney was informative, compassionate, and spent as much time as Janet needed to talk to her about everything that had happened. For some original victims postconviction attorneys became unexpected allies. Millie Maxwell's experience is especially illuminating. Because the system officials were no longer communicating with Millie and her family, she had no source of information or answers to her questions, no way to find out what would happen next in the criminal charges related to the death of her father. The postconviction attorney contacted her; he informed her that the young men may be innocent. "When he had called it was just like, 'Wow, well maybe he knows something that we don't know' because at that time the justice system had shut us down. It was like boom somebody's charged for the case in the crime and that's it, it's over with. I think that's what they thought it was going to stop at and end. But then these boys started fighting for their own freedom and saying that they were pressured into taking these pleas or that they were threatened by the justice system that if they didn't take the plea." She describes this postconviction lawyer as "really supportive"—he provided her with information that no one else had given her. He hosted a meeting for her family to learn as much as possible about the case and to answer their questions. He was considerate, helpful, and respectful and ultimately earned Millie's trust. "I would say the best support for us as far as somebody helping us would be the Innocence Inquiry Commission, for me. Because that's where I learned the majority of what really went on with this case." (The North Carolina Innocence Inquiry Commission is described more fully in chapter 10.)

Some of these participants recalled the local innocence projects attorneys who said that the *flawed system*, not the victims themselves, produced the wrongful conviction. This was especially salient to the rape survivors who had participated in flawed eyewitness-identification procedures. This is, in a sense, the first step toward finding solace and understanding for what had happened and how the miscarriages of justice occurred. Janet Burke's case is an example: "[The innocence project attorney] was really trying to get me to focus on when I picked [the exoneree] out was there something in that *process* that went wrong. And you know I had spent a whole lifetime trying to forget all of those things and here I was obsessing over trying to remember how and why I picked him out of that picture ID." By emphasizing the flawed process, the original victims can accept that the anguish and guilt they feel are in fact misplaced; it was not their responsibility to conduct the lineup procedures. Furthermore, referring to the flawed process is more precise when outlining how wrongful convictions can occur.

Several participants talked about their contact with innocence projects connected to their cases. It is important to recognize that innocence projects around the country have attorneys on staff and may also have social workers, policy reform advocates, and others. Innocence projects exist in most states and are formally independent. The Innocence Network facilitates collaboration nationally and internationally.[2] Some participants in this research had stressful experiences with innocence projects and were extremely apprehensive about communicating with them. A particularly traumatic aspect of Debbie Jones's case was when the wrongly accused defendant threatened to kill her at one of their first court proceedings. She recalls it vividly. After he was exonerated and released, she feared that he might carry out that threat. When asked by the local innocence project to tell her story at their public event, she included this detail. She later received a call from a staff member at the innocence project requesting that she not relate that detail again in the future. This had a chilling effect on Debbie, and she became angry with the innocence project. "I was so angry! How dare you tell me to change my story to suit your feelings? Nope. And I knew right then and there I will not do [public] talks anymore." Ultimately, Debbie called another attorney who works in postconviction litigation to seek support. The response she received was supportive, reassuring Debbie: "'You tell your story.' She was awesome. And I told my story and I don't know what they said to [the exoneree] but he still came and he still talked, we did talk a lot after that. And I think maybe it does upset him that I tell that part of my story but I am not changing my story to suit somebody else's needs."

Because lawyers operate within the legal system, they have a unique view of how a case unfolds. Prosecutors, in particular, can provide critical information to crime victims along the way. Still, lawyers have enduring impacts on how original crime victims experience the justice process, at every stage. Defense attorneys have an ethical duty to represent their clients, and that might cause more harm for crime victims in these cases. Postconviction attorneys also can be a source of information so long as providing that is within the ethical parameters of duty to their clients.

Wrongful Liberty: Actual Perpetrators and Additional Victims

When a wrongly convicted person is incarcerated, the actual perpetrator is not (Baumgartner, Grigg et al., 2014; Norris, Weintraub et al., 2020), generating the problem of wrongful liberty that shapes additional traumas for victims. One impact the original victims confront is the identity of the actual perpetrators; and another is to grapple with additional victims who were harmed by the actual perpetrators when the wrongly convicted original defendant was incarcerated. The circles of harm (Thompson and Baumgartner, 2018) ripple throughout these cases. As the devastation of wrongful convictions unfolded in the lives of these victims, the actual perpetrators of the violence were unimpeded in whatever violence they would inflict on additional victims.

In four of these homicide cases, the actual perpetrators have not been identified, so it is impossible to know what other crimes they may have committed throughout their wrongful liberty. It is not known who killed Jacqueline Harrison, Jacquetta Thomas, Noreen Malloy, or Kathy Wilhoit. The actual perpetrators have confessed to killing Millie Maxwell's father, but they have not been prosecuted. In the homicide cases of Ginger Blossom and Peggy Sanders / Christy Sheppard the actual perpetrators have been identified and prosecuted. In contrast, the rape cases all produced the identity of the actual perpetrators through DNA evidence, but for Penny Beerntsen, Debbie Jones, and Karen M. the statute of limitations had expired while the wrongly convicted men were incarcerated, so their actual perpetrators cannot be prosecuted. Discovering the actual perpetrators, for those who now know, was tumultuous. Christy Sheppard and Peggy Sanders learned that Glenn Gore was the man who raped and murdered Debra Sue Carter during a court hearing, when they also found out that Gore had just escaped correctional custody. They attended a hearing, only to learn that "he was on the lam."

Tomeshia Carrington-Artis was relieved and confused to learn the identity of the actual perpetrator through a DNA match: "They had the right guy, who CODIS had hit on, but I didn't even know his name; they wouldn't tell me anything. I didn't see a picture, I didn't know a name. They couldn't tell me anything because we had to go to court again and I still had to testify and they did not want anything to be said that I knew this information at the time. So I didn't know who I was going to court against. I didn't know what he looked like. Now I'm not sure of anything, nothing."

For Debbie Jones, the identity of her actual rapist was not known until several months after the exoneration of the wrongly convicted man, which caused suicidal ideation.

We didn't find that out until three months later. But you are living, trying to process that it's not [the exoneree] but I can't. I see [the exoneree] in my face raping me and I hear him and now these twenty-three years later I hear him saying, "If you go to the police I will kill you." And in court I see him saying, "I will kill you when I get out bitch," and it is all melting together that it is the same person. And it sounds the same. But this stupid piece of paper is telling me of the DNA evidence. I don't care about the DNA. I don't care. He gets out, and they explain CODIS to me. I am trying to work and trying to survive. I am suicidal: contemplated many days how could I kill myself with the least amount of pain. And what stopped me was my children. I can't put that pain on them.

Some of the actual perpetrators were prosecuted, but some were not. Michele Mallin's actual perpetrator sent letters to officials taking responsibility for the crime against Michele, while the wrongly convicted man was in prison. But the letters were ignored, and the wrongly convicted original defendant died in prison.

Oh I think it is terrible. I think they should have investigated it. I mean I think DNA was starting to be done about that time. I mean it wasn't in the eighties where they couldn't have done anything about it. Now they could test it. Obviously it's a common knowledge way of investigation. But back then I think it was started in the nineties. They just [ignored] it because the Lubbock Police Department thought they knew better. Which they didn't. So that kind of upset me that they didn't do anything. I mean I would have rather gotten a call then that we got the wrong guy but [the exoneree] is getting out of prison and at least he would've been able to live his life and I would've been able to tell him how sorry I was that happened. I didn't like it at all.

Had these victims received timely, professional, trauma-informed care during the process, it might have been less damaging.

While many of these actual perpetrators were identified and convicted, they committed more crimes in the time between the crimes against these participants and their arrest. Norris et al. (2020, p. 370) point out that many actual perpetrators are "repeat offenders." Hundreds of additional crimes are committed by actual perpetrators while the wrongly convicted are incarcerated (Norris et al., 2020). Penny Beerntsen described subsequent harms, most likely by the actual perpetrator, after the wrongly accused man was in jail. "It's almost like someone is watching the house because I'm home for like ten minutes I get a phone call and that was in the time when there wasn't cell phones but there was a public phone at a nearby gas station.

So if someone was watching the house and then it was discovered that my assailant often stalked his victims and called his victims. So I'm guessing it was [him] who was calling me."

A painful and terrifying aspect of these victims' experiences was learning that other people were harmed by the actual perpetrators while the wrongly convicted people were in the custody of the state. Recall that these survivors depended on the system and cooperated with the investigations in order to prevent this violence from occurring to other people. Subsequent victimizations were preventable, and these original victims often felt guilty and betrayed by the system that they expected to protect them and others. Regina Lane is a subsequent victim of the actual perpetrator who killed Deborah Sykes. A few months before Regina Lane was abducted and raped, Sykes was murdered by Willard Brown in Winston-Salem, North Carolina. The police arrested Darryl Hunt and charged Hunt with Sykes's murder, but Regina's mother-in-law was convinced that the person who killed Sykes had also abducted and assaulted Regina: "My mother-in-law believed that she had helped solve that crime and I truly believe that she did too. And she always thought that even though she was dying of cancer during all this time."

Jennifer Thompson was one of several women attacked by Bobby Poole that night.

> The only thing I did know in the hospital was that [another woman had] just been raped and that we were pretty certain that it was the same person. It was days later that I found out that she had physically tried to fight, and what he had done to her. That's when I learned that she was not able to give a really good description other than the clothing. And, there had been a woman before me right across the street where he attempted to break into her home and she called the police. Again it was the same thing, he had punched his arm through the kitchen window so she noticed the same white stripes blue sleeves, white knit gloves, African American male.

After Jennifer Thompson shared her story publicly in *Picking Cotton*, another woman contacted her:

> Bobby Poole went on to create a lot of harm. In April of '85 his last victim screams, and a neighbor called the police and the police were coming towards the apartment I think Bobby Poole was running and he was shot. So it was that victim that had read the book and got in touch with me. We actually met for a drink one evening and I had never talked to her before. I was really nervous because I thought gosh she's going to blame me for leaving Bobby Poole on the street. And she

may be very angry at me and she wasn't. She said thank you so much for writing this. This helps explain so much of what had happened.

Janet Burke expresses a sense of personal, though misplaced, guilt for the wrongful liberty: "That was probably so hard for me was knowing that people counted on me and I got it wrong. There were people, there were young girls, really young girls, younger than me that were hurt after [the wrongly accused man] was locked up because I got it wrong. And so that's really hard for me and I felt like I let so many people down." And Karen M. later learned that "after he raped me, he raped a child in Norman, Oklahoma, when he was a city employee. She was a fourteen-year-old girl so within months after raping me, because I was wrong identifying him he broke into a home and kidnapped a young girl, pulled her from the house, held her at gun point by the neck, raped her I think he sodomized her. I didn't know any of this until a year and half ago. And if I hadn't been wrong this fourteen-year-old child wouldn't have been kidnapped and raped by [the actual perpetrator]."

It is clear that these victims feel a singular crushing and misplaced guilt and shame, wrongly carrying the full responsibility, when in fact it belonged to the system whose flawed procedures created these disasters. This experience shatters their faith in the system they believed was meant to aid them in the worst moments of their lives. (Chapter 8 explores the shame/guilt impacts more fully.)

THOUGHTS ON THE LEGAL SYSTEM

It is painful to endure these crimes, the trials, the exonerations, and then the aftermath. By this time in their experiences, the survivors were disillusioned. They no longer believed in the promise of justice, and they felt betrayed or shamed by the system. It was not an avenue for repairing the harms or addressing their traumas. Furthermore, many felt a sense of individual blame and sole responsibility for the flawed procedures employed by the system. It is, in fact, the legal system that is responsible for the tertiary trauma. This chapter concludes with their thoughts on the legal system. They describe a sense of personal responsibility and experience of being demonized and being abandoned by the system officials who should have kept them informed, lost trust in the system, and harm inflicted by the system itself. And last, they share their views on whether the system works.

Consistent with the views of many of these participants, Penny Beerntsen urges that the public hold system officials instead of crime victims accountable: "We're taking responsibility, being vulnerable and putting ourselves out there so don't demonize us. I think people get angry, and they get angry at the victims. We should be angry at the original perpetrators. We should be angry at the flaws in the system that allow it to happen."

As the mother of a homicide victim, Peggy Sanders describes being ignored and not kept informed by system officials on any developments in her daughter's murder investigation. "I needed more information. I needed more because I still don't know what all was supposed to happen. They kept so much from me. Just like the day it happened. And they just kept so much from me. I just pray about it. That's all I can do."

In the now cold case homicides, the harm by the system is evident. Like others in the Wilhoit family, and as the sister of an exonerated death row survivor and sister-in-law of the murder victim, Nancy Wilhoit Vollertsen says, "It's really affected my belief in our criminal justice system. The trust that I used to have that it works all the time has been destroyed. I mean I would never have that back. In my particular case the wrongfully convicted person was my brother, a family member. I certainly saw how it destroyed his life. He lost everything. Not only was his wife murdered, but he lost his mental health, his physical health, his home, his livelihood, the opportunity to raise his children. He lost everything. And in my particular case I became his caretaker in our family."

Millie Maxwell feels harmed by the system because evidence connected to her father's murder was destroyed and/or ignored. Sean Malloy is angry that the murder of his sister was not properly investigated, which is "sickening" because now his family will never have the answers they need. And Yolanda Thomas, whose sister was murdered, describes the harms by the legal system on her sister's children, who were put into state custody and raised by extended family members without additional support. This has long-term impacts. "This affected her children! These kids needed counseling."

When asked, "Does the system work?," these participants said "no" in several ways. Millie Maxwell's immediate reply was "not like it should" and then she elaborated,

> I think it should provide some kind of support system for the victims. Like at least come in, talk to them and ask them what it is that they're looking to get out of whatever the situation is. Whether it's closure, comfort, whatever they need at that time especially going through the trial and everything else. They don't do that. I'm sure they have advocates that could do that but that's usually not one of their first needs. I think they look more like, "Oh we have to catch the person that did this and then we have to solve this case and close it up and get on with it." And they don't dot the i's or cross the t's and make sure that everything is suitable for the victim's family or the victims. I think they

should at least come to us and say, "Are you comfortable, are you happy with the way we've done this or is there anything else that we can do?"

When asked the same question, Christy Sheppard responded,

The criminal justice system is the only system that I know of in this entire country that we are so resistant to look at the flaws in it. If there's a plane crash there are people dispersed immediately to find out why it crashed. We've got to make it safer, we've got [disasters like the] Oklahoma City bombing. Committees are [formed] in days and they want to get to the bottom of it. But when it comes to the criminal justice system, no. It works just fine and dandy. You need to leave it alone. In theory, it's a good system. But it's a human system and so it has to evolve. There has to be movement and there's not.

Janet Burke, rape survivor, acknowledged changes and advances in forensic evidence that require the system to change and evolve too. And even with the advancing technologies of DNA testing and other forensic evidence, there is still a chance of getting it wrong: "So we're still broken. We have to have a system. I still believe in law enforcement, even though it is often wrong. We just need to do better because now we know better. [Q: Do you feel like as a victim of a crime the system served you well?] No. I mean that's no. It's not even a question. No."

Ginger Blossom, whose twin brother was wrongly convicted of murdering their parents, also has concerns about the system not serving victims well based on how evidence was collected and interpreted in her case. "[Q: So does the system work?] Well no. Not really, no." For Regina Lane, the system did not work as a subsequent victim of the actual perpetrator. She feels the system is haphazard. "There's no consistency, there's really no consistency. It just doesn't ever seem like there's any path for how things need to go."

With lost faith in the system survivors must live with debilitating regret and rage. Karen M., rape survivor, says, "I wish DNA had been there in 1982 because this never would've happened. I'd give anything, I would. I never would've pointed to his picture, when I only had what maybe six pictures in front of me that were crappy pictures. I would never do it again without DNA because DNA is what proves guilt." And Sean Malloy, whose sister was murdered in a robbery, concludes with the following: "It did fail us. The district attorney should have [done more]. He was a bureaucrat and he didn't want to fight it. They should've got everything in a row. They should've had everything neat and orderly."

For system officials who work on these cases, the timing and process of notification of postconviction claims of innocence can reduce the added trauma for crime victims and survivors, when officials follow professional and trauma-informed practice. Suggestions for this process are shared in chapter 10.

Conclusion

As Walklate (2012) points out, in an adversarial system the state becomes the institutional victim of crime. By supplanting the direct victims of crime and their survivors, the legal system seeks to win against an adversary believed to be responsible for hideous crimes. The collision course of the legal process brings these original victims in contact with the wrongly convicted in a process that consumes years of their lives. They see each other at hearings, read newspaper stories about themselves and each other, they learn about key investigative or legal developments from media coverage or in unexpected ways. Perhaps they desire the exonerations (as in the Wilhoit family, for example), or perhaps they are dubious about the claim of innocence (as in Debbie Jones's rape case, for example). Or perhaps they are simply confused, frustrated, and angry and do not know what to make of it all (as in Andrea Harrison's family).

Politicians and state officials offer promises that reporting crimes to the police is a refuge away from the harms; that they can find the culprit and implement justice on behalf of the victims. This cultural narrative is so pervasive that it has become folklore. When people are forced into the criminal legal system because they have been victimized by crime, they are going through some of the worst experiences in their lives: murders and rapes (in these cases). The expectations are that the police will care about their suffering (and many do), that the investigation will produce an accurate outcome (and most do), and that the perpetrators will be stopped from harming others (and that can happen). But in cases of wrongful convictions and exonerations, those expectations and that faith are shattered. Instead, crime victims in these cases are left feeling solely responsible for the system's errors, frustrated and confused by how this all happened, relieved that the innocents were released, and yet horrified by the additional crimes committed by the actual perpetrators. The primary and secondary traumas of the original crimes are compounded by tertiary traumas of wrongful convictions, exonerations, and aftermath. Along the way, there is some support and comfort offered, but not enough. And when comfort and answers are provided, they come from unexpected sources. In the next chapter, the elements of tertiary trauma are examined.

CHAPTER 7

Elements of Tertiary Trauma

WHEN KAREN M. LEARNED about the exoneration of the original defendant in her rape case, she was shocked. Fortunately, DNA evidence convinced her that he had not been the man who raped her all those years ago. Unfortunately, the flawed eyewitness-identification process caused her to feel entirely responsible for the error: "I'm white and when I see pictures of both [the exoneree and the actual perpetrator] I see similarities but I never compared African American men. I wish I'd never reported it." The crime she experienced was extremely traumatic; the first trial and conviction also caused her additional trauma. Now the exoneration revealed the flaws in the investigation and the broader cultural pressures that impacted her experience: sexism and racism. The intersectional waves of trauma resurface again and again and again.

Situating tertiary trauma within the lens of intersectional feminist analysis (Collins, 2019; Crenshaw, 1995; Potter, 2006) produced an opportunity to examine multiple layers of harm. Beginning with the traumatic impacts of institutionalized sexism and racism in their cases, this chapter examines how their experiences were shaped by sexism and racism, particularly for survivors of African American women homicide victims and for white women who were raped by Black men where different Black men were ultimately exonerated. These survivors were all harmed (in multiple ways) by racialized and gendered systems of power. Ten of the fifteen exonerations involved cross-racial dynamics that were salient to their experiences. Thirteen of the fifteen exonerations involved elements of sexism, especially where sexual violence was included in the original crimes. Because racism and sexism are intersecting systems that reinforce each other and the original crime victims experience them as co-occurring harms in their experiences, the data are presented in conjunction. The chapter concludes with an examination of institutional betrayal as a feature of tertiary trauma.

Complex trauma (Litvin et al., 2017) has multiple dimensions where the trauma survivor must cope with the complexities of each layer every day as they move toward resolution and possibly healing. The domains and subdomains of complex trauma, as measured by Litvin et al. (2017, p. 605), include the following:

a. reexperiencing trauma (intrusive dreams, flashbacks, distress when exposed to cues)
b. avoidance (avoiding internal and external cues to the trauma)
c. sense of threat (hypervigilance and exaggerated startle response)
d. affect dysregulation (heightened emotional reactions, apathy, dissociative responses, violent outbursts, recklessness and self-destructive behavior)
e. negative self-concept (includes self-blame and feeling worthless)
f. disrupted relationships (difficulty with launching or maintaining relationships)

Previous chapters documented how these participants experienced the complex layers of primary and secondary traumas that included surviving violent sexual assaults, often while threatened with a weapon, or the murder of family members that completely altered their lives in profound and uncontrollable ways. Victims described the exonerations in their cases as reopening the wounds of the original crime that produced many agonizing effects, a loss of control of their lives, and a sense of helplessness in the investigations. They described how their families were impacted by these events and that their self-perception was severely damaged. In two cases, the families welcomed the exonerations of their loved ones; in most cases, the survivors feared and were anguished by it. In all cases, elements of tertiary trauma include frustration and confusion, betrayal and deception, guilt, shame, and powerlessness. Tertiary trauma is conceived as an extension of complex trauma and expands into explanations by these participants of their frustration, confusion, sense of betrayal, powerlessness, and ultimately misplaced yet crippling guilt and shame. Tertiary trauma includes a collision of institutional sexism and racism that are present in these cases and connects to historical legacies of gendered mistreatment and racialized harms.

Layered atop the complex trauma of the original crime, and secondary traumas associated with the investigation, the trials, and the aftermath, the participants in this research shared that the wrongful convictions and exoneration processes themselves were traumatic. For those who were family members of the murder victims and the wrongly convicted, the exoneration process was a relief to the terrifying ordeals that included losing their murdered family members and another family member being accused, wrongly convicted, and condemned to death; still it inflicted additional harms. For those who were mourning the deaths of their family members and believed that the exonerated person had been rightly convicted, the exoneration process brought mountains of frustration and confusion and ultimately a sense

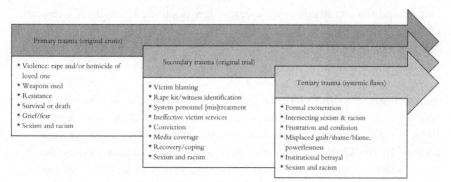

Figure 3. Grounded Theory of Tertiary Trauma from Exonerations

of betrayal. And for the participants who are rape survivors, the exoneration process brought crushing confusion and a debilitating sense of shame, guilt, and blame. Through all of this, these participants needed the truth, hoping it would bring resolution to their shattered recovery process.

Primary trauma seeps into and impacts secondary trauma, and then the tertiary trauma of systemic failures that caused the wrongful convictions becomes the repository for excruciating residue accumulated through this decades-long experience. Figure 3 displays the ongoing impacts of continuing and compounded traumas.

INSTITUTIONALIZED SEXISM AND RACISM

Sexism is a system of power that inflicts oppressive conditions on women and girls at the same time that it empowers men and boys to anticipate entitled access to advantages over and above what women and girls can anticipate. Sexism shapes our social world in historically relevant patterns, where women have been legally invisible, politically disenfranchised, and economically marginalized (Mooney, 2020; Stanko, 1985). Men historically held a legal "right" to beat women and girls to maintain control over them in domestic spheres (Dobash and Dobash, 1979; Pleck, 1987). Women and girls were regularly subjected to brutal violence, often justified by a sexist social climate that saw women and girls in very limited roles (Mooney, 2020). Sexism gives support to "rape culture," where women are often blamed for the victimizations they endure (Caringella, 2009). Similarly, women may also be seen as responsible for their own demise if or when they are victims of homicide, especially if they were believed to be involved in risky activities (Lloyd and Ramon, 2017; Richards et al., 2011). Women and girls are dehumanized under these conditions. Given systemic racial oppression, women of color experience disproportionately more disenfranchisement than white women. Intersecting oppressions of sexism and racism are the scaffolding of American culture and the architecture of American law (Collins, 1990, 2019; Crenshaw, 1995); they profoundly shape the experiences of wrongful convictions for original crime victims.

Racism and sexism are "intersecting systems of power" (Collins, 2019, p. 39) that frame and inform how these victims experienced and understand their ordeals of crime victimization and legal processes thereafter. In fact, "racism and sexism readily intersect in the lives of real people" (Crenshaw, 1995, p. 357), though scholars and activists tend to focus on either racism or sexism. In the United States, racism is a form of systemic oppression that shapes every aspect of our social world and produces a social caste system with myriad manifestations (Wilkerson, 2020). Particular to racialized oppression of African Americans, these manifestations include formal and informal segregation, stigmatization and criminalization, the propagandization of the fear of Black men, and the exploitation of Black men and women. In the United States, evidence of racial disparities in criminal sentencing, including capital punishment, is abundant (Pierce et al., 2014; Sered, 2019). Especially gruesome tentacles of systemic racism include lynching, where gratuitous violence against Black men and women broadcasts messages that any perceived insult against white people, and particularly white women, could be subject to lethal violence (Wilkerson, 2020). For Black people, the messages are clear: stay in your subjugated place and do not veer away from the limitations enforced by those with social and political power; doing so may jeopardize life and limb. Ultimately, the lesson is that to be an African American is to be dehumanized. When learning these painful realities, Black men and women, boys and girls, develop coping skills to aid their survival and accumulate a lifetime of traumatic memories from seemingly insignificant microaggressions to flagrant and hostile exclusions. The stress of coping in this hostile caste system can be lethal in itself (Wilkerson, 2020).

Systemic racism is documented in research on wrongful convictions and exonerations. According to the National Registry of Exonerations, 47 percent of the 2,813 exonerations documented since 1989 are Black exonerees.[1] Patterns of racial bias identified in known exonerations show that "innocent black people are about seven times more likely to be convicted of murder than innocent white people" (Gross, 2017, p. ii). Furthermore, "a black prisoner serving time for sexual assault is three-and-a-half times more likely to be innocent than a white sexual assault convict" (p. iii). Among the explanations for these racially disparate patterns in exonerations, Gross identifies cross-racial eyewitness identification, especially in sexual assault cases with white women victims and Black exonerees. Additional explanations include several elements of systemic racism, such as investigation procedures impacted by bias. Smith and Hattery (2011, p. 91) analyze racial bias patterns in exoneration cases as well and conclude that these "systematic procedural errors could have been avoided." Johnson (2021) analyzes the pathways into wrongful convictions in sexual assault cases based on race and shows that stranger rapes of white women by Black men are at risk of wrongful convictions. This research examines gendered and racialized dimensions of wrongful convictions and its impact on the victims of crime who participated.

An element of tertiary trauma, as several participants described, includes their struggles with racism and sexism that infected their cases. Racialized and gendered patterns are present and impact the original crime and its investigation and therefore the exonerations. Realizations of racial bias generated more harm for many original victims. The analysis presented here is both abductive and inductive (Charmaz, 2014). The impacts of systemic racism and sexism include cumulative harms from childhood and preceding experiences of oppressive conditions. A compelling example of cumulative harms of systemic racism is Dwayne Jones's childhood experience that shaped his life and his awareness of racism.

> I come from an ugly place. They spit on me walking to school. Milledgeville, Georgia. It's not a good place. My people are still there. I went there last year—I was finally able to walk in the bakery that I wanted to walk in when I was a little kid. . . . I cried when I went in there last year. . . . I walked into that bakery and I told the lady, "I've been wanting to come in here ever since I was seven years old. [Back then] a white lady and a white man told me to 'Get off of the sidewalk!' and I said, 'Ma'am, today I'm walking in your bakery.' I said, 'I'm leaving here tomorrow to head back to New Jersey.'" She said, "Come on in I'm glad you came." She gave me two dozen doughnuts, and I brought them back to New Jersey. I walked out with a tear in my eye but I couldn't wait to get home and tell my wife that I went into that bakery after forty-something years.

Confronting old wounds of racism is both painful and liberating. For Dwayne to reclaim the right to buy baked goods in his ancestral southern hometown took bravery and strength. When his domestic partner, Jacqueline Harrison, was murdered and she was portrayed as a "promiscuous party girl," racism was again palpable by deploying the "Jezebel" trope in suggesting she contributed to her own death. When the exoneration occurred and there was little effort to reopen the investigation, both Dwayne and his daughter, Andrea Harrison, were frustrated:

DWAYNE: We want our bottom line ma'am.
ANDREA: The right person [should] be held accountable, whoever Mr. X is, he needs to be identified. Now unfortunately it has been thirty years and people pass away every day.

These two experiences, decades apart, exemplify similar frustrations for both
Dwayne and Andrea. African American people often experience exclusion
and oppression in ordinary microaggressions and persistent abuses (Wilkerson, 2020) that render their existence insignificant and insubstantial. Their
lives do not matter, or so it feels. Growing accustomed to this, then, it is
unsurprising that the homicide of their loved one also resulted in a sense of
being rendered insignificant and insubstantial. Dwayne and Andrea view the
homicide investigation as inadequate, the portrayal of Jacqueline Harrison as
an insult to her memory, and the lack of action in reopening the investigation
as another indicator of being treated as insignificant and insubstantial. Systemic racism and sexism, evidenced in how Jacqueline was portrayed, coexist
in this case, leaving them all feeling dehumanized.

Yolanda Thomas, whose sister Jacquetta Thomas was murdered in
North Carolina, contextualized the racialized contours of her sister's murder based on a lifetime of experience in the city and state as an African
American woman. When she first learned the details of her sister's murder
and that a white man had been accused of the murder, she was dubious.

> It was crazy. Like how did this happen because that white man didn't go
> into southeast Raleigh by himself and kill my sister. I'm just trying to
> process they arrested two people. And now the Black guy is off and the
> white guy has been arrested. I don't understand that. The white guy
> couldn't have gone over there without an escort. So they're telling me
> this white man has been charged and sent to prison for life and the Black
> man is off?! So, there was no way it made sense to me that they charged
> that white man for killing a Black woman in a Black neighborhood. No.
> No, there's no way. It was never about her because she was nothing any-
> way. She was a "prostitute." It was never about her.

This devaluation of Black women in general, and among homicide victims
specifically, highlights the coexistence of both systemic racism and systemic
sexism (Potter, 2006). It also is an element of tertiary trauma for original
crime survivors in cases that result in exonerations. It is not surprising,
therefore, that in these two murder cases the actual perpetrators have not
been identified nor prosecuted.

Millie Maxwell, who is African American, perceives the prosecutor as
having racially biased motives while prosecuting the wrong men for her
father's murder. "I think it was the district attorney himself not liking these
particular boys for previous crimes, or whatever they did before. That's not
for him to judge what somebody did before and what they've already been
punished for or whatever their time was. I think that's where the racism
played in. He was a white district attorney and he was well known and had
been district attorney in this town for a long time." Reconciling the impact

of racial bias throughout their experiences within and beyond the criminal legal system is difficult. In Millie Maxwell's case, the men who murdered her father have confessed but have not been prosecuted. So tertiary trauma leaves a vacuum of trust, based on frustrated efforts to be seen and treated with respect.

Systemic racism and sexism are especially evident in the wrongful convictions in rape cases. There are complex and nuanced responses to interracial rape cases that reveal intersectional experiences. At the convergence of antiracism activism on the one hand, and feminist activism on the other hand, "the primary beneficiaries of policies supported by feminists and others concerned about rape tend to be white women, and the primary beneficiaries of the black community's concern over racism and rape tend to be black men" (Crenshaw, 1995, p. 368). For the six white women rape / sexual assault survivors whose cases resulted in the wrongful convictions of Black men, this convergence produces an explosion of intersecting agony that leaves them feeling solely responsible for the entire system of racial injustice after having been subjected to dehumanizing victim blaming during rape prosecutions and in daily culture. The convergence, coupled with the exoneration, invalidates the harm they experienced in the original crime and converts them into unwitting accessories to racialized injustice.

Thus, the white women victims of sexual assaults whose actual perpetrators were Black men faced the devastating task of reconciling how racism shaped their experiences after the exonerations and compounded the long-term trauma of systemic sexism that impacts most rape victims (Caringella, 2009). There are specific and permanent facts that cannot be shifted: they had been assaulted and raped by Black men and did everything they could to cooperate with the investigation after reporting it to the police. Jennifer Thompson recalled her mother's first response was to ask if she had been raped by a Black man, which was jarring: "The perpetrator being black never factored in to it for me ever, personally. To me, it was a violation of my body." Michele Mallin, who is from Texas, where southern racism is common, said, "I don't really ever remember thinking about it from a racial standpoint. It could have been a white guy and I would have been just as upset." Sexist and racially charged responses of other people were part of their experiences.

Janet Burke articulates the conundrum of cross-racial witness identification and what she has come to learn about the inherent flaws in the procedures used at the time:

When I identified a Black man, with me being a white female, I'm not as in tuned to African American facial features, you know distinction between the skin tones and colors, you know and all those things. So as much as race is not a piece of this it is a piece of it, but it's not in a "because you're a Black man I chose you" you know type of thing. It's not about that. It's not about you know I'm white and they're Black. It's just not about that but it does play a piece in the identification process.

She went on to describe an experience where the exonerated man was interviewed on a radio program where an African American radio host cast this experience as "another example of a Black man who's been convicted by a white woman" and how the exoneree just didn't go down that path with the host. "Yeah and it was hard for me to sit and hear that, because I just really felt like this was a horrible situation from the start and [the exoneree] will tell you, 'You were raped. I mean that was nothing you did, this was something that happened to you and we got caught up in.' And I just try not to go down that road even though race does play a part. It's a hard thing to look at."

Debbie Jones experienced an immediate racialized response to her rape at the hospital for the forensic rape examination,

> There was predominantly Black people in there. The whole place erupted as I walked through. They start screaming at me and they say, "This bitch, F her! What is going on! This is wrong! I've been sitting here for hours with my baby and you're gonna take this white bitch back before me?!" So I have just been raped and now I am being completely abused as I walk back to get a rape kit. The cops just push me through and told me to just keep going. But that is all I can hear is people calling me vulgar names.

As described earlier, these women also experienced harms when strangers commented on media reports of the exonerations or when they would receive racially charged and sexist death threats. Like many of the rape survivors, Jennifer Thompson reported receiving hate mail and death threats. Janet Burke mentioned previously that her daughter was outraged by the racialized and sexist comments people posted on news coverage of her case. And Tomeshia Carrington-Artis, the only African American woman who is a rape victim in an interracial rape case, reported racist and sexist comments through the media as well. She described comments on social media and news articles online saying, "You Black b-tch sent the wrong guy to prison, her family needs to be burned up and yeah; that n———needs to go to prison, stuff like that."

The tertiary trauma of feeling singularly responsible for the racialized harms another experienced, after having been subjected to gendered harms as victims of rape, is nearly unbearable. The legal system they turned to for relief produced a more traumatic impact for them. The system let them down, and society blamed them for the errors, generating frustration and confusion.

FRUSTRATION AND CONFUSION

Using Herman's definition of trauma (1997, p. 33) and Litvin and colleagues' (2017) conceptualization of complex trauma, tertiary trauma includes deep frustration and confusion. Trauma results in senses of powerlessness, loss of control, lack of connection and meaning, and threat of annihilation (Herman, 1997). During the exoneration process, these participants were not in control of the process, or how their experiences were represented in the legal system or by the media. While some, like Debbie Jones and Jennifer Thompson, had compassionate assistance from the police, who helped them through the ordeal, and Millie Maxwell, Penny Beerntsen, and Janet Burke had unlikely support from the postconviction attorneys representing the wrongly convicted men, they were still powerless as to the timing, the claims, the media coverage, and the outcomes. This is especially vivid when Penny Beerntsen stormed out of a hearing after hurling an expletive at the judge. No victim wanted the wrong person incarcerated for the crimes they endured. The fear of annihilation was vivid and real for Debbie Jones, especially since the exoneree issued a death threat against her during an early hearing in their case. She responded to this threat, upon his exoneration, by taking steps to protect herself and her family. Peggy Sanders and Christy Sheppard, upon hearing that the exonerees were being released, also learned that the actual perpetrator who killed Debra Sue Carter had escaped correctional custody that morning. The fear of the violence resurfacing was as real as their frustration with the entire fiasco of the court process.

For the Gauger and Wilhoit families, the exonerations meant that their families would not endure another tragic bereavement in that neither Gary Gauger nor Greg Wilhoit would be executed for crimes they did not commit. Still, their frustration was intense. Ginger Blossom recalled a sense of betrayal: "Yeah the good guys, the ones that are supposed to be on your side are actually the bad guys. And in the meantime when we finally do get back to the farm and whoever killed my parents, the murderer or murderers we didn't know they are still at large and we are living here." Ultimately, the Gauger family has learned the truth about their parents' murders. This is not the case for the Wilhoit family. They experienced frustration over not knowing who was responsible for the death of their family member. For both families, though, nothing prepared them for the monumental task of welcoming home their exonerated loved ones and assisting their reentry to society (Westervelt and Cook, 2012).

Frustration was common during the exoneration process, and they report experiencing many symptoms of trauma throughout the ordeal, including hypervigilance, nightmares, sleeplessness, and flight, fight, and freeze responses. Tomeshia Carrington-Artis fled, Penny Beerntsen fought, Karen M. froze. All of these responses fluctuated and shifted over time; they were not static. Millie Maxwell's frustration was drenched in confusion about who killed her father and what the courts were saying. During the home invasion, several men burst into the house, hiding their faces with bandanas. The investigators set their sights on one group of young men (group A), while another group of young men (group B) were more likely to be responsible. Millie recalls,

> And that's what the confusion was when we got down there. It was so much confusion with group A, because it was this person said this and this person said that. This person went to [one place] and this person said such and such. And then you have people in halfway houses, people at the nightclubs, people at different apartment complexes and this person runs into that person, this person said that. It was just like whoa! You're trying to keep up and jot notes. And it just got to the point where I went to [request the transcripts]. They sent me transcripts. They sent me everything.

Confusion often generates fear among those who are uncertain about their predicament. Debbie Jones certainly experienced this confusion and fear after the exoneration due to the death threat she got from the wrongly accused man at his original trial. "I took [the exoneree's] threat that he was going to kill me seriously. It was almost as bad as the rape itself."

For Regina Lane, a subsequent victim of the actual perpetrator, the aftermath of Darryl Hunt's exoneration brought into sharp focus her efforts to compare her experience with Willard Brown to the abduction, rape, and homicide of Deborah Sykes: "There are times I feel a little deceived. It's just disappointing to know that we were that close. . . . It happened on February 2 of '85 and by March 1986, you know, there was the lineup and it didn't make any sense why they couldn't find Willard Brown. I mean he lived so close to the police department and even where I was taken. He was just so close in that vicinity. It's not like they had to travel three hours to find him. [and I] think about Linda and Kathleen [the next victims of the actual perpetrator]."

Misplaced Guilt, Shame, and Powerlessness

Some experienced a crippling experience of misplaced guilt, shame, and individual blame for the wrongful convictions, particularly among those who provided eyewitness identification during the investigation and at the original trial. The slurry of emotional impacts are layered on top of the primary trauma of being victims of rape / sexual assault and then subject to the secondary trauma of the investigation and trial; the third layer of harm from the exoneration includes perceiving oneself and being portrayed as "perpetrators of an injustice" rather than a victim of crime. Disentangling these distinct emotional impacts is nearly impossible, but they all are identifiable. Victim blaming is common in the legal system, and rape culture includes messages that rape victims are responsible for their own victimization (Campbell, 1998; Campbell and Raja, 1999, 2005; Caringella, 2009). In these cases, mostly white women raped by Black men, the rape / sexual assault survivors are "good victims" of stranger rape, who followed the system's protocol of reporting to the police and cooperating with the investigation (Johnson, 2021). The police, and later prosecutors, investigated using the procedures commonly used at the time. These participants are not responsible for the outcome of the wrongful convictions. Still, the crushing and misplaced guilt and shame stem from them being seen as the main culprit—alone—in the system of errors (Simon, 2012). It is in fact the legal system, its policies and practices, that produces wrongful convictions, whereas these victims are blamed for "mistakes" that are actually byproducts of systemic failures.

When this misplaced guilt is internalized, a deep sense of shame can take root. Shame, according to Brown (2006), is an "intensely painful feeling or experience of believing we are flawed and therefore unworthy of acceptance and belonging" (p. 45). As such, when people feel shame, they believe that there is something wholly unworthy about themselves as a consequence of that shame. The feeling is debilitating, crippling, and difficult to overcome. Shame often leaves people feeling trapped, powerless, and isolated (Brown, 2006) yet surrounded by expectations to engage in the world that damaged them so severely. The sense of shame can become a defining feature of someone's self-identity, particularly when they are unable to break through that shame to move toward healing. These "unwanted identities" (pp. 46–47) may become so painful that isolation, unworthiness, and powerlessness overwhelm those who experience shame.

Jennifer Thompson has spoken publicly and written about this crushing avalanche of misplaced guilt and shame:

> You feel powerless, you feel out of control because it's not my decision. I didn't want to have to do this. So that sense of loss of control again, loss of power and all of that, comes back but in a totally different manifested way. I pointed my finger at that man. And I swore on the Bible, in front of his family, he was called the worst menace to society that this judge had ever seen, in front of his mother. Then I'm starting to

learn what prison was like, and that people are killed in prison, they are raped in prison. On top of that you actually prayed for that to happen to that man. You condescending, self-righteous person. You could pray to God to have an innocent man raped and killed. So there's a part of me where I acknowledge that the harm done to [the exoneree], while I know it was the state, I put the blame on me for many many years, many many years.

There was no counternarrative to challenge Jennifer's unfortunate self-blame. She was told in many ways that the error made in the identification process was her mistake alone and therefore she was individually responsible for the wrongful conviction in her case. This message came from academic research, lawyers, and media coverage where the concept of "mistaken eye-witness identification" emphasizes how victims can get it wrong, when in fact research showing that policy and practice produce erroneous results is less salient in the public discourse. A close companion to shame, then, is guilt. A sense of guilt also cripples people (Brown, 2006). Guilt emerges from a painful acknowledgment that one's behavior harmed others and thus imposes a moral obligation to repair the harms whenever possible. As a result, guilt can be an avenue toward connecting to the person harmed. The trauma bond is forged in painful life experiences where both original victims and exonerated people might benefit from acknowledging their conjoined traumas.

Penny Beerntsen's experience illuminates how guilt couples with shame: "I mean obviously I was still the victim of a horrible assault but in many minds I was also a perpetrator of a huge injustice. . . . I thought I had forgiven myself but the guilt would just resurface." The (misplaced) guilt felt by these participants includes their concerns about the impact on the exonerated persons and their families. The survivors acknowledge that these wrongly convicted men missed the opportunities to build a family, to build a nest egg, and to move forward in life within their communities. Therefore, the guilt felt by these participants includes a sense of responsibility for the children of the wrongly convicted having to live without their fathers and with a damaged extended family surrounding them. Debbie Jones expresses this:

You know why it's bad? Because you go through this thing and it's horrible, it's a nightmare and you relive it and now you're going back to every tiny little detail from twenty-three years later trying to figure out where there was a misstep. How did I miss it? I now have to relive it but with a layer of guilt. And you find out that [the exoneree's] dad died while he was in prison and now his aunt died while he was in prison and you find out he's never had children and he's missed twenty-three years of his life and why? Because you absolutely identified him. And, again, you can tell me all day long that it wasn't my fault and it doesn't feel like it wasn't my fault. And you have the guilt and the shame and then I found out also that because we had not identified the right person a girl a year later had been raped by [the actual perpetrator].

When the shame and guilt are so big, so expansive, and so profound, the traumatic effect can be very damaging. None of the research participants saw this disaster impacting themselves alone. Rather they acknowledged an impact on their communities as well, and the possibility (and in some cases, the reality) of subsequent victims of the actual perpetrators. Karen M., rape survivor from Oklahoma, says, "It wasn't only the fact that I was wrong. It compounds to where hell sounds good you know? I almost sometimes say I wish he had [killed me] because it almost would've been easier, you know?" And then she goes on to say,

I wish I had never reported it. I wish I had never ever made that mistake because that ruined my life more than the rape I think. I would never do it again. It changed me. I've had many, many years to just wish really I wasn't here. And I love my husband, I love my family, I love his family, I love my animals but yeah I mean quality of life you know it speaks a lot for quality of life. I've survived. I have gotten through. I haven't had quality, I haven't had happiness, I haven't had children you know this is a big guilt, the guilt over it.

INSTITUTIONAL BETRAYAL

The emotional slurry of complex trauma includes a deep and enduring sense of institutional betrayal (Smith and Freyd, 2013, 2014) especially among the homicide survivor participants. When people face excruciating violence and turn to social institutions, such as the criminal legal system, for redress and remedy, they anticipate effective and reliable assistance. As Regina Lane notes above, it turns out her effort to draw connections with the Sykes homicide in the same city resulted in her being "disappointed" and in other victims being harmed by the actual perpetrator: "I just felt unimportant unfortunately." The betrayal felt by Yolanda Thomas, whose sister was murdered, includes elements of racism: "They did my family wrong on behalf of my sister, yes that's betrayal. That is betrayal. It's not even about her being important enough you know? People say they just they did this because she was Black or because they labeled her as a prostitute."

Millie Maxwell felt betrayed by the district attorney, who was "covering up things, hiding things and things not coming out because we should've known about the [tip] call too, immediately that day." Andrea Harrison and

Dwayne Jones perceive the police did not conduct a thorough investigation into Jacqueline's death because of "who she was" and "what she was into" as a "promiscuous party girl," which harkens to both racist and sexist cultural tropes. As Jacqueline's partner and father of her daughter, Dwayne Jones feels bitterly betrayed: "I feel that way because they didn't finish the job. And they should finish the job." For Sean Malloy, the sense of betrayal connects back to the original investigation into his sister's death: "They should've buttoned up the case and this should have never happened."

The original trauma of losing a loved one to murder, then the ordeal of the investigation and trial compound the post-exoneration experiences for original victims. They are launched into a retrospective examination of their agonizing loss, the violence they and/or their loved ones experienced, and then come to realize that the original trial did not produce the justice they once believed in. In that retrospection, the memories and images of violence are matched by the recollections of the investigation and trials. They are harmed afresh because now those memories are contaminated with the new, more accurate understanding of what happened to them and their loved ones. While the more accurate information provides answers to the questions about who committed the crime, it raises new painful questions about how the system failed them.

The concept of institutional betrayal (Smith and Freyd, 2013, 2014) emerged from academic research on the policies and practices of social institutions responding to sexual assault and other forms of trauma. It is defined as "trusted and powerful institutions (schools, churches, military, government) acting in ways that visit harm upon those dependent on them for safety and well-being" (Smith and Freyd, 2014, p. 575). The impacts of institutional betrayal include a decline in the physical and mental health of trauma survivors and a reluctance to seek additional support or redress from the specific social institutions and others for fear of more harms. Institutional betrayal includes analysis of clergy sexual abuse and military sexual assaults. The church and the military contributed to and then failed to repair the damage of those traumas. Applying the concept to instances of wrongful convictions and exonerations is appropriate because the legal system is a behemoth government institution that is responsible for investigating and prosecuting crimes. "Although institutional betrayal tends to have a broad impact, for the individual experiencing the betrayal the problem may appear at first to be an isolated incident" (Smith and Freyd, 2014, p. 579). Participants in this research initially believed their personal troubles with exonerations were isolated cases: rare, no policies or programs to address their needs, no one else they knew had been through this. The legal system that was supposed to ascertain the truth failed to do so, causing immeasurable harm for themselves and for the exonerated people and their families.

Yet the legal system remains their only avenue toward understanding how their nightmare happened.

Social institutions, such as the legal system, may be elevated to positions of prestige or vaulted to nearly heroic status and may face the dilemma of losing prestige if the damage is not minimized and thus risk losing public support. It is in the interest of the institution to downplay the harms, deny compensation to those who are wrongly convicted, and lay responsibility for the harm on the victims to whatever extent possible (i.e., the victim made a mistake, etc.). Therefore, the rhetoric of "mistaken witness identification" may be translated into the eyewitness/victim being singularly responsible for the flawed outcome. Women of color are portrayed as "promiscuous party girls" and prostitutes, thus contributing to their own murders. Homicide victims' families are dismissed as siding with their wrongly accused family members and then are kept uninformed about the investigations. Other homicide victims' family members may be ignored by the legal system officials and exploited by the media.

When institutions acknowledge the harms they have visited upon the people they were supposed to protect, they may use the concept of "bad apples" according to Smith and Freyd (2014, p. 581). This is true in wrongful conviction cases. Recall that of the fifteen total cases, official misconduct is present in six, false or misleading forensic evidence is present in seven, flawed eyewitness identification is present in nine, perjury or false accusation is present in six, and false confession is present in three. For example, we can definitely point to specific technicians involved in Jacquetta Thomas's homicide investigation as bad actors,[2] yet the fact remains that their work was reviewed by the legal system and was upheld as reliable for seventeen years. The "contaminated orchard" (Westervelt and Cook, 2012, p. 274) harms the original victims of crimes as well as the wrongly accused.

CONCLUSION

The complex trauma (Litvin et al., 2017) experienced by these participants has been described in detail. They experience tertiary trauma that includes institutionalized racism and sexism and expands into frustration, confusion, guilt, shame, powerlessness, and betrayal. Consequently, the tertiary trauma nearly destroyed the victims. They felt responsible for additional suffering, when they were mainly searching for redress in their own suffering. Despite the reality that the legal system takes over control of the situation upon receiving the police report and conducting the investigation, many survivors felt abandoned, with the responsibility for the "mistake" that resulted from the flawed witness identification process. And for the homicide victim's family members, many felt betrayed by the promise of justice—that the system would take their loss seriously and find the truth.

Acknowledging systemic racism and sexism in their cases also generates fresh layers of trauma.

During the tertiary trauma, the victims are unable to escape the triggers of their original harms. Given media reports about the claims of innocence and everyday reminders of their journeys (birthdays, anniversaries, seasonal mood swings, etc.) they are forced to remember. There may never be answers to their questions about who killed their family members, or if the actual perpetrators will ever be prosecuted. Their sense of self may be forever altered by the shame or guilt associated with participating in such a tragic outcome. Victims learn they cannot depend on the legal system to get it right, even when everyone is trying to do the right thing. The trauma continues. The wreckage in their lives reoccurred. Where do they turn? How do they cope? What does the system do to serve them better?

CHAPTER 8

Shattered Grief, Loss, and Coping

WHEN YOLANDA LEARNED the terrible news that her sister Jacquetta Thomas had died, she was devastated. As the investigation unfolded and the police arrested a white man, she was doubtful about its accuracy. Still, she had her life in the military and her children and extended family, including Jacquetta's children, to raise; it was a hard and hectic time. She missed her sister; she was sad and frustrated by the impacts on her family, especially the children. There was not much time or space for grieving. Life is greedy that way, demanding so much effort and attention to get through each day. Yolanda attended the postconviction process to represent her family and to support the exoneration. She did not anticipate the avalanche of grief it would produce: "The day I dealt with her death was the day he got off. So just remember that; that was when I felt grief." After years of denial and avoidance, Yolanda's suppressed grief was finally able to surface; the conjoined moment of release for the wrongly convicted man created space to grieve the loss of her sister.

The exoneration process can open decades-old wounds, particularly when insufficient information and support are offered. The victims/survivors in these cases had been processing their grief and loss since that time, to varying degrees. Because of the way they were ignored, dismissed, or forgotten, the exoneration exploded whatever productive grief they had achieved and inflicted fresh wounds. This chapter presents inductive and abductive (Charmaz, 2014) analysis of the grief, loss, and resolution experiences these participants described. Moving toward resolution and integration is a difficult journey that is rarely ever complete. A vital ingredient to resolving the grief process is to know the truth about what happened to them and/or their loved ones. The exonerations revealed that the process of grief they had endured since the original crimes, trials, and (wrongful) convictions was based on inaccurate, incomplete, and unreliable information. Their grief journeys were shattered and required this new information to be integrated into an entirely new grief process. Additional pain was attached to the new grief process due to the tertiary trauma: misplaced guilt, shame, and institutional betrayal, which could have been lessened (but not eliminated) with sufficient victim-centered support.

According to the Mayo Clinic, "Grief is a strong, sometimes overwhelming emotion for people, regardless of whether their sadness stems from the loss of a loved one or from a terminal diagnosis they or someone they love have received."[1] Ordinarily, the overwhelming emotions associated with grief erupt and then are processed by the grieving person over time, perhaps many years. Elizabeth Kubler-Ross (1969) outlined the five stages of grief: denial, anger, bargaining, depression, and acceptance. While thinking about grief as a linear process has saturated our culture, it was not intended to be perceived as a journey through one stage on to the next, in a progressive path toward acceptance. Rather, grief journeys typically weave in and out of these stages and continue for the remainder of a grieving person's life.

Inspired by pioneering research examining the stages of death, dying, grief, loss, and meaning making (Kessler, 2019; Kubler-Ross, 1969; Kubler-Ross and Kessler, 2005), the current research reenvisions grieving, loss, resolution, and meaning making as a braided fabric with many interwoven strands that may, ultimately, create an integrated resolution or healing. Kubler-Ross and Kessler (2005) express dismay that their *stages* have been misconstrued to mean sequential journeys toward a conclusion; they meant for their theory to be descriptive, not prescriptive (Kessler, 2019). They argue that grief is messy and does not occur in a fixed sequence or pattern toward conclusion. When people experience traumatic losses, such as those described in this research, they endure a tangle of painful corresponding events and emotions that they must integrate into their new understanding of the ordeal. The strands woven into the braided fabric include the emotional progress one might make while grieving as well as events that relate to and compound the loss. The emotional strands include anger, depression, denial, bargaining, acceptance, and meaning making (drawing from Kessler, 2019; Kubler-Ross and Kessler, 2005), as well as the corresponding events that create additional losses, lost/destroyed relationships, lost communities, lost futures. Some strands are hard to discern when and where they begin, but they do begin in the tangle that is grief. To disentangle the strands of complicated grief, this analysis draws from Maercker et al. (2016, p. 189), who identify an "unremitting preoccupation with the loss" as a feature of the complicated grief process. Visualizing grief as a braided fabric of interwoven strands, the grieving person may, on any given day, experience depression as the most salient strand and then experience bargaining as the most salient strand on another day. A corresponding loss might occur that unravels the grief process such that anger and depression resurface. None of strands in the braided fabric disappear; they remain woven into the whole experience and may unravel with new information or events linked to the original loss. The braided fabric itself may transform the grief process into a connection from the original loss to the meaning one can make of that loss (Kessler, 2019) and may generate healing and posttraumatic growth (Tedeschi and Calhoun, 2004). Grieving includes other strands as well: information about how their loss occurred surrounds the grief process and becomes part of the woven fabric. As knowledge about their loss shifts, changes, and is clarified, the grieving process is impacted.

Complicated grief is attributed to traumatic loss through bereavement. It "compromises the survivor's functioning in occupational, familial, or broader social roles [and] include[s] shock, disbelief, and anger about the death; loneliness and isolation; a feeling that a part of the self has also died; and the sense that the future holds little prospect of purpose or fulfillment" (Maercker et al., 2016, p. 189). Bordere (2017) documents that, beyond bereavement, sexual assault survivors experience grief and loss in the aftermath of their assaults, including lost sense of self, security, and truth in themselves and in others. The loss of fundamental bodily sovereignty inflicts a grief process that is largely unrecognized by society. Bordere argues "that sexual assault is a non-death loss and bereavement experience and should be classified as such in research and practice" (p. 32).

To theorize complicated grief as experienced by original victims in exonerations requires an acknowledgment that the initial grief process was interrupted and broken by the exoneration. The initial losses associated with the violent death of their loved ones or the violent assaults on their bodies launched their grief process as related to these crimes. Embarking on the initial grief journey required these victims/survivors to experience the anger, denial, bargaining, depression, and acceptance in varying degrees and with individual paces over multiple years following the crime. They had no choice but to live with it in order to carry on. Their coping fluctuated from strategies of avoidance to strategies of incorporation and could shift from one day to the next. The initial grief process either depended on an understanding of the violence that shattered their lives drawn from the court process or rebelled against the court's understanding of the violence. Some knew that the courts got it wrong, some suspected the courts got it wrong, and some believed that the original convictions were accurate. Their grief process included these different positions with respect to the original conviction.

The post-exoneration grief process forced a new task: processing the new information about the crimes they experienced. In homicide cases where family members were wrongly convicted, the grief process of their murdered family members could continue with the courts acknowledging the error. In homicide cases where the exoneration produced new evidence and the identity of the actual perpetrators, the grieving family members then had to reorient their grief process based on this new information. In homicide cases where the exonerations left an unsolved cold case, their post-exoneration grieving process generated a sense of frustration and betrayal; their loved one's death was no longer an important concern to the authorities.

In rape / sexual assault cases, the initial loss of bodily sovereignty launched a painful grief process that required them to integrate the identity of the men who they believed assaulted them. But in the post-exoneration grief process, they had to reconcile the wrongful conviction for which they felt singularly responsible with the new information based on DNA evidence. The post-exoneration grief among the rape / sexual assault survivors demanded they make sense of the flawed process that produced the error and possibly see themselves as part of a new injustice. They also had to reconcile the identity of the actual perpetrators once that was revealed and the harms done to additional victims. Whatever progress they made on their initial grief journey was destroyed by the exoneration: it had to start over, with new information and added layers of anguish and confusion.

LOSSES

The participants in this research discussed their losses and grief processes as not sequential and in nonlinear layers. Therefore, a loss associated with the post-exoneration grief process is braided back to the agony they felt in their initial grief process but with new contours. The findings reveal compound losses and corresponding events, childhood losses, emotional devastation, and efforts to commemorate their losses in meaningful ways. Children are at a higher risk of developing complicated grief when they are victimized (Maercker et al., 2016). The participants in this research who were children at the time of the original crime matured within broader emotional milieus of grief and loss. Krissy and Kim Wilhoit (fourteen months and four months old, respectively, when their mother was murdered), Andrea Harrison (three years old when her mother was murdered), Christy Sheppard (eight years old when her cousin was murdered), and Tomeshia Carrington-Artis (twelve years old when she was raped), experienced profound losses that were foundational to their emerging identity. For example, while discussing her mother, Andrea Harrison shared memories of seeing her mother's picture on the television news:

> [My mother] was coming home from work and my sister and I were getting in the car with my aunt and my grandmother and my younger cousin. We were going downtown for dinner or something like that and we asked her, "Hey, mommy are you coming?" And she said, "No

y'all go ahead." I gave her a kiss. She went in the house and we got in the car and drove off. And [then] that Tuesday morning, [I was] eating cereal at the kitchen table—my grandmother had like a little black-and-white TV and a picture of my mommy's face was on the screen. My grandmother had a green rotary phone and the phone starts ringing immediately. She made us go into our rooms downstairs to play. She's on the phone, crying, talking. And after that it was kind of blurry. I remember the day of her funeral because I wasn't allowed to go. They sent me across the street. My grandmother made me stay with one of her friends. I just sat on the couch looking out the window like where is everybody going and why can't I go. It took forever for anybody to come back home and that was kind of it. But of course at three you're not really thinking. She's supposed to be around here but she's not around. I didn't know what any of it meant until I got older.

While we discussed happy memories of her mother, I asked if she looked like her; Andrea replied, "I don't know." The loss of such a foundational sense of identity is hard to capture.

For Krissy and Kim Wilhoit, losing their mother while they were fourteen and four months old left empty spaces in their lives. Krissy recalls, "We were young enough to have no memory. All we remember is our [foster parents] and Daddy Greg. Visiting with him and having fun but nothing that really keeps us up at night. I feel bad about everything that happened to [our mother] but we didn't know her." And Kim recalls, "But that makes it sad in itself. Greg and I always connected in a way, that I'm a lost soul like he was. I always felt loved enough by my [foster] parents, but I've always felt like I didn't fit in. I always had a harder time of not knowing [our mother] or a whole lot about her."

Millie Maxwell and Sean Malloy were in their late teens at the time their family members were murdered. They describe losses such as being denied the opportunity to view the body, not celebrating the usual milestones completing high school, and losing the will to succeed in school. Millie wanted to see her father's body, but she could not: "I didn't get to see him the night that he got killed and I wanted to go to the hospital but they wouldn't let me go and see him. The officers and the people at the hospital persisting that it was so bad that they wouldn't let anyone back there. So grandma insisted that I not go but they weren't letting anybody back there. I think they had to cut his clothes off of him because they were so covered in blood and different things but it hurt my feelings."

In reflecting on his lost high school experience due to the murder of his sister, Sean Malloy explains, "My whole senior year was just terrible. I mean I don't even remember much. You're supposed to love your senior year.

You're Mr. Hotshot. I don't remember shit about my senior year. Nothing. . . . I broke up with my girlfriend. I was so dark inside. Anybody that will get close I would just [yell] 'leave me alone, why would you want to be around me, why, leave me alone. Everybody just leave me alone.' I pushed a lot of people away. I screwed a lot of friendships up, really bad." Most of these participants were adults when the original crime itself interrupted major portions of their lives. Several struggled to complete college. Karen M. articulates a profound loss: "[I lost] being a productive citizen, being comfortable in my own skin, being comfortable out in public, being comfortable around Black men, being comfortable around my own peers, that I grew up with. I felt like a failure. I'm embarrassed. I've never been to a high school reunion and I was popular in high school and [at] college [they] never saw me again. . . . I'm scared to death to this day in my mid-fifties you know if I hear something I'm terrified."

Several participants described more losses connected to the original crime and the exonerations such as loved ones who died of cancer or heart attacks. Some of the participants themselves also developed serious health challenges of their own: Millie Maxwell has had several strokes, Karen M. has suffered serious cardiac problems, and Debbie Jones continues to experience medical problems that require surgery and extensive care. Peggy Sanders struggled with alcoholism and ultimately was hospitalized for psychiatric care: "Girl, I came unglued." After several years with no arrest in the case of her daughter's murder, the police requested her permission to exhume Debbie's body to test a bloody hand print. This reignited Peggy's grief process and drove her over the edge to where she was hospitalized in a psychiatric unit.

GRIEF

Victims often experienced the exonerations as compounding events that severely interrupted the grief process and required them to start all over again. Yolanda Thomas's grief had been "frozen" (Boss, 1999) by her continuing doubts about the accuracy of the original conviction in the homicide of her sister. She provides an example in the opening to this chapter. Due to the exoneration, Yolanda was able to begin grieving her sister's death as well as other events in her family related to her sister's death and, woven into that, the parallel reality that an innocent man was incarcerated for seventeen years, losing all of those years with his own family.

Ginger Blossom celebrated her twin brother's return home and grieved the loss of their parents in tandem. She helped her brother confront the extensive losses associated with his wrongful capital conviction (Westervelt and Cook, 2010, 2012). Ginger said, "This is always hard because I still miss them. I won't talk about them. I'm too much like my dad, but I wish I was more like my mom." Her original grief process unfolded under extremely difficult conditions: "If mom had been here she would be doing that stuff for Gary so I had to take her place. I had no time to grieve. I felt like if I cried I would never put myself back together. I had to keep going. I had no time to grieve. Running the farm, running the business, trying to get my brother help. I just had to keep going. It was crazy." To commemorate her parents' lives, Ginger says, "The farm was always really special and it's like they're still here. It's still really special. [Q: Do you have a special marker that marks your parents' lives here or is it the whole of it?] It's here. The whole farm."

Sean Malloy's early grief process was expressed as prolonged anger, which he had not experienced before. A detail that continues to haunt him is that he had planned to stop by Noreen's work before her shift ended that night, but he did not get there.

> But you know I kept saying: just going to stop in and see her. That bugged me for years. I wondered, what would I have done? We both would've been shot. You know that killed me for years. The whole summer I was just numb and starting fights. I never started fights when I was a kid. I was picking fights with monster guys. It was about two weeks after Noreen died, we all used to hang out at this one pizza shop and this guy comes by and he's a little jerk. I let loose. I just let him have it that was the first fight.

Sean was also observing his parents grieve Noreen's death: his mother "smothered" his father and "[she] died in 1998 of lung cancer. We always said she died of a broken heart. She was never the same." When the exoneration happened, the Malloy family had to reconcile the cold case with the losses of Noreen and Mrs. Malloy. For Sean, the grief strand of anger now resurfaced, and it intertwined with a deep sense of betrayal that the promise of justice was stolen from them by an incompetent investigation. So as the state steals the original crime, it also steals the exoneration and leaves in its place a sense of despair that gobbles up relationships and families.

The braided fabric of grief now includes the tangled emotions of corresponding events (deaths, health scares, exonerations), making resolution even more challenging. Compounding the experience is a sense of "disenfranchisement" of the losses (Doka, 2002). Disenfranchised grief is disconnected from the typical social supports available to grievers. Doka defined is as "The grief that persons experience when they incur a loss that is not or cannot be openly acknowledged, publicly mourned, or socially supported" (cited in Corr, 2002, pp. 39–40.). For the participants in this research, grieving after exonerations is untethered to social support systems, cultural acknowledgments, and understandings. Certainly no rituals exist for crime victims whose original trials result in exonerations or for them to receive an accounting of how this happened. These victims report there is nowhere to turn with that grief. For homicide victims' survivors, the post-exoneration grief is disenfranchised in that their loved ones' death may not be resolved, that there is no system of support available where they can find solace and understanding. "A bereaved person is one who has been deprived, robbed, plundered, or stripped of something" (Corr, 2002, p. 45). And this theft of the grief process, the theft of the right to know who did this to them and why, and the lack of supports to help untangle the messy strands of grief are debilitating.

Resolving Grief

When asked what she needed to feel whole again, Millie Maxwell replied,

> First it would be closure, like just knowing that the truth, yeah. Either you know these people did it or you don't. But I think the family is pretty much exhausted with the fact of it keeps coming up every year or every other year or every other month in the paper. It's reinforming you and reinforming the town and everybody about what went on in the case, you know what I'm saying? To keep it as a live open case but you keep running into dead ends. There's no closure behind it at all and it's almost sad because now there's a new district attorney and he's having to learn all over again.

Andrea Harrison and Dwayne Jones concur. Andrea put it succinctly: "I want the truth. I want the case to be closed with the right person." Dwayne elaborated that they "need to let someone else investigate what they didn't investigate."

When the truth is revealed through DNA evidence, or through other means, and that convinces officials to release the person who was incarcerated for these crimes, the braided fabric of grief unravels. An entire strand of the grief process has been torn out and left the survivors in tatters. Those who supported the exonerations, and especially those whose family members were wrongly convicted, are immensely frustrated because they knew that it was a miscarriage of justice, but they were powerless to stop it. Their grief process then included strands of intense frustration, being silenced, ignored, and bereaved. For those who believed that the original conviction was accurate, the discovery that their original belief about the crime was wrong added strands to the grief process of misplaced guilt, shame, and a sense of betrayal by the system. The crippling grief process is very difficult to navigate and manage. Coping with these realities is another process that coexists with the legal issues. It impacts how people experience the ordeal.

It is not an optional process; in order to continue living through trauma, one must adapt with coping strategies that can vary.

COPING AND RECOVERY?

Coping strategies shift as the situations shift and change. As such, coping should be seen as a situational adaptation that produces avenues toward avoidance or incorporation of the trauma. The human condition generates much emotional pain; that is unavoidable, and that pain often changes who we are and how we live. It may repel us from certain places, certain people, or specific situations. It may impel us toward them instead, and it frequently shifts and changes. Nonetheless, the need for belonging and connection is a foundation for social life and well-being. We all need to feel that we fit in a group, a family, and a community. These crime survivors often felt that connection was severely ruptured; they then had to develop new ways of living that would both protect them from further harm and create a new sense of well-being and wholeness where possible. Krissy Wilhoit exemplifies this for herself and her sister: "Kim and I both have this in common and I don't know if it's anything to do with what happened or we're just like this but we're very hungry for love. We need to feel loved. We tell each other fifty times a day I love you. I do it with my kids. Sometimes I drive my husband nuts but we just always feel this need to feel loved. And when we were kids we would always tell our [foster] mom and dad, 'We love you!' And they'd say, 'We love you too.'"

Coping with the ordeal begins immediately with the assault or attack or learning of the crime against a loved one. These participants described their immediate reactions during the attack in classic trauma response terms. Jennifer Thompson recalled herself becoming "fierce" while the intruder was in her home; Regina Lane managed to escape her attacker and run to safety; and Ginger Blossom immediately returned home to Illinois when her parents were murdered. The initial trauma response often presents limited options: flight, fight, or freeze. As days turn into weeks and weeks turn into months and years, the coping strategies expand and become a new way of living. Coping can lead to healing and can produce resiliency.

Situational coping strategies are in fact trauma responses. For trauma survivors coping with tertiary trauma, over and above primary and secondary trauma, being in control of the spaces, places, and people in their lives requires adaptability. Two broad strategies of coping identified among exonerated death row survivors are also evident among these original crime victims impacted by exonerations: avoidance and incorporation approaches. "Strategies that rely on the avoidance approach are more defensive, aimed at reducing or avoiding negative consequences of the trauma" (Westervelt and Cook, 2012, p. 137). And "the incorporation approach to coping focuses on

the survivors' efforts to master their circumstances after the trauma and create or move toward constructive outcomes for themselves and others"
(Westervelt and Cook, 2012, p. 135). Echoing this previous research, readers should not presume that one approach is better or more effective than the
other. Both of these broad approaches reflect options available throughout
the process of recovering from the trauma, and a particular person may opt
for avoidance strategies one day and be ready for incorporation strategies the
next day. It is evident that early coping strategies are most accurately classified as "avoidance approaches." Post-exoneration, and particularly after
having reconciling contact with the exonerated person, "incorporation
approaches" were more common. Still, these participants adapt their coping
strategies depending on the situations they encounter daily.

SITUATIONAL AVOIDANCE

The avoidance strategies include social isolation, substance use, refusing
to discuss the experiences, and moving away from home. It is important to
acknowledge that avoidance tendencies are emotional necessities that can be
strategic decisions based on a survivor's emotional capacity in the moment.
Choosing to leave, avoid, or evade a probable agony may certainly be the
safest option among many difficult options and trauma triggers. These adap-
tations are often linked to the coping strategies from the original crime and
return after the exoneration. Social isolation experienced by Tomeshia
Carrington-Artis resulted from emotional barricades she felt:

> I have a wall up and I just function like a drug addict that goes to work
> every day. I just function. I don't breathe. Because [addicts] do what
> they have to do for nobody to question them or something to try to
> keep that secret. [Q: You need to keep it buried inside of you?] Yes,
> because I go through stages where I dissociate myself from that twelve-
> year-old little girl. I go through times where I feel like, what was that
> twelve -year-old little girl doing that made her stand out for her to get
> attacked? Why her? Sometimes I can't forgive that little girl and it's like,
> I don't breathe. I don't relax. I'm always on guard.

Being on guard is perpetual for Karen M., and it leads her to being
reclusive and hypervigilant around her home. "To this day, I guess. My
husband travels a lot on the road and is gone a lot. I can't tell you how many
times I get up and walk the house and check things and if I hear something
unusual I'm up all night and I'm fifty-three years old you know. It will
never go away. It changed me, it changed me fundamentally, and it changed
the course of my life." She rarely socializes outside of her home or apart
from her extended family. Janet Burke withdrew from university and from
most social activities: "[I] started staying home a little bit more a little bit

more withdrawn from friends, . . . my life just came to a halt for a year, I decided to leave the [job at the] church and took a new job at a child care program."

Rather than just isolating themselves socially, these participants also chose to avoid discussing their experiences. Janet Burke recalls, "I think everybody's thought was 'Well if we don't talk about it it'll just go away and Janet will be fine.' And certainly whether it was the initial rape or whether it was the exoneration process, it's not dinner party talk. It's not something that people want to hear about. So I think I just kind of kept pushing it down to the point I wasn't fun anymore." Tomeshia Carrington-Artis explained that "my dad and I don't talk about it; I don't talk to anyone about it. I feel like they don't know what to say to me." And Peggy Sanders reached a saturation point: "There was so many times there I just shut it off, you know that's enough, didn't want any more. And then I'll come back and do better and do better but then sometimes I just shut it off."

Penny Beerntsen also describes an avoidance response when she refused to discuss her experiences with reporters or documentarians, particularly since Netflix released of *Making a Murderer*. Every time she speaks publicly, it may generate additional pain and attention for the family of Teresa Halbach, whose murder is the subject of the documentary, and the exonerated man in Penny's rape case has been convicted of murdering Ms. Halbach. It is another agonizing position for Penny to navigate: how best to use her voice with a sense of responsibility for the impact of her voice on others.

Several participants described their use of alcohol and/or drugs to escape/numb the pain of these ordeals. Substance use is an avoidance strategy to cope with indescribable loss. Janet Burke explained, "I used alcohol way too much, it was a way to kind of escape but yet it always ended poorly, it always ended with me in tears."

Peggy Sanders described her substance use as so severe that ultimately she was committed to a psychiatric hospital:

Bad bad bad bad drinking and all I did was make a fool out of myself. I haven't had a drink in seventeen years because I had to quit. I was bad. I'll tell you how bad I got, I'd get to missing her so bad that I'd get off work, I would get a thirty pack and I would just hit the roads driving. And that song "Help Me Make It through the Night." I would roll my windows down and just sang. I pray no one knew about that, they would say put her away because she's crazy. And then before I'd go home I would go out there and lay on that grass. [Q: Lay on her grave?] Yup. I woke up out there one morning at five o'clock and I thought, I got to get out of here. I spent the night with her about three times out there and I think that's just crazy.

An element of situational coping is to change the situation if possible. Several participants moved away as a strategy of avoidance. Peggy Sanders sought clinical care in a rehabilitation hospital twice. Sean Malloy enlisted in the Navy after he finished high school, and Jennifer Thompson moved to New York for a period. Karen M. combined substance use and moving away: "I moved to Baton Rouge. It's the only time I ever left and tried to blend in with people that did not know me, did not know my life, my history. I did drugs. I didn't care if I died. I didn't even tell my family this. [Q: So would you say it was kind of escapism?] Honey, I couldn't escape enough, I wanted to die. I tried to die at times." And for Yolanda Thomas, moving to Alaska meant leaving North Carolina behind, missing her sister, feeling concerned about the exoneree in her case:

> I can tell you as beautiful as Alaska is I find myself saying I wish [my sister] was here. All the things I've experienced, all the places I have been. I remember from when I went to Africa I thought of her and I said I wish she could be here. But, all of these things have been on her behalf. She has been here with me. In North Carolina I didn't want to deal with [the exoneration] anymore. I want people to leave [the exoneree] alone and let him be. If they mess with him they mess with me, and it's vice versa. I told his mom our lives will forever be intertwined. We can't change that, so moving to Alaska was part of that, to get away from that.

Tertiary trauma generates a nonlinear coping response, where the painful developments in their cases often serve as trauma triggers. Reliance on avoidance strategies creates emotional distance from the tertiary trauma to survive the unimaginable agony again and to shield themselves from additional harm.

SITUATIONAL INCORPORATION

Strategies of incorporation are necessary steps in the direction toward healing for these victims and survivors. Situational coping strategies may include three broad types: direct contact with the exonerated person, experiencing a turning point toward acknowledging the harms of wrongful convictions, and finding meaning through faith and/or public advocacy. Incorporation approaches encourage integrating the traumatic experiences into one's identity, life goals, and sense of purpose, to do something productive and constructive with that pain. Ginger Blossom supported her wrongly accused twin brother. The Wilhoit family were all devoted to the exoneree's release and had maintained contact with him throughout the legal ordeal. For this group of murder victims' family members, incorporation strategies included welcoming the wrongly convicted loved one back home, despite limited support. Yolanda Thomas was actively involved in the exoneration, and she maintained contact with the exoneree and his family.

Incorporation approaches to coping started for some participants prior to the exonerations in their cases. Penny Beerntsen describes a turning point that occurred when she attended a restorative justice workshop and retreat. The presenter shared his understanding of a victim's journey toward healing. She felt validated: "It was winter, I got my cross-country skis, I went to the spot where I had been assaulted and I said, 'You don't have any power over me anymore!' And it was kind of an epiphany. I don't have to stay angry. I can, it's not to say that I never had another angry moment, obviously I did, it's not to say the next day I woke up walking down the primrose path, obviously it was a journey but that was a real kind of crucial moment."

Christy Sheppard's turning point inspired her commitment to pursue a formal education in criminal justice, which was due, in large part, to what her family had endured. She began college prior to the exoneration and wrote research papers about her cousin's murder. "One of my last criminal justice classes I wrote a big paper about Debbie's case and it was a two-part paper. I got an A on it." In this experience, the turning point acknowledges the conjoined harms among original victims and exonerees in these cases. When Christy was facing publicity about her cousin's homicide and the exonerations of Ronald Williamson and Dennis Fritz, she reached out:

> I cannot make one more move until I call Dennis Fritz. Will he talk to me? I waited several days. I was in my office and I almost wore that rug out, pacing. Calling him was worse than calling [Ron's sister] because [she] had had contact. I called Dennis and he answered and my voice immediately began to start cracking and I said, "Mr. Fritz." I said, "This is Christy Shepherd, I'm Debbie Carter's cousin," and he said, "Yeah?" I said, "There's a lot going on with this and I need you to know" . . . and I started to cry. "I need you know from Debbie's family that we know you didn't do this." He started crying. He said, "You don't know how much that means to me," and we were just like crying and talking and I said, "I'm so sorry," you know? And it just felt so bad and nobody ever said to him that they were sorry and now it's us that having to do it.

Incorporating coping strategies can include meeting with the exonerated person. Jennifer Thompson, after consenting to media interviews about her experience with flawed eyewitness-identification procedures and being consumed by misplaced guilt and shame, worked with the detective to arrange a personal meeting with Ronald Cotton, the exoneree. She explains her effort to compartmentalize and then integrate her experiences:

You take it and put it in a little box, close that lid and stick on the shelf somewhere and that's that. I've shelved that but it's seeping out, it's leaking, and you're ignoring that. Because I haven't dealt with it, and it's kind of growing in the dark. It's just this moldy mess manifesting itself in other parts of my life. So I can honestly say that I didn't begin putting the pieces together or even attempting to heal until Ronald and I met in 1997 and that had been thirteen years. That was the first time I ever took the box out.

In an act of incorporation, Janet Burke was invited to present an award to Jennifer Thompson at a luncheon for the Mid-Atlantic Innocence Project, whose postconviction lawyers represented the exoneree in Janet's case. The exoneree would be there, and in order to give the award to Jennifer, Janet knew she had to meet him before the public event. By moving toward incorporation, Janet could express her feelings about the wrongful conviction and transform her relationship with him closer to healing from their parallel trauma. She describes the situation as a turning point; when asked which approach worked better for her, she replied,

> Because I think the self-pity, the withdrawing, the dependence on something else, or even someone else prohibits you from really doing what you need to do. Whereas embracing it you just you take the good, you take the bad, and you use it and you just work through it because it's not all good and it's not all bad. It really is saying it's okay. This is really bad at this moment but there's got to be a positive that comes out of it. I mean it's these unexpected things that just happen and I don't think when I say I've embraced things and it's positive and I'm moving forward.

Andrea Harrison articulates a turning point in that "embracing" her experience is a strategy to move forward with optimism, though not including contact with the exoneree. It is a Herculean effort:

> It's been a challenge. I've taken the negative of this and rolled it into a positive with the different things I'm trying to do. I don't allow the negative of it to weigh on me as much anymore. I'm able to talk about it more openly and freely like when people say I can't believe you can just openly talk about it like that. If I'm not walking in my truth, and I'm not embracing all aspects of it, then I'm letting it take a hold of me. And the power that I allow whoever took my mother from me when I was younger growing up causing me to be depressed and things like that, the power that I allow that situation to hold over me I don't want that anymore.

Acknowledging and accepting the impact of these experiences often includes pursuing therapeutic care. Several participants described how important counseling was for their recovering process. Penny Beerntsen was particularly keen on ensuring that she sought counseling and was able to find a practitioner who helped. Andrea Harrison pursued therapeutic care through artistic and creative expression projects highlighting violence against women. She said, "So I was nineteen or maybe twenty, I started attending Art Institute and while I was doing a project called the national Clothesline Project.[2] Everybody that did a shirt they told us to go talk to one of the counselors. That was my first time talking to somebody about it. After that I realized I need to talk about this a little more which is what prompted me to write the book." The culmination of this project for Andrea was her book, *The Black Butterfly* (Harrison, 2005), wherein she writes a fictionalized account of a young child abandoned by her mother. There are important echoes in the first-person narrative when the main character, Nicole, thinks, "We had no idea what would be next in this crazy life we were living. All we could do was keep living. Nothing was expected and everything was unknown" (p. 13). Her main character becomes a young woman, still wondering where her safe place would be. Again, her character Nicole thinks, "I had gone through a lot and I would probably be a burden to them, *like someone's child they didn't know what to do with*" (p. 50, emphasis added). Turning to creativity, for Andrea, meant that she could integrate this loss into her identity in the world as an artist, to share her voice in a way that matters to her, and could inspire others, to build community and pay tribute to her mother's life.

This form of incorporation includes finding meaning from the wreckage of the original crime and the exoneration process. Regina Lane shared her experience to promote her Christian faith and to help others facing traumatic life events: "It has given me a stronger platform to stand on to tell my story and to give glory to God for how He was there with me. There's something about going through something horrible, because we all face traumatic things in our life, but being able to share that with other people and especially women being able to share what you lived through, how you survived, what you did to survive, it brings our hearts closer together. There's a bond that takes place there, and it's a beautiful thing."

Regina also turned to writing; her memoir, *From Victim to Victory: The Story of Regina Lane, the Integon Victim of Winston-Salem* (Lane and Felker, 2012), shares her faith and her experiences. Throughout her memoir, Regina consistently leans on her faith to help her incorporate this terrible ordeal: "God used my suffering to prepare me to help other suffering people. I know what it feels like to be abducted; I know what it feels like to be brutalized; I know what it feels like to be victimized" (p. 70). And "my purpose is to help others through my experience. By telling my story, I may be able to connect with victims who are struggling to find the answers and strength to live" (p. 146).

Several participants found meaning in their faith traditions; Penny Beerntsen appreciated the pastoral care she received; Millie Maxwell valued her church community; and Ginger Blossom felt spiritual connections to her deceased parents as consequence of her friends and community. Krissy Wilhoit also finds meaning in this situation as an inspiration for how she is raising her own children. Janet Burke finds meaning in acknowledging that if this attack did not happen she would not have the family she has now, and if the exoneration did not happen she would not be able to make a difference in helping to reform the legal system.

Public advocacy based on their experiences is another coping strategy of incorporation; it acknowledges the harms they endured and those inflicted on the wrongly convicted men as well as presents the urgency of legal system reform. It renders their suffering meaningful to the broader public debates about crime and justice. Consistent with activism and public advocacy that these victims/survivors describe is a desire to raise awareness, to join other groups, to provide victim advocacy in prisons, to oppose the death penalty, and to honor their lost loved ones. Penny Beerntsen became devoted to raising awareness about eyewitness-identification procedures among law enforcement and collaborated with Professor Gary Wells: "This was fairly quickly after the exoneration. We traveled around the state training law enforcement. I would tell the personal story of the identification process gone wrong and then Gary Wells who as a scientist relates very well to laypeople. He's got a good sense of humor and can make the science very understandable, would talk about here's what we can do to lessen the likelihood."[3] Unfortunately for Penny (and others), this public advocacy may also expose them to more tertiary trauma: being demonized by the public. Penny continued,

> The victims that are criticized are the ones who have come forward or have been identified. And most of us came forward because we wanted to say there are errors being made and I was involved in one of those and we have to stop this. We're taking responsibility, being vulnerable and putting ourselves out there so don't demonize us. I think people get angry at the victims, when we should be angry at the original perpetrators. We should be angry at the flaws in the system that allow it to happen. And we should make changes to lessen that likelihood, but why would any victim choose to identify the wrong person deliberately because that means the actual perpetrator is out there.

Five of these participants became advocates against the death penalty. Ginger Blossom and Yolanda Thomas joined anti-death-penalty nonprofit organizations devoted to serving the needs of murder victims' family members and promote human rights and reconciliation. Nancy Wilhoit Vollertsen became involved in Witness to Innocence, a nonprofit organization devoted to providing peer support for exonerated death row survivors and their family members and to advocate against the death penalty.[4] Christy Sheppard served on the Oklahoma Death Penalty Review Commission, and although the commission did not officially support abolishing the death penalty, they recommended an extended moratorium on executions and acknowledged that innocent people had been sentenced to death in Oklahoma.[5] As a result of her experiences and her work in prisons, Jennifer Thompson advocates for death penalty abolition as well: "The men that I've met on death row, the crimes they've committed they were seventeen, eighteen, nineteen, and twenty and they're now in their forties and fifties and they're not the same people. The death penalty does not allow for any restorative justice or reconciliation. It doesn't allow for us to recognize that people can be redeemable and can be rehabilitated and contributing members of society even if we keep them locked in prison. They can still contribute."

Making contributions is a strategy of incorporation that can lead to cultivating resiliency. For the participants in this research, their journeys toward healing and wholeness are documented in the next chapter.

Conclusion

Grief and loss are woven throughout the tertiary traumas of these original crime victims. They have lost loved ones, lost their sense of security, and lost their faith in the legal system to serve and protect them and have endured extended depressions, intense frustrations, and confusion along the way. The stress of these circumstances harmed their health and the health of other loved ones and complicated their coping and recovery. The tertiary traumas generate these losses and thus require more grieving after the initial grief unraveled. Their grief can show up one day as depression and another day as bargaining; it may present itself as avoidance or as anger, but grief does not conclude with acceptance. Their initial grieving is based on an understanding of what happened to them and their loved ones that, as it turns out, was inaccurate. Had they experienced a strand of acceptance during the initial grief process, losing it unraveled the interwoven braided fabric of grief. Thus, they lost the progress they may have made in their initial grief. Their post-exoneration grief includes more accurate information and requires them to make sense of how this could have happened while reflecting on the details of the original crime, original investigation, and original conviction in their minds to locate the moment when it went wrong. For some, it was the moment of the flawed eyewitness process. Coming to terms with the moment that produced a flawed outcome inflicted additional grief on these survivors and transformed their identity from someone who was harmed to someone who contributed to the harm that another was forced to endure. For others, finding the moment when the error began to occur is more elusive, leaving the retrospective excavation of how this happened immensely frustrating and enraging. The institutional betrayal felt is an added layer of harm from the tertiary trauma generated by wrongful convictions.

Coping with these realities is uncharted territory, as acknowledged by the detective who informed Debbie Jones of the DNA results in her case: "We don't really know what you're going to need." As with exonerees, these original crime victims experienced parallel harms that were so overwhelming they sometimes engaged strategies of avoidance and at other times engaged strategies of incorporation. It is rare that they talked about one overriding strategy, and mostly they depended on coping approaches depending on the situation. As a trauma response, situational coping may involve substance use or moving away or somehow altering the situation by changing the self in relation to the situation. Coping during tertiary trauma must be nimble, particularly as the case unfolds and in the aftermath of the exoneration because the triggers to the earlier trauma are everywhere and they never know when a trigger will explode in their day. Actively seeking information and contact with the exonerated person in their cases is a coping strategy that helped produce more incorporation approaches. Like grief, coping strategies are strands braided together with information that may alleviate or complicate misplaced guilt and shame or may compound a sense of betrayal. And their interwoven, integrated grief may unravel without warning.

PART THREE

 Healing, Repair, and Reform

PART 3 CONCLUDES this research by examining aspects of healing from these traumatic experiences, repairing the harms expressed by these participants and reforming the system. Chapter 9 examines how these participants described their emotional recovery. A major theme that emerged from the coded data is the central role of Jennifer Thompson and the nonprofit organization Healing Justice, which she founded in 2015. Using restorative justice practices, Healing Justice provides peer support to people directly harmed by wrongful convictions and exonerations, including original crime victims and exonerees. Restorative justice and peer support demonstrate that resilience is shared among those who have survived these experiences and that healing is possible through connection to others with shared experiences. From a trauma-informed framework, Jennifer's work with Healing Justice exemplifies the "tend and befriend" trauma response.

Chapter 10 compiles policy reforms to prevent, mitigate, and make reparations for miscarriages of justice for victims of crime. Inspired by insights from the original victims who participated in this research and coupled with current policy debates and initiatives relating to wrongful convictions, the chapter includes efforts to reform witness identification processes, conviction review units, compensation, and other ideas.

CHAPTER 9

Healing Justice

JENNIFER THOMPSON was unexpectedly launched onto a national stage of activism when she became the first crime victim featured in major news platforms discussing wrongful convictions. The flawed eyewitness-identification procedures were vividly demonstrated in her experience. Unfortunately, too often it was framed as her "mistake" that caused the wrongful conviction. But Jennifer has a knack for turning trials into triumphs. She focused on changing the narratives of wrongful convictions that exonerees and crime victims are all harmed, creating space for healing to start or continue through peer connections. She started Healing Justice, a nonprofit organization that promotes healing using restorative justice and advocates for policy reform. After attending the first ever restorative-justice-based healing retreat that included exonerees and original crime victims, Tomeshia Carrington-Artis said, "I do, I love them. I can call Jennifer for that motherly [talk] to calm me down. [Bobby] is my brother. Mr. [Pat] is like a father figure. [Darnell] and [Juan] are like uncles. I mean all of them play a part in my life, I'm ready to go back because I could be me. They don't judge, they know what I've been through, they don't question, they understand me and I do I love them."

Tomeshia has found a family of others harmed by wrongful convictions. The exonerated men she mentioned (Bobby, Pat, Darnell, and Juan are pseudonyms) also attended the restorative justice retreat that Jennifer Thompson organized. Their parallel journeys into and through wrongful convictions created the opportunity for their healing to be connected to each other as well. This chapter explores how these original crime victims pursue healing the wounds of their traumatic experiences. It is a quest outside of the legal system, which, for many, began with connecting to the exonerated people in their cases, as described previously. This avenue toward healing may feel inaccessible for some, particularly when the original crime is now cold or when the victims may retain a belief in the original conviction. Many participants, inspired by Jennifer Thompson's bravery and resilience, pursued connections to her for peer support. Highlighting restorative justice practices, this chapter explores how the participants described their general needs for healing. Jennifer Thompson's resilience exemplifies how traumas may inspire survivor missions (Herman, 1997).

JENNIFER THOMPSON AND HEALING JUSTICE, 501(C)(3)

On August 27, 2020, Jennifer Thompson received the following email from Theresa Newman, Duke University Charles S. Rhyne Clinical Professor of Law and co-director of the Wrongful Convictions Clinic: "Jennifer, I trust you know/saw that you and Ronald [Cotton] play a central role in Judge Wynn's extraordinary concurring opinion in the *en banc* decision for Ronnie Long today.[1] When I saw how your story impacted Judge Wynn's thinking about eyewitness identification, I started imagining how wide a circle of influence you have had by sharing your story. Thank you for being the change agent you are. It makes such a difference in people's thinking and lives."[2] As a change agent, Jennifer Thompson has made herself vulnerable to public attention, sometimes with terrible consequences that include death threats, hate mail, and derogatory comments from strangers. She has bravely shared her experience and voice to advocate for crime victims, for improvements to eyewitness-identification processes, for the abolition of capital punishment, and for exposing the circles of harm that wrongful convictions create. She tirelessly advocates that original crime victims, exonerated individuals, and their families are *all harmed* by the original perpetrator of the crime and by the flawed processes in the legal system generating erroneous convictions. The cascade of harms includes the subsequent victims of the actual perpetrators for whom "wrongful liberty" is a by-product of wrongful conviction (Baumgartner, Grigg et al., 2014; Thompson and Baumgartner, 2018). In fact, this circle of harms approach translates into a wide "circle of influence" as Newman writes, whereby Jennifer's willingness to share her experiences attracts people who benefit from hearing her story. Some of these people are in positions of power within the legal system.

It is impossible to overstate the impact of Jennifer's story for those who have lived through these ordeals themselves. In 1984, Jennifer was asleep in her apartment when Bobby Poole broke in, dug through her personal belongings, and sexually assaulted her. During the assault, Jennifer paid careful attention to his appearance, vowing to recall his face. She escaped the intruder, called police, and endured the humiliating forensic rape examination (twice). Subsequent to the investigation and flawed eyewitness-identification procedures, Ronald Cotton was arrested, prosecuted, convicted, and incarcerated. Years later, after DNA testing, Ronald was exonerated, and Ronald and Jennifer published *Picking Cotton: Our Memoir of Injustice and Redemption* in 2009. One of the most compelling elements of Jennifer's story is the experience of judgmental victim-blaming reactions throughout her ordeal. Some of the judgmental responses emerged immediately after she was attacked and can be traced to sexism and rape culture; some of it erupts from racism associated with interracial sexual assault cases, some from the blame she experienced for the flawed eyewitness procedures that she did not control. The scrutiny was rarely kind, inflicting compounded harms that extended her trauma over decades. In April 2015, Jennifer and Ronald received the Special Courage Award from the U.S. Department of Justice's Office for Victims of Crime.[3] This was the first time in U.S. history that an exonerated person was acknowledged as a victim of crime, joined by the original victim. The decades-long journey of trauma and survival forged a pathway toward resilience, but was never easy. Resiliency is "hardiness" that includes "finding a meaningful purpose" and "the belief that one can learn and grow from" these experiences (Miller, 2018, pp. 176–177).

Also in 2015, Jennifer founded the nonprofit organization Healing Justice to serve original crime victims, exonerated people, and their families in the aftermath of exonerations, using restorative justice and peer support methods.[4] Healing Justice also engages in education, training, and policy reform efforts, which are explained in more depth in chapter 10. The executive director of Healing Justice is Katie Monroe, an attorney who provided postconviction representation to her now exonerated mother, Beverly Monroe.[5] Using restorative justice and peer support methods, Healing Justice is the only organization serving both exonerated people and original crime victims, and their families, in exoneration cases. A cornerstone of this work includes regular healing retreats, where original crime victims, exonerees, and their families can find common healing in connection to each other.

Some of the participants in this research shared their experiences of learning about Jennifer, reading *Picking Cotton*, and becoming involved in Healing Justice.[6] *Picking Cotton* itself is more than a book; it is a lifeline to those navigating the painful impacts of tertiary trauma. By reading Jennifer's story, they learn that while they feel isolated and alone, there is at least one other person who has survived a similar ordeal too. That hopeful example is an avenue of connection, conversation, and support and an on-ramp to the healing journey.

Inspired by Jennifer Thompson's book, Karen M. went to meet the exoneree in her case when she saw that he would be speaking at a public venue near her home. Without a facilitator or an officer with her, she prepared by writing him a letter, putting it in a card, and giving him a copy of *Picking Cotton*. She arrived at the venue and

> touched him on the back of the shoulder and I said [his name]. He looked at me. And I said, "Can I talk to you for minute please?" And he

says sure. He followed me up the stairs. He had no idea who I was. I said, "I'm Karen." I took a few steps back because I didn't know what he would do and I just started sobbing and we hugged and he said, "Karen, I forgave you a long time ago." I couldn't quit crying and he just literally hugged [me]. I thought this man wanted to kill me for twentysomething-odd years you know? He kept saying, "Wow it's you," and it was beautiful, it was the kindest sweetest moment. And when I handed him the envelope, I said, "It's *Picking Cotton*." He said, "Are you serious?" And I said yes. He says, "I can't believe you're giving me this book."

In that moment, Jennifer Thompson's story became a mechanism of conjoined healing, a peace offering, for Karen and the exoneree in her case.

Reading *Picking Cotton* or hearing about Jennifer's story is a watershed moment for victims in wrongful conviction cases across the country. In North Carolina, Tomeshia Carrington-Artis remembers struggling until someone suggested she connect with Jennifer:

I just started crying and he said I know this lady that I need you to get in contact with. At first I was nervous and then she initiated the conversation and I felt like I could talk to her and calm down. [When] she told me her experience and what happened her, it left the door open for me to talk about what happened to me. It helped tremendously. I visited her and we talked and we talked and I could get everything out how I was feeling, how I was handling things. I knew I could talk to her because she has been through it and I wouldn't be judged.

Also, in North Carolina, Millie Maxwell heard about the book but did not have a copy. She connected with Jennifer by phone through a mutual acquaintance: "Even when I've had busy weeks and I can't get back up with her I'll get a message from her saying, 'I was just thinking about you and your family and how you're doing.' I could tell she's a really sweet person. She is because at the time she was getting ready to go and do some kind of event. And she still made sure she got that book sent to me. So, I think there are some good people in the world and some people who really do care."

In Virginia, Janet Burke reached out to Jennifer through email and did not expect a response. When Jennifer replied very quickly, Janet was surprised and relieved to have another person who understood her experiences. "I just took a shot, I mean what are the chances that I get email back? What are the chances of that? Who really reads emails from these books and then she did."

In Texas, Debbie Jones, rape survivor, was feeling alone and isolated. She contacted Jennifer through the publisher's website:

I knew there is one person in this world who can help me, who knows what I am going through. I went to her publisher's website and I emailed blindly. I said, "I'm really needing help getting through what she has been through and I need to talk to her." It was late at night I think when I emailed, and first thing in the morning I get this phone call and it is Jennifer. She called me, and I just started bawling. I needed somebody to tell me it was going to be okay. There was nobody in this world, there was nobody.

In Wisconsin, Penny Beerntsen says Jennifer is a vital source of peer support who helps with releasing some of the misplaced guilt and shame she felt: "It was coming full circle; Jennifer said all these helpful things to me about you did the best you could it's not your job to decide what evidence is presented or to decide who is a suspect."

It is not only rape survivors for whom Jennifer's story matters. In Oklahoma, murder victim family member Christy Sheppard also offered her thoughts on what has helped her:

Jennifer starting Healing Justice and I didn't know any of that was going to take place, but wanting more of that. I think it is huge for the victims to get to be a part of the process, not a spectator or pawn or whatever. But also to decide in the process of what's going to make me feel better about this. I've said everything that I needed to say, you said what you needed to say, I got to ask all the questions I needed. I've cried, wallowed in all this. Now I need to be able to walk through the rest of my life as unwounded as possible.

Healing Justice offers an opportunity to participate in healing retreats, to be heard, to meet other people with this lived experience, to make a difference, and to be involved in justice reform efforts. Janet Burke summarizes her views: "It really has everything to do with Jennifer giving me the ability to make a difference. That's what brought me back. I don't know where I would be if I didn't have that opportunity because it's hard. The guilt is incredible, So having that opportunity to kind of make a difference is huge."

Prior to launching Healing Justice, Jennifer organized the first ever retreat for people with direct experience with wrongful convictions and exonerations: it included exonerated people and original crime survivors. Tomeshia Carrington-Artis attended: "[Jennifer asked] would I be interested in going, she wants me to come. I said yes, and we flew out there. They paid for everything and it was so nice. I was the youngest victim there so I was the baby of the group and I loved it because I could be the baby, I could be that twelve-year-old little girl and I could be the adult. I was safe and I could be 'Meshia. I just loved it I mean, that's my family, I can be me

with them." After recognizing how she was broken by trauma, the difficulty of reconnecting with the internal authentic self (that twelve-year-old
little girl), to nurture and grieve that loss collectively provided Tomeshia a
powerful avenue toward healing. The retreats, hosted by Healing Justice
and led by Jennifer Thompson, provided some of these participants opportunities to reconnect with themselves as well as to meet and connect with
each other. Despite some initial hesitation about going, Debbie Jones recalls,

> Healing Justice is what I needed. When [Jennifer] first opened Healing
> Justice and she [suggested I] look at this, "You need to look at my web-
> site and you need to participate," but she had ties with the Innocence
> Project and I thought this was an Innocence Project deal. I didn't real-
> ize that it was about the victims. And it totally is and I had to see that
> for myself because let's face it, when you are a product of domestic vio-
> lence, child abuse, rape, exoneration, you have zero trust. So I had to
> come and see for myself. But restorative justice is so important to me. I
> need my voice to be heard. I need [people] to hear and see me that I'm
> okay. Because they are going through exonerations right now and they
> need to see that I am going to make it.

Not all of the participants in this research were familiar with the work
of Healing Justice. Nancy Wilhoit Vollertsen, for instance, was very active
with the nonprofit organization Witness to Innocence, which serves exonerated death row survivors and their families, but she had not participated
in a Healing Justice retreat.[7] Krissy and Kim Wilhoit attended a retreat after
our conversation. Sean Malloy and his father connected with Healing Justice after our meeting. Andrea Harrison and Dwayne Jones have participated in Healing Justice retreats since our conversations.

WHY RESTORATIVE JUSTICE?

"If crime is about injury, then justice should be about healing," according to Professor John Braithwaite (personal communication, 2001). The
adversarial legal system harmed the victims of crime who participated in
this research. Though some found support and meaningful assistance from
system-based officials, others did not. All of the participants described in
painful detail how their experiences in the legal system caused additional
harms even when system officials treated them respectfully. Restorative justice offers a collaborative paradigm for pursuing repair of the injuries due to
crime victimization. Therapeutic restorative practices (see Miller, 2011, for
an extensive review and discussion), specifically, promote victim-centered
healing. For example, victim/offender-mediated dialogue improves victims'
satisfaction by providing them with answers to questions that can be given
only by the perpetrator of the harm (Miller, 2011). Within therapeutic

restorative justice, victims of crime are at the center of concern. Sered (2019) lists several types of needs for crime victims:

a. "validation that what happened to them was wrong" (p. 23)
b. a "coherent narrative" about the events (p. 24)
c. "survivors want what they say to have an impact" (p. 26)
d. "survivors want access to the resources they need to heal and be safe" (p. 27)
e. "survivors want to be safe" (p. 28).

Central questions from a restorative justice paradigm include the following: Who was harmed? What do they need? Whose obligation is it to repair the harm? To answer those questions in the context of original crime victims in cases that result in exonerations, clearly the original crime victims are harmed, the wrongly convicted original defendants are harmed, and their families are harmed. Furthermore, the harms extend beyond the original crime and original conviction; they continue throughout the postconviction claims and the aftermath of exonerations. The needs of those who have been harmed are complex and center on the requirement for a truthful understanding of the original crime. Additional postconviction needs include victim-centered support, trauma-informed medical care, therapeutic care, financial and family assistance, and legal support before, during, and after the exoneration. The obligation to repair the harm stemming from the adversarial legal system includes providing answers to the original victims, taking responsibility for the systemic flaws that produced this outcome, providing adequate continuing support, and of course compensating both the victims and the exonerated. Daly argues that restorative justice is a mechanism that can help attend to victims' "justice interests" that "widens to embrace others in a justice activity" (2017, p. 109). Those interests affirm Sered's view of victims' needs, and include participation in the justice process, having a voice for truth telling while seeking justice, validation for victims to be believed and understood (free from victim blaming and without the burdens of guilt or shame), and vindication where the offender takes responsibility for the harms. Of course, these victims are interested in the outcome of any and all court procedures related to their cases, and they should be informed of each event and offered an opportunity to attend. National and state victims' rights require they be provided these opportunities and protections.

A mechanism commonly used in restorative justice is the circle process (Pranis, 2005), where participants engage in a facilitated dialogue process. "Peacemaking circles use structure to create possibilities for freedom: freedom to speak our truth, freedom to drop masks and protections, freedom to reveal our deepest longings, freedom to acknowledge mistakes and fears, freedom to act in accord with our core values" (Pranis, 2005, p. 11). Devices used in these facilitated circle processes include a communal centerpiece, a talking piece, articulated values, shared guidelines, and consensus-building resolutions. The circle process often involves the person who is responsible for the harm that the victims experienced, with supporters, a facilitator, as well as the victims. However, the circle process and practice has expanded to include using this technique in affinity groups that have a type of experience in common—the circle process is used to prepare prisoners for release (Baker, 2020; Walker et al., 2006; Walker and Hayashi, 2007), and victim impact circles are used within prisons (Crocker, 2015). Furthermore, the circle process is a common feature used in many schools that are transforming their learning environments away from punitive models and toward restorative practices in an effort to combat the school-to-prison pipeline (Gonzales, 2012; Schiff, 2018). And restorative justice can be an effective tool for promoting racial justice (Sered, 2019) and gendered justice (Goodmark, 2018).

The healing retreats at Healing Justice were developed by Jennifer Thompson based on a training program with Sujatha Baliga of Impact Justice that Jennifer, Katie Monroe, Britt Stone, and I attended.[8] Healing Justice is the only organization whose mission is to serve the original crime victims, exonerated people, and their families, as well as criminal justice professionals (police, prosecutors, victim advocates, and judges). The retreats typically include original crime victims/survivors, exonerees, and their families. In some instances, the original victim and exoneree from the same case are present. The conjoined harms, the parallel hell, are fulcrums for healing by connecting survivors in deep dialogue and forging strong bonds of compassion, empathy, understanding, and enduring friendships. Healing Justice has developed retreat weekends exclusively for original crime victims/survivors and their supporters. The retreats occur over several days, including a facilitated circle process. Also, expressive art projects are incorporated for participants to share their emotions.[9] The retreats include fun and games, s'mores around the campfire, music, and more. Meals are provided, and participants eat together in a relaxed family atmosphere. The circle process itself is an opportunity for people to share how they were harmed and what they need to feel whole again and for them to be involved in providing that wholeness to each other.[10] In addition to the retreats, Healing Justice has hosted a virtual circle process to maintain contact with original crime victims and exonerated people who have come to know each other through the retreats. By maintaining contact, the Healing Justice family provides support to each other at any time.

Penny Beerntsen was well-equipped for the circle process offered at Healing Justice because her experience with restorative justice predates the exoneration in her case. She became involved in victim-impact circle processes as an advocate for reform. She volunteered in prisons to tell her story of victimization and listened to prisoners share their experiences as well. She became a certified facilitator for crimes of severe violence. Participating in the Healing Justice retreats was impactful for her: "I think it has given me a sense of we are all the same. We all make mistakes that we all deserve a second and maybe third and fourth chance. That everybody has a story to tell and that if we listen and understand other people's stories we are much less apt to demonize them and we are much more likely to support them in their efforts that change. In today's political climate, I think there's a need for restorative justice and healing circles more than ever. I think it has made me less quick to judge people."

Healing Justice retreats have lingering positive impacts. For example, Tomeshia Carrington-Artis attended several retreats: "When I came back I was a little more relaxed with checking doors and windows. Telling myself okay I just checked it and I don't need to check it again. I have to be more confident in myself to know that nothing bad is going to happen every day. Nothing bad is going to happen to my kids every day. I need to relax. I need to let my husband love me and get to know me. I haven't had any breakdowns since then so, it's great progress." Healing in connection to others similarly harmed is possible, especially when it is coupled with compassion, listening, empathy, expressive arts, and play.

TEND AND BEFRIEND

It is essential for restorative justice mechanisms to operate in a trauma-informed climate (Bath, 2008). The setting needs to include an assurance of safety, the opportunity for connections, and resources for managing emotions in the midst of implementing restorative justice process. Taylor (2002) argues that the traditional trauma responses of fight or flight are incomplete conceptualizations of how people respond to trauma. There is, she articulates, another way, and it is especially common among women, to "tend and befriend" those who are traumatized. Humans are neurologically hardwired to tend others, creating and maintaining social bonds that are necessary for survival. In essence, the tend-and-befriend strategy creates a "glue" (Taylor, 2002, p. 99) to adhere these social bonds so that humans might be "less rattled" (p. 112) by stressful events when tended by others. The tend-and-befriend response, therefore, taps into a fundamentally altruistic inclination, based in compassion and understanding: "Our capacities to bond with others, to empathize with their experience, and to feel emotions vicariously have enabled our species to minister to total strangers as well as to kin" (p. 159). Jennifer Thompson's approach to her traumatic experience certainly fits this model, where she invests in tending and befriending others who are harmed by wrongful convictions. Tending others promotes healing, connectedness, and courage to become publicly engaged in shaping policy reform. "Social ties are the cheapest medicine we have. . . . When we invest in them, we reap the benefits for generations to come" (p. 199). The shared trauma experiences for crime victims, and the conjoined trauma for original victims and exonerees can provide an opportunity for healing in connection to one another and may create a kinship of mutual support (or glue, to use Taylor's concept) forged in the tertiary trauma of wrongful convictions and exonerations.

POSTTRAUMATIC GROWTH AND RESILIENCY

In addressing the need for emotional repair, these participants talked about self-care, healing with exonerees, apologies, forgiveness, and peer support as adaptive strategies. Current research on the impact of trauma documents "posttraumatic growth" and resiliency (see Miller, 2018). Ai and Park (2005) state that while much research centers on pathologies or maladaptation, scholars now address possible personal growth gains and resilience that may be exhibited by survivors. The importance of documenting how posttraumatic adaptation may generate growth and resilience is undeniable. Emerging from positive psychology, posttraumatic growth and resilience broadens our knowledge about trauma and its impacts and includes "the human capacity for transformation in even the direst of circumstances" (Ai and Park, 2005, p. 247). Features of posttraumatic growth and resiliency may include shifting priorities, reframing family relationships, improving self-care, and serving others who may also be experiencing similar challenges. Scholars are clear that posttraumatic growth is a journey, not a destination, and that it "ebbs and flows" (Miller, 2018, p. 19). Sociologically, social institutions (such as families, faith communities, the legal system) may provide buffers and supports for posttraumatic growth, and/or they may be sources of additional harms. When survivors construct meaning, it transforms their experiences into lessons for social change and is an avenue for survivors to "reestablish themselves as people of value with something to contribute" (Westervelt and Cook, 2012, p. 149). These survivor missions (Herman, 1997; Westervelt and Cook, 2012) are "adaptive strategies" (Miller, 2018, p. 109) toward the posttraumatic growth and resiliency, which are exhibited by the participants in this research.

Resilience is individual, contagious, and shared. Acknowledging their conjoined injuries aided these participants to cultivate resilience together, particularly because it acknowledges the need for self-care. Self-care is exhibited by Kim Wilhoit, who depends on medication to manage anxiety. "I've been on medication off and on since I was a teenager. Right now I'm on a good one it helps my depression and my anxiety. I'm an anxious person." And for Regina Lane, self-care means that "you compartmentalize those things within yourself. As much as you don't want that kind of baggage in you, you hold on to those details. I can be a detailed person but I never expected for twenty-five years later for that to come out. Many people never knew what happened to me because I didn't talk about it. I felt like it was a closed portion in my life and there was nothing else I could do." Self-care may also involve seeking peer support, which helps to generate collective efficacy (Miller, 2018, p. 131). Janet Burke articulates for many the importance of peer support in the process of developing resiliency: "I think it's the support of the people, knowing that even though they may not be right there with me, they agree with what I'm doing and they support me in doing it. That's the first piece."

HEALING WITH EXONEREES

As seen in Karen M.'s offering of *Picking Cotton* to the exoneree, many victims shared their connections to the exonerated individuals in their cases. Part of acknowledging the harms for many of these original victims is the impact of the wrongful conviction on exonerees who were convicted of harming them and their families. They shared the injuries of that ordeal with the exonerated individuals. In the process, their healing journey may be a conjoined endeavor. Connecting with exonerees is scary because it requires vulnerability for the victims to pursue it and because there is no guarantee for how it will go, if agreed to. These original victims had ups and downs in their contact with the exonerees in their cases; and for many, the connections provided significant progress toward healing. For those whose family members were wrongly convicted of murdering family members, they were devoted advocates for their wrongly convicted loved ones while also grieving the loss of their murdered family members. They remained in contact with their brothers and recalled visiting in prison. Upon release from prison, they returned to the family. In Ginger Blossom's family, her exonerated twin brother worked to rebuild the porch of the farmhouse during that early stage of his post-exoneration time. This provided them time to adjust and move toward repairing their lives. Her brother continues to work the farm with his wife Sue Gauger, and Ginger now runs the import business. Ginger finds comfort in being able to see Gary every day. In family situations, the conjoined harms of the wrongful convictions required healing and recovery that definitely involved family support and relationships. The Wilhoit family worked toward healing and wholeness by maintaining strong relationships with each other, and especially for Krissy and Kim to reconnect with their exonerated father. They made the most of those opportunities to share time together.

Welcoming, embracing, and shared healing may exist in some of these circumstances. Where the actual perpetrator is revealed during the exonerations through DNA evidence or other information and the original crime victims have accepted the exonerated person is actually innocent, the desire to connect may be slow to arrive, but it did arrive for several participants. It is vitally important that the initial meetings between the original victims and the exonerees be mutually desired and facilitated by a trustworthy person. As discussed previously, Debbie Jones was nervous about meeting the exoneree in her case; he had threatened to kill her during one of their early court sessions. She needed reassurance that meeting him would be facilitated by a police officer, in uniform and armed, in case things went badly. She "needed that peace" and ultimately had that meeting with the exoneree.

The other rape survivors described their initial contact with the exonerees as "healing" or as the start of their healing journeys that included apologies, forgiveness, and understanding that the rape victims were the originally harmed person and that the actual perpetrators and the flawed system were responsible for the pain they both endured. Penny Beerntsen's meeting with the exoneree concluded with a hug: "I went over to [him] and I said so only he could hear and I said, 'Can I give you a hug?' He didn't answer he just grabbed me in a big bear hug and I whispered to him 'I am so sorry,' and he said it's okay Penny it's over. [It was] incredibly healing. That is what kinda launched me on the journey of saying if he can forgive me I can learn to forgive myself."

Apologies and Forgiveness

Given the fact that the flawed system generated the wrongful convictions, it seems odd for victims to apologize to the exonerated individuals in their cases. Crime survivors are not responsible for the procedures used in crime investigations, nor are they responsible to decide what leads to follow, which suspects and fillers to include in a lineup, what evidence to include, how to process evidence, or how to interpret evidence. Furthermore, crime survivors are not responsible for charging decisions made by legal system officials, court rules of procedure and evidence, systems providing representation for indigent defense, or court schedules; all of these factors play important roles in generating wrongful convictions. Still, the popular media coverage, the legal system vernacular, and some advocates' rhetoric often imply that crime victims are responsible, at least in part, for making mistakes. Many of the participants in this research unnecessarily internalized the damaging sense of responsibility, almost to the point where they felt uniquely responsible for the entire flawed process. Therefore, in the aftermath of the exonerations, many crime victims felt compelled to offer personal apologies to the exonerated individuals in their cases, as a means of pursuing healing for all involved.

A central component of the healing process for these participants is the experience of giving and receiving apologies. During their first in-person meeting following Ronald Cotton's exoneration, Jennifer Thompson describes her apology to him as a uniquely emotional event,

> When he walked through that door, I looked at him and I thought, this is the man that I mistakenly accused of raping me thirteen years before and trying to articulate how sorry I was. Eleven years were gone and all I have to offer is words. And when he started to cry and said that he had already forgiven me years before. Something inside of me cracked, like physically cracked. All of a sudden my spirit began to find its way back for the first time. It's hard to explain. I can't really define that moment. There's relief, there's love, there's warmth, there's stuff that I never experienced before in my entire life.

Even though wrongful convictions are not their fault, for victims to apologize to the exonerees may be a healing gesture on their parallel journeys. These moments must develop naturally in each situation and should be victim-driven, whenever the crime victim is ready and interested in having such a meeting. Several victims who participated in this research chose to do this. Tomeshia Carrington-Artis explains, "I wanted to apologize because I felt like I needed to apologize for me and that he needed to hear my voice."

Some apologies are complex and multidirectional. It is appropriate when system officials offer apologies to crime victims, though such apologies were rare and welcome; Tomeshia recalls the judge "called me into his chambers and then he called [the exoneree] and even the attorney called me in the jury room and apologized. He said that was his job but he felt bad, he hated it for me being a child having to go through this all over again, and he wanted to apologize. And he talked to me for a long time in the back, he was very apologetic."

Millie Maxwell was "glad" that a justice system official apologized to the exonerated men accused of killing her father and that "they could get their life back," but neither she nor her family received an apology or acknowledgment of the pain they endured. It is in these aftermath moments, in the process of recognizing the wrongful conviction and when charges are dropped, that we see again the parallel experiences of these victims and the exonerees. Sharing these painful ordeals and arriving at a place to acknowledge the conjoined systemic harms is possible when the actual perpetrator is identified; then both the original victims and the exonerees may begin to move closer to healing.

But not all of these original victims received apologies. Peggy Sanders remains upset that the state never apologized to her: "I couldn't believe it. They always kept things from me, hide things from me. They should apologize to me for this and they never did. And I still think about it. But they're blaming me, and I still think about that. They never did apologize to me and I think they should have. There's so many things [they should apologize for]. I don't get anything and that's why I like to do this [speaking out], I guess." And the Wilhoit family similarly did not receive an apology for their ordeal, Nancy Wilhoit Vollertsen recalls: "What I wanted for Greg from the state of Oklahoma was for somebody to say that they were sorry. But, that never happened. And now it breaks my heart that he's gone and will never hear that. I have a real problem with that, that he never heard anybody say they were sorry. I guess it wouldn't have changed anything, except it would have restored my faith in the system a little bit."

Forgiveness is intimately entwined with apologies and is a companion on the healing journey that these participants described. The act of forgiveness started for most of these participants during the initial meeting with the exonerees, but it did not end there. Embracing forgiveness included being more gentle with themselves by overcoming the shame and misplaced guilt they often felt for their role in the flawed system and, when possible, forgiving the actual perpetrators. Due to the crushing shame and guilt felt by some of these original victims, the need to release that burden requires "speaking shame" (Brown, 2006, p. 49) and self-forgiveness. As Debbie Jones articulates, "Because forgiveness is to set a prisoner free and realize that the prisoner is you. What I learned is nobody is holding me prisoner, I am holding myself prisoner. And I was tired of being held prisoner." An element in the shame and guilt experience is the sense that one is unique in the world. These survivors know no other people whose cases resulted in wrongful convictions and exonerations, so they have no one they know from whom to seek support. The lived experience of these cases is a lonely and frustrating ordeal. Seeking out others who have had this experience is nearly impossible. Serendipity often dictates the possibility of connecting to others who have been through similar experiences. Support can play a key role in helping to cultivate self-forgiveness. Initially, Penny Beerntsen had to broaden her search for support to survivors of different types of ordeals:

> I remember feeling like I'm the only person this is ever happened to. I mean intellectually you understand that there's all kind of rape survivors out there but get a sense of how can the world keep turning when this terrible thing happens to me. And you get self-absorbed in a way and part of that is because you're trying to heal and you don't have the energy—but I have found in subsequent years if I start feeling sorry for myself or that the best thing in the most healing thing I can do is exactly what I feel like not doing. When I feel like pulling the covers over my head, what I need to do is go out and get into the world. Be with

someone and be available to hear other stories not necessarily of assault. I think when you're with others and you have a broader worldview it helps you realize that yeah what happened was terrible but it's survivable and you can learn from it and become stronger from it. So be supportive and be supported by other people.

Developing a support system for trauma survivors is never a solitary enterprise (Herman, 1997). It requires relationships built on trust, understanding, and compassion. Finding peer support among other survivors of similar traumas may be a strategy to move toward recovery (Boss, 2006). Miller (2018) identifies peer support and mentoring as a platform for developing resilience and posttraumatic growth among formerly battered women. Similarly, peer support for the victims/survivors in the current research benefited from the peer support model that structures Healing Justice's work. It provides opportunities for them to reach out to each other and assist during tough days. It provides recurring gatherings of others with similar experiences to meet, talk, share, and grow together by helping each other.

CONCLUSION

This chapter offered insights into how original crime victims might begin a healing journey by connecting to each other and possibly connecting with the exoneree. In this chapter, the work of Healing Justice played a central role in shaping the healing experiences of several of these participants. By acknowledging the conjoined harms of the crime victims/survivors along with the exonerated individuals in these cases, Healing Justice is unique in that it offers peer support to all who are harmed by wrongful convictions and exonerations. However, the work does not end there. Healing Justice is also involved in shaping policy reform at the state and national levels to improve the support of crime victims and survivors throughout the postconviction process and particularly in cases involving claims of innocence and exonerations. Chapter 10 explores those reform ideas and offers some conclusions for scholars and practitioners.

CHAPTER 10

Repairing and Restoring Justice

CHRISTY SHEPPARD's family has been through hell ever since her cousin Debra Sue Carter was killed in 1982. Their primary trauma was horrendous, as the details of the rape and murder of Debbie were too gruesome to understand. Peggy Sanders, Debbie's mother, struggled to maintain her composure after losing her daughter. Their secondary trauma expanded their pain to the flawed investigation, the lack of contact from the police or district attorney, and then the excruciating fiasco surrounding the decision to exhume Debbie's body. And then came the initial trials that, years later, finally produced convictions, one death sentence and one life without parole. Finally, their family might be able to recover. Learning years later that the men convicted were in fact innocent launched their tertiary trauma. Christy has been actively involved in advocating for reform in Oklahoma. The tertiary trauma that hit her family could have been prevented had there been a more careful investigation at the beginning. The agony of tertiary trauma could have been mitigated had there been suitable support and resources through the process. The tertiary trauma could have been rectified with acknowledgment of the harms and reparations made to the family. Peggy and Christy and their family have involuntarily occupied front-row seats to the legal system at work. They have seen its failures, have endured the crushing consequences of its errors, and have tried to advocate for system reforms and repairs so that other families are spared this hell.

"Criminal investigations are prone to produce evidence that contains substantial errors, which the adjudicatory process is generally incapable of correcting" (Simon, 2012, p. 3). Scholars and practitioners estimate the error rate, or the frequency of wrongful convictions, as either low (1 percent or less) or high (5 percent or more) (Gross, 2017). The error rate is not zero. The legal strategies used to collect, present, and review evidence for accuracy are complex and operated by humans (Simon, 2012). Policy reformers debate strategies to push those rates as close to zero as possible, but error cannot be eliminated. Therefore, acknowledging that more wrongful convictions and exonerations will occur in the future and preparing to support crime victims and the exonerated in the aftermath of these legal disasters are prudent.

When asked to discuss their ideas for systemic reforms, these participants expressed their understanding that justice reform is complex, difficult, and—to some extent—beyond their experience and expertise. Several expressed concerns about the systemic inequalities, such as sexism and racism, that fuel the problems in the system. Those whose experiences included capital punishment shared their thoughts on abolition. These participants desire criminal justice reform that includes preventing wrongful convictions—none of these participants advocated to keep wrongly convicted people incarcerated as a remedy to the harms they endured. Most of their ideas revolve around their individual experiences that created frustration and harms. Their ideas are organized into three broad categories: prevention, mitigation, and reparations. Prevention recommendations explore how these participants express the desire that no one else should experience these ordeals. Related to mitigation, these participants describe ways to help alleviate some of the harms they have endured. For reparations, these participants express their desire for system accountability and for efforts to repair the damage to them and to others. These categories are not mutually exclusive; in fact, they often overlap and coexist. This chapter also presents some final thoughts from the participants, overviews of policy reform in specific areas, and recommendations for additional policy reform.

Overall, to start the conversation on reforms, Regina Lane, rape survivor and subsequent victim of an actual perpetrator, observed two important realities: the inconsistencies within and throughout the legal systems and the troubling problems of racial inequality. "I think there are a lot of hard working people in the criminal justice system, but everything seems so different depending on who you are." She elaborated that "if you can pay for an attorney then he'll probably get you off or probably get a reduced sentence for you or something. But, there's no consistency, there's really no consistency. And see how different it is for one person compared to another." The presence of inconsistencies and inequities in the system is a disservice to crime victims. The common goal of the legal system is to prosecute successfully those charged with crimes and to incarcerate those convicted of crimes. The main focus of winning lies underneath an allure of seeking justice, where truth is less important as a measure of success than securing convictions (Simon, 2012), such that factual accuracy may become a casualty itself. In his searing exploration of investigation procedures, Simon concludes that the courts' "marginalization of factual accuracy is manifested most bluntly by its subjugation to competing interests . . . notably, bureaucratic considerations—over the protection against false verdicts" (2012, p. 212). In the ordinary way investigations are conducted, where courts ratify the processes and outcomes of those investigations, Simon exposes this "low regard for factual accuracy" (p. 213) that becomes an avenue, ultimately, of institutional betrayal for crime victims and unlikely to end in the current legal system.

When the system is wrong in capital cases, as is true in several of the victims' experiences covered in this research, the potential calamity of executing an innocent person is very troubling. The lore of the death penalty is that it provides closure to victims' family members after homicide (Miller, 2006). Public rhetoric and political campaigns have used the death penalty as a cudgel for political support (Cook, 1998), arguing that on behalf of murder victims the state has a legitimate claim to kill those convicted of the worst crimes, that it is in the best interest of the state to conduct executions, and that the system is "fair and accurate" (Miller, 2006, p. 3). With the rise of "law-and-order" politics in the 1980s, particularly with the Dukakis presidential campaign in 1988 and the now-infamous Willie Horton ad (see Cook, 1998, pp. 35–36), murder victims' families became fodder for the argument to continue implementing capital punishment. The lure to victims' rights advocates included achieving finality in the violent crimes they endured. Segments of the victims' rights movement embraced this public passion and willingly gave voice to pro-death-penalty sentiments gaining favor. Seldom did death penalty supporters acknowledge the increasing numbers of exonerations from capital crimes, which are "a serious challenge to the legitimacy of both death sentencing and the criminal justice system" (Miller, 2006, p. 4). Several victims who participated in this research had direct experience with capital punishment in their cases, and some had become involved in death penalty activism due to their experiences.

Some participants described the death penalty as a factor in their cases or as a cause for their activism. Ginger Blossom and the Wilhoit family experienced loved ones who were murdered and other family members who were wrongly convicted and sentenced to death for those homicides (Westervelt and Cook, 2010, 2012). After the murder of Debra Sue Carter, Christy Sheppard and Peggy Sanders experienced the wrongful capital convictions that resulted in one man being condemned to death and another condemned to life without parole, while the actual perpetrator was free. An example of "lethal leverage" (Vick et al., 2021), the men wrongly accused of killing Millie Maxwell's father were threatened with the death penalty in order to secure a false confession. Millie acknowledges that "they were pressured into taking these pleas or that they were threatened by the justice system that if they didn't take the plea, they would get the death penalty so it almost seems like what they did might have been the best choice for them." The presence of capital punishment as an option may in fact contribute to an increased risk of wrongful convictions (Vick et al., 2021).

After initially supporting the death penalty, several have become advocates for death penalty abolition. Peggy Sanders and Christy Sheppard were early supporters of the death penalty for the men convicted of killing Debra Sue Carter. While Christy was in college, enrolled in a criminal justice class, her professor arranged a tour of the prison, including death row. Tending toward chitchat, she was on the tour and chatting with her classmates, when her professor asked,

"Do you know what you're looking at? This is death row." And he said, "Right up there sits Ron Williamson right now." This is his life, this is what he does. They don't come in contact with any other human. They can go to the showers. They can talk to their lawyers. When they're transported, they're double guarded, guards on each side and they're shackled behind their backs and on their feet. And I can remember thinking, "Good, I hope he is miserable." And we go to the death chamber. And I wanted to see that, I wanted to know what would happen to him and it was very sterile, very white, bare, clock on the wall. That table looks like a crucifix, with the arms out. There is that second room with the glass and you see where the tubes run out. They showed us where the executioners stay and the three tubes that come out of the wall that would feed into the IVs. The professor is telling us the process. I'm asking all kinds of questions. "How do you become an executioner? How do you pick those people? How does this work?" I remember thinking, I want to be here, I want to watch him die. I want to watch. All of that sadness means something. I want him to suffer. I remember feeling very, I don't know if satisfied is the right word but I feel better. I know what's going to happen.

Since then, Christy's views on the death penalty have evolved. The evolution included the exoneration of Ron Williamson and Dennis Fritz and meeting other exonerees and murder victims' family members over the years. Eventually, Christy published an op-ed arguing against the death penalty in a particular case in Oklahoma.[1]

In Illinois, Ginger Blossom's twin brother was wrongly convicted of murdering their parents and condemned to death. She recalls when "he was sentenced to die it was like that's when you kick into the hyper mode because the clock starts ticking. And I didn't know how long the process is but you feel this urgency. It's hard." When asked about her views on the death penalty, Ginger replied, "What is the point? One of the things that murder victims' families face, they say every time they have to live through all of this, when the sentencing comes on, and they watch them [die] it still doesn't bring them closure, well no it doesn't. Closure comes from you. It doesn't come from external stuff."

Nancy Wilhoit Vollertsen has become a vocal activist against the death penalty based in large part on her family's experience with wrongful conviction. She did public speaking with her brother Greg in various places, telling their family's story of his wrongful conviction and exoneration. She has served on the Board of Directors of Witness to Innocence, which is a national nonprofit organization devoted to abolishing the death penalty and providing peer support to exonerated death row survivors and their families.[2]

Initially supporting capital punishment, Jennifer Thompson became involved in death penalty abolition through exonerated death row survivors who were agitating to stop an execution in Texas. She used her experience as an original crime victim in a wrongful conviction case to urge people to work on preventing violent crime and stopping injustices in the first place.

> As an anti-death-penalty person, I see my activism as in trying to diminish the harm, not perpetuating the harm. And creating a conversation: one of the problems that I find with the death penalty that bothers me so much is . . . we do a terrible job of taking care of our folks prior to when they commit these crimes. We wait until afterwards and then we just lock them up and put them away to try to kill them. So part of my death penalty conversation is about really restorative justice, how do we become better people, and how do we address these issues we have third-graders who are struggling and falling through the cracks, how do we provide mental health services to people who are sick, how do we help poor people and homeless people drug addicted people. So that's the broader picture definitely for the death penalty. How do we stop it before it starts?

Ultimately, though, "capital exonerations expose the state's fallibility" (Miller, 2006, p. 128). While some citizens are willing to allow innocent people to "fall through the cracks" and be executed (Cook, 1998, pp. 192–193), public concern about erroneous executions has undermined support for capital punishment in the United States (Baumgartner et al., 2008). For these victims, then, a conversation about reforming or abolishing capital punishment fits within a broader goal of preventing harms of wrongful convictions. Additional efforts to prevent, mitigate, and repair wrongful convictions are worth considering.

PREVENTING WRONGFUL CONVICTIONS

Gould writes, "For the broad recognition that wrongful convictions occur, too little has been done to prevent them" (2014, p. 1). Pointing to efforts at reform in some jurisdictions, Gould includes reform to DNA testing and eyewitness-identification procedures, which have resulted in some failures and limited progress. There is no question that exonerations generate public attention through dramatic media coverage. Correct and accurate prosecution of crimes in the first instance is far less newsworthy but no less important to original crime victims and survivors. Henry and Jurek (2020) report that the prosecutors they surveyed used DNA evidence in sexual assault cases to identify the guilty person in stranger assaults, to corroborate the victim's version of events, and to support a plea bargain with the accused and spare the victim a trial. Their particular ideas for preventing wrongful convictions begin with victims being at the center of concern because they are the originally harmed people in these cases. Christy Sheppard says, "After doing policy work all these years I truly believe we are not going to reach justice reform in this country unless it is victim-led. That's the only way." In order for that to work, the system needs to stop blaming victims across the board. Penny Beerntsen agrees, and offers more depth: "We really need to make systemic changes. It's a system that involves humans, and human errors. There will probably always be people wrongfully convicted, not every case is a DNA case obviously. I would not take it as a case that the system is working. We should be angry at the original perpetrators, we should be angry at the flaws in the system that allow it to happen. We should make changes to lessen that likelihood."

By supporting victim-centered prevention efforts, these participants endorsed improved and expanded scientific testing whenever possible, including DNA testing, eliminating "junk science" techniques. DNA testing is a vitally important tool used in criminal cases to test for accuracy when biological evidence is preserved. The first DNA exoneration in the United States occurred in 1989, when Gary Dotson was relieved of all legal responsibility for a 1977 rape conviction (Norris, 2017, pp. 47–50). That case marked the beginning of the modern innocence movement, and in fact was the starting point for the National Registry of Exonerations (NRE), a list of known exonerations. The NRE reports that postconviction DNA testing contributed to 20 percent of known exonerations since 1989, and it was used in thirteen of the fifteen exonerations represented in the current research.

Forensic science reform, writ large, includes bite mark evidence and emerging fire science and has exposed "junk science" in many wrongful convictions (Olney and Bonn, 2015; Scheck et al., 2000). The reform movement started over thirty years ago, before the advent of DNA evidence. There has been an expansion and refinement of DNA testing in criminal cases where biological evidence is available (Cole, 2014). In fact, "it has played a revolutionary role in correcting the wrongful convictions of hundreds of factually innocent people" (Weathered et al., 2020, p. 59). Reforming forensic science in criminal investigations includes standardizing regulations at state and federal levels and improving scientific standards for collection, testing, and gauging accuracy. DNA testing at the postconviction phase contributes to exonerations in fewer than 35 percent of the known exonerations by year (Norris, Acker, et al., 2020). DNA testing can contribute to *prevention* of wrongful convictions, however, only when used during the original investigation and trial. Twenty years ago, Scheck et al. (2000, p. 351) recommended, "DNA testing should be done within seven to fourteen days of a crime to make sure innocent suspects are not incarcerated and to improve the chances of catching the guilty." Therefore, it is vitally important that evidence used in a criminal proceeding be preserved for the purposes of appeals and improved technologies for testing the accuracy of results. Failure to preserve evidence denies the victims access to the truth about what happened to them and their families. If an exoneration results in a cold case (such as in the deaths of Noreen Malloy, Jacqueline Harrison, Jacquetta Thomas, and Kathy Wilhoit shared by their family members), access to the original evidence is vitally important to resume the investigation. Because the need for the truth never expires, the preservation of evidence should be routine practice in the legal system on behalf of crime victims.

More than four hundred crime labs in the United States employ over thirteen thousand technicians to run scientific tests on forensic evidence (Garrett, 2017). Crime labs expanded due, in part, to the war on drugs (to test substances found on criminal suspects) and to the rise of DNA-based exonerations. While crime labs are expected to meet federal guidelines, they are regulated at the state level and may, on occasion, work with federal crime labs to test evidence. Forensic evidence, when properly tested, presented by prosecutors, and challenged by defense attorneys during court proceedings, can be the linchpin in a criminal conviction. This ultimately depends on appropriate handling of the forensic evidence, such as a clean lab setting to prevent contamination and ethical practices throughout the testing process. Still, errors occur in crime labs that go beyond the "bad apple" problem (Garrett, 2017, p. 984). Therefore, forensic testing during the investigation prior to the original trial, on its own, is not sufficient to prevent wrongful convictions. Scheck and Neufeld argued that "when an airplane falls from the sky, . . . a post-mortem usually takes place as a matter of course," yet, "when inmates are released, . . . an opinion is rarely even written to mark the event" (2002, p. 251). Two decades later, we now have an important and serious examination of the genesis of wrongful convictions and the need to reform forensic evidence processes in order to prevent them.

In 2016, the Obama administration received a report on *Forensic Science in Criminal Courts: Ensuring Scientific Validity and Feature-Comparison Methods* from the President's Council of Advisors on Science and Technology (PCAST, 2016). Their goals were to review the scientific standards for using and evaluating forensic evidence in criminal cases with an eye toward preventing wrongful convictions. The report finds that DNA-based exonerations from single-source samples (common in rape cases) are scientifically valid and acknowledges that DNA-based exonerations "reflected a systemic problem—the testimony was based on methods and included claims of accuracy that were cloaked in purported scientific respectability but actually had never been subjected to meaningful scientific scrutiny" (PCAST, 2016, p. 26). Among their many recommendations, the council advocates for increasing the scientific rigor of forensic evidence testing that includes advice from and consultation with the National Institute of Standards and Technology. "It is especially important to create and support a vibrant academic research community rooted in the scientific culture of universities" (PCAST, 2016, p. 127). PCAST also recommends that scientists develop "objective methods of DNA analysis" (p. 129) as well as access to the forensic databases not commonly accessible by researchers. Their recommendation to the U.S. attorney general and to the judiciary includes making reliable forensic evidence more available in the court processes. Ultimately, the goals of justice should include identifying the true perpetrators, releasing the wrongly accused, and providing original victims with accurate information about their cases.

DNA testing, however, may be a "double-edged sword for the innocence movement" (Gould, 2014, p. 5). When properly collected, tested, challenged, and presented to juries, it can be the definitive evidence in a criminal case where biological samples are available. Gould states that "as DNA evidence is (fortunately) used more regularly in criminal investigations today, the exonerations of tomorrow will likely come from cases without biological evidence, which are much harder to prove" (2014, p. 5). The trend toward declining numbers of DNA exonerations presented on the NRE supports this prediction and makes the preservation of all other evidence vitally important to an accurate result.

A major reform arena for these participants is eyewitness-identification procedures reform to prevent wrongful convictions. Michele Mallin, rape survivor, urges reform on identification procedures: "Well I think they need to have better police practices to find rapists. Just like they shouldn't have done the photo lineup and putting in the picture just to make me pick it, and things like that. Just to have consistent things that they do and do it right and don't try to lead the victim because we don't want the innocent to go to prison for our rapists. That's not what we want. We want the guilty to be convicted. But I think they need to have better practices to get the right guy."

According to the NRE, flawed eyewitness-identification procedures contributed to 28 percent of known exonerations since 1989 and to

67 percent of documented exonerations in sexual assault cases and in 26 percent of homicide cases.[3] Eyewitness-identification procedures used in nine of the cases in the present study were from the 1980s, when they were rudimentary and deeply flawed (Cutler and Kovera, 2010; Cutler and Penrod, 1995; Loftus, 1996). Modern acknowledgment of flawed identification procedures began with Loftus's first edition in 1979; in the preface to the second edition, she describes letters she received from prisoners searching for relief and claiming innocence (Loftus, 1996). She also outlines the increasing use of expert testimony and appellate court rulings regarding these issues. Because the presence of an eyewitness in court pointing to the defendant as the person responsible for the crime is powerful evidence, and powerfully flawed, the legal system must confront the techniques and utility of this evidence. Loftus (1996) provides scientific research about how memory may be contaminated; about the difficulties of recognizing people, particularly cross-racial strangers; and about how the legal system depends on eyewitness testimony without fully understanding its limits.

Cutler and Penrod (1995) examine the vulnerabilities of eyewitness-identification procedures. Their findings expand awareness of witness-specific research where stressful conditions that often accompany witnessing or experiencing a crime can further undermine the accuracy of witness testimony. High levels of stress or arousal, "such as that felt by an individual under extreme danger or duress, debilitates perceptual skills" (Cutler and Penrod, 1995, p. 104). Wells and his colleagues (2020) offered four recommended reforms for eyewitness-identification procedures:

1. double blind procedures
2. pre-lineup instructions to the witness that the perpetrator may not be present
3. one suspect per lineup
4. asking the witness to state how confident they are in their identification (reviewed and updated in Wells et al., 2020)

The Innocence Project endorsed these reforms and added a recommendation that eyewitness processes used should also be documented. These reforms have been adopted in twenty-four states.[4]

Cutler and Kovera (2010) synthesized research findings into a series of best practices for experts using eyewitness-identification processes to increase the probability of accurate results. Particularly, they outline factors that may impair accurate results such as own-race bias, stress, and the presence of a weapon during the crime, all of which are part of the experiences of several original crime victims in the present study. Cutler and Kovera warn practitioners to be aware of the weaknesses of photo array lineups, live lineups, and cross-racial identifications, and they support blind administration.

Reforming eyewitness-identification procedures to reduce the probability of errors is central to preventing the harms for victims. A comprehensive research review with updated and expanded recommendations for reforming eyewitness procedures shows that between 23.7 and 27.9 percent of cases may generate unreliable results (Wells et al., 2020, p. 5). The updated recommendations for continued reform of Wells et al. (2020, p. 8) now include the following:

1. pre-lineup interview with the witness to capture important details
2. evidence-based suspicion of suspects
3. double-blind process (consistent with 1998 recommendations)
4. lineup fillers should not make the sole suspect conspicuous (consistent with 1998 recommendations)
5. lineup instructions to witness (consistent with 1998 recommendations)
6. immediate confidence statement from witness (consistent with 1998 recommendations)
7. video recording of procedure
8. avoid repeating identification procedures
9. avoid show-up procedures

Presumably, with these scientifically grounded reforms of eyewitness-identification procedures in place, we might see a reduction in errors associated with these investigative techniques over time. The NRE presents a chart that displays the year of conviction, and it suggests there may be a decline in exonerations with eyewitness evidence used during the original convictions.[5] It may be decades more before scholars can empirically examine whether eyewitness procedures are less often contributing to new wrongful convictions. For example, through the 1980s, new sexual assault convictions ranged from a low of five new convictions in 1980 to a peak of twenty-four in 1990, all of which resulted in exonerations, according to the NRE. Since their peak at twenty-four, new sexual assault convictions that have resulted in exonerations have declined to fewer than four since 2007. This may be a result of other claims of innocence not yet resolved, rather than a consequence of more accurate convictions due to reforming eyewitness procedures. Still, when victims participate in an investigation and provide eyewitness evidence, they are now more likely to experience a nonsuggestive, double-blind procedure that is documented and recorded. Prosecutors are more likely to use DNA evidence to corroborate witness evidence, though there is much room for growth in this area (Henry and Jurek, 2020).

Reforming eyewitness-identification procedures may also have a racial justice element. As with many of the cases in the current research, six of the original victims in sexual assault victims were white women who had been raped by Black men. "Most innocent African American defendants who

were exonerated for sexual assault had been convicted of raping white
women. The leading cause of these false convictions was mistaken eyewitness identifications—a notoriously error-prone process when white Americans are asked to identify black strangers. As with murder exonerations,
however, the leading cause is far from the only one. We see clear evidence
of racial bias, ranging from unconscious bias to explicit racism" (Gross,
2017, p. 2). Therefore, reforming eyewitness-identification procedures and
requiring corroborating evidence for a conviction may help promote a less
racially biased justice system, even though these "estimator variables" are
not under the control of the system (Wells et al., 2020). None of the original rape victims in this study intentionally identified the wrong men. The
errors belong to the process, and the process belongs to the legal system.
One step to be taken immediately is to be diligent in referring to the "flawed
eyewitness process." To cease using the phrase "mistaken eyewitness identification" is important because it implies responsibility on victims who give
evidence and is additionally destructive to them. Every reform effort should
include that blaming victims for outcomes that result from a deeply flawed
process is inappropriate.

Official misconduct is present in 54 percent of exonerations overall,
according to the NRE. It is a contributing factor in 39 percent of sexual
assault cases and in 71 percent of homicide cases and is present in six of the
victims' cases in this research. It is difficult to disaggregate prosecutorial
misconduct alone because that category of contributing factors includes
police, prosecutorial, and judicial misconduct. The American Bar Association Criminal Justice Standards outline the ethical obligations of prosecutors (Allen, 2018): "The prosecutor should seek to protect the innocent and
convict the guilty, consider the interests of victims and witnesses, and
respect the constitutional and legal rights of all persons, including suspects
and defendants" (cited in Allen, 2018, p. 2). The district attorney is obliged
to disclose evidence to the defendant prior to trial. Prosecutors can "do a lot
to prevent wrongful convictions through avoiding one-sided investigations" (Killias, 2013, p. 70). The district attorney's duties require them to
review the evidence gathered during the investigation with "a fresh set of
eyes" (Petro and Petro, 2013, p. 95), decide on the criminal charges for the
accused, determine if the evidence can withstand the scrutiny of juries and
courts, and ultimately authorize prosecuting the case. Most often, cases are
resolved through plea bargaining, and the evidence is rarely reviewed by a
jury or judge.

Unfortunately, with an adversarial system in the United States, the
desire to win overrides the desire for truth among prosecutors. Petro and
Petro (2013) argue that law schools should prioritize the duty to seek the
truth more than is currently practiced. The fact remains that prosecutorial

misconduct is present in many criminal convictions, some of which are resolved through exonerations. Violations of ethical rules and legal requirements can certainly contribute to wrongful convictions, and none more so than failure to disclose exculpatory evidence to the accused, known as *Brady* violations. A report from the King's County District Attorney's Conviction Review Unit (KCDA–CRU, 2020) identified prosecutorial misconduct as the most common form of official misconduct contributing to wrongful convictions. The legal system tends to protect prosecutors with immunities against legal action. In order to prevent wrongful convictions, prosecutorial immunity must be overhauled so that misconduct can be identified, reviewed, and remedied. Bar associations and court precedence, on their own, are insufficient to ensure prosecutorial integrity and ethical practice. Recommended reforms for prosecutors to prevent wrongful convictions are to follow the required ethical and legal duties to disclose exculpatory evidence, to ensure that investigations are conducted with best practices to produce reliable results, and to require corroborating evidence for eyewitness testimony. While victims were mentioned in the report when describing the crimes they experienced, they were not central to the proposed reforms or needs of stakeholders in the recommendations.

We will not have a 100 percent accurate system for crime adjudication; innocent people will continue to be erroneously convicted, and victims of crime will continue to experience the traumatic impacts of our flawed legal system. We may be able to reduce the percentage of cases that result in erroneous convictions; and to the extent that this can be done, our efforts will be well spent. Preventing erroneous and flawed convictions would spare the original crime victims the compounded agony of misplaced guilt and shame that is inappropriately imposed on them as well as the sense of institutional betrayal that often follows exonerations. The plight of crime victims is often overlooked in the research and policy reform in this area, but it should be far more central. Justice system reforms to prevent wrongful convictions on behalf of crime victims could be a compelling foundation, especially when factoring in subsequent victims of the actual perpetrators whose wrongful liberty is a by-product of the flawed investigation and flawed prosecution. Maintaining a flawed system is a disservice to crime victims; reform and repair are needed to prevent future victims from experiencing these ordeals.

MITIGATING WRONGFUL CONVICTIONS

Exonerations will continue. The participants in this research offer some important ideas for mitigating some of the excruciating impacts of these experiences for future cases, such as a victim-centered process, victim outreach, and victim notification. Michele Mallin was adamant that when the actual perpetrator began writing letters to confess to raping her, the investigation should have continued so that the wrongly convicted man might have been released. Instead, he died in prison prior to his exoneration.

> I think it is terrible. I think they should have investigated [the confession letters]. I think DNA was starting to be done about that time. I mean it wasn't in the eighties where they couldn't have done anything about it. Now they could test it obviously; it's a common knowledge way of investigation. But back then I think it was started in the nineties. I believe Jennifer said that Ronald Cotton was tested that that's when her case came out in the nineties so why couldn't they have done that for Tim Cole? But they didn't. They just [ignored] it because the police department thought they knew better. So that upset me. I mean I would have rather gotten a call then that we got the wrong guy but he's getting out of prison. At least he would have been able to live his life and I would have been able to tell him how sorry I was that happened. I didn't like it at all.

For the cold case homicides, of course, the continued need for investigation is vitally important to the surviving family members. Andrea Harrison and Dwayne Jones want to know who killed Jacqueline Harrison. Sean Malloy is angry that his father will "go to this grave" not knowing who killed Noreen. Yolanda Thomas will likely never learn the truth about who killed her sister Jacquetta. The Wilhoit family, particularly Krissy and Kim, have received no follow-up investigation into the murder of their mother. As another example of conjoined harms, particularly when the case is unresolved, the criminal accusation continues to follow the exoneree in their post-exoneration lives (Westervelt and Cook, 2012).

When claims of innocence are unfolding in the courts, these victims/survivors urge officials to notify crime victims in those cases using a victim-centered outreach approach. Receiving cold calls from postconviction attorneys is very jarring. Being approached by innocence network advocates can generate high levels of anxiety. Still, for these cases, receiving truthful and accurate information is vitally important to understanding, accepting, and moving forward. Yolanda Thomas prefers that victim outreach ideally come from an independent source, if possible. "It should be an outside agency who is not connected to the case in any way, who's not going to benefit." Yolanda also connects the victim's needs to the needs of the wrongly convicted person; the parallel harms collide in this process, and both are entitled to accurate information and resolution. During the outreach to the next victim/survivor, she says, the person calling should "say 'I am here for you. It's not about the justice system, it's not about the right, the wrong, the end result. I am here for *you*. You tell me what you need and I'm your [person]. I'm here. If you don't understand I'm going to speak up and tell them to slow down. If you need a break I'm going to say we got to take a break and go in the hallway and cry until you get yourself together. I am that person.'" This suggestion from Yolanda reflects the experience of her case going through the North Carolina Innocence Inquiry Commission, which is described in more detail later in this chapter.

Being seen as an important person in the case is a component of being respected. System officials could express that they understand that the victim is a central stakeholder in the process and its outcome and deserves information about the case early and throughout the process. That ideal is not reflected in Peggy Sanders's experience, where being ignored was part of the problem: "I needed more information. I still don't know what all was supposed to happen, they kept so much from me. Just like the day it happened. [Q: You mean the justice system?] Yes. And now it's going to stay just like it is and I'm just going to stay the way I am and just pray about it. That's all I can do."

For the homicide victims' families who had other family members wrongly convicted, the process unfolded without much information coming to them. Nancy Wilhoit Vollertsen recalls that notifications of events or connections to services that might help them were not offered. "My dad could not get [the lawyer] to return their phone calls. They were frantic. They didn't know what to do." Without an advocate, the family was left to its own resources. An independent victim advocate who could aid them in understanding the byzantine legal process, the legal language, and the next steps could benefit people in these cases. Williamson et al. (2016) affirm that original crime victims in wrongful conviction cases ought to have independent legal representation provided to them as they navigate exonerations. Legal and victim advocates assisting in these cases should be professionally trained in trauma-informed care and aligned with neither the prosecution nor the defense. The victims in these cases would be served better by someone who could offer insights about the process and information about the case, translate details of the evidence that may be confusing to the victim, and serve as a buffer during the process. The costs associated with hiring people to serve in this role should be borne by the legal system in the county of original jurisdiction and not by the victims themselves.

Though "little is known about them" (Webster, 2020, p. 247), conviction review units (CRUs) are vital tools to reduce the harms of wrongful convictions for all key stakeholders—including the original crime victims. According to the NRE, the numbers of CRUs in the United States are expanding every year.[6] Malavé and Barkai (2014) outline how CRUs operate using checklists and front-end and back-end efforts to address wrongful convictions. The checklist process helps to identify "red flag areas" (p. 193) in cases they review on the front end of their process to "guard against wrongful convictions." On the back end, CRUs review postconviction claims, also looking for red flags and aspects of witness testimony (single witness identification without corroboration is a red flag). Prosecutors can provide an "additional safeguard" (Webster, 2020, pp. 257–258) against wrongful convictions, because they can aid in exonerations when the evidence warrants that action. Prosecutors can vacate convictions and order new testing, among other things, to review claims of innocence. CRUs in prosecutors' offices are authorized to reinvestigate old cases where innocence is claimed and can open cold cases that have developed from exonerations. But it is not a smooth process either. Webster (2020) documents that the process of conviction review is similarly marred by system biases and emphasis on procedural rather than factual errors.

An interesting model of reversing wrongful convictions is the North Carolina Innocence Inquiry Commission (NCIIC) established in 2006.[7] It is "the first state process dedicated to innocence review in the United States" (Mumma, 2014, p. 250). As the agency is neutral within the state, the "claimant . . . must waive all protections normally afforded a person on trial and agree to cooperate with the commission" (p. 261). With eight commissioners representing a balanced array of stakeholders including victim advocates, the commission reviews claims of innocence, investigates the claims, and facilitates the process for review before a three-judge panel. The claimant cannot argue procedural violations and must limit the review to new evidence of innocence that was not presented to the original jury. The professional staff reviews and investigates claims as neutral fact finders and, if warranted, recommends a hearing. As of September 30, 2020, the NCIIC has received 2,881 claims, producing 12 exonerations. Once exonerated, the claimants are officially declared innocent and released from state custody. NCIIC exonerees' compensation claims are expedited. Crime victims are represented on the commission, and the original victims in cases that go to a hearing are contacted and supported. In this research project, we have heard from Yolanda Thomas and Millie Maxwell that they found answers to their questions through the NCIIC proceedings, with the support of the NCIIC staff members and postconviction attorneys involved in their cases.

The arduous process of review through CRUs or the NCIIC may produce anxiety for the original victims but ultimately can also offer essential insights into the details of the crimes they endured. By providing answers, the process may offer resolution. When errors are present, acknowledged, and reversed, the harms of wrongful convictions are mitigated for the exonerated persons, and *perhaps* for the original victims, so long as the victims receive respect, support, and the truth throughout the process. When victims feel misplaced shame and guilt for their role in the wrongful conviction, they also feel responsible for the many years of freedom deprived to the exonerated person. An element of reducing that sense of shame and guilt is for the CRU process to avoid displacing system responsibility on the victims. Furthermore, when the exoneration process also produces the identity of the actual perpetrators, the victims then gain a more accurate understanding of their experiences, which can then aid their journey toward healing and repair. Because of this possibility, evidence collected during a criminal investigation should be preserved indefinitely to ensure new testing can be authorized when appropriate.

Prosecutors can have a role in reversing wrongful convictions, though the "prosecutor's modal response to postconviction innocence claims appears to be either resistance or ambivalence" (Webster, 2020, p. 259). Given prosecutors' ethical obligation to seek justice, not just to secure convictions, the process of reviewing claims of innocence, in concert with the postconviction attorneys, is complex and delicate. The institutional climate of the prosecutor's office factors into how they respond to the challenge; some perceive trial work as the most important job of a prosecutor, and therefore see conviction review, like appeals, as less interesting (Webster, 2020). Webster's recommendations for reform within prosecutor's offices include developing triage strategies for reviewing cases, based in part on the seriousness of the original crimes. Since most claims of innocence are reviewed after the wrongly convicted person has exhausted the appeals process, Webster recommends that claims of innocence proceed prior to or as a part of direct appeals, as in Wisconsin, for example. For original victims in these cases, having a resolution sooner might have the advantage of occurring within the time frame of the statute of limitations so that actual perpetrators (once identified) may be prosecuted and additional subsequent victims might be avoided.

Postconviction attorneys who represent prisoners claiming innocence can also help to prevent victims from being additionally harmed. Though their legal obligation is entirely to represent their clients in their investigations of these claims, attorneys may need to contact the original victims. When this is done, outreach should be victim-centered, trauma-informed, and collaborative with prosecutors and victim advocates trained in postconviction issues. The experiences documented in this research indicate that victims do not want innocent people to be incarcerated for the crimes they endured; and when the system begins the process to review claims of innocence, the victims have a right to know about the process, the evidence, and the possible outcomes. Making the decision to notify the victims in such cases, before the outcome is known, is difficult. It will vary in each case with its unique features, making a hard and fast recommendation on the timing of notification hard to determine. When a postconviction claim of innocence case is moving toward exoneration, victim notification is important and needs to precede news coverage so that victims can brace themselves for the news when it appears. While notification and information should always come from trained professionals in the system, some victims shared positive experiences regarding their contacts with the postconviction attorneys who provided them with accurate information and with an opportunity to listen, learn, and participate in the process to the extent possible.

In 2017, Healing Justice, funded by the Office for Victims of Crime (OVC), developed resources to improve services to original victims in post-conviction processes.[8] The project was led by a multidisciplinary advisory committee, including police officers, prosecutors, researchers, victim advocates, and crime victims.[9] The project brought together original crime victims from around the country for a listening session in Washington, D.C., in 2018. The listening session provided original crime victims time to share their experiences and needs with system officials. The project also funded a survey of practitioners' experiences with postconviction claims of innocence, to learn about their agency protocols for working with victims in these cases and identify services available in those agencies. Healing Justice produced eight guiding principles, guidelines for practitioners, a sample agency policy, and assistance for original victims.[10] The resources for victims includes password-protected videos of original crime victims sharing their stories so that other victims going through the postconviction process can listen, learn, and reach out to Healing Justice for support.

Healing Justice recommends that practitioners follow eight guiding principles that include strategies for contacting original victims:

1. establish contact with the victim early
2. provide victims with choice and respect victims' rights
3. convene a multidisciplinary notification and support team
4. address victims' safety, privacy, and confidentiality concerns
5. offer referrals to emotional and psychological support services
6. be prepared to address media coverage
7. be truthful and don't overpromise
8. stay informed and knowledgeable about cultural, physical, and other diversity

Practitioners who contact original victims in these cases should become very familiar with the guidelines developed by Healing Justice and OVC and follow those guidelines closely. First, when innocence claims start, and before media coverage occurs, the victim should be contacted by an independent victim advocate or by someone associated with the original investigation who had a good relationship with the original victims and survivors (for example, the detectives who aided Debbie Jones and Jennifer Thompson). All contact with original victims should be guided by trauma-informed care and victim-centered considerations. Original victims should always have a choice in how/when/where to meet and should have ample time to receive answers to their questions.

Second, the initial contact letter or phone call should contain only basic facts that there is new information and invite the original victims to call back to a specific person with a direct phone line to arrange a personal meeting. Suggested language can be found in the Sample Agency Policy produced by Healing Justice.[11] Practitioners should be patient in awaiting a reply, in case the original victims are wary of contact; however, if the media pressure is likely to become intense, reaching out again may be necessary.

Third, the independent victim advocate should then call the victim to initiate a discussion and answer questions. In the unique cases that proceeded through the NCIIC, such as the homicide case of Millie Maxwell's father, she recalled the postconviction attorney hosted a meeting with all of her family members.[12] He answered their questions and remained in close contact with them throughout the NCIIC process. In Yolanda Thomas's case, the staff members of the NCIIC also served as vital sources of information and support through that process. The victim advocate should not predict or promise an outcome of the case but should always be honest and provide realistic information about the next steps and the likely timeline.

Fourth, if the process requires the victim to provide a DNA sample, as was the case for Debbie Jones, the process itself should be fully explained to the victim as well as the range of possible outcomes from the DNA testing. It is not appropriate, at this point, to promise a particular outcome of the DNA testing. Ultimately, these steps should be an effort to prepare the victim for the possibility that an exoneration might occur.

Fifth, given the inevitable hearings and media coverage, victims should be accompanied by the victim advocate. The advocate can ensure they are treated respectfully throughout the process, can alert the victim to possibly difficult evidence being displayed in the hearings, and can communicate with the lawyers about the victims' needs.

Sixth, it is essential that the victim not be portrayed as having caused the legal system failures that led to the erroneous conviction; they need to be reassured that the system erred, not them. The victims will likely have many questions as they recollect the original investigation, and those questions should be answered by people who can help them make sense of the confusion they may experience.

Seventh, if and when the victim wants to meet with the exonerated person, every effort should be made to facilitate that meeting. Yolanda Thomas met with the exoneree prior to his release; Jennifer Thompson met with the exoneree two years after he was released. Janet Burke met with the exonerated man several years after his release, as others did. It is not required for victims to meet with the exonerated person, though. If they wish to do so, and the exonerated person consents to meeting, it should be facilitated by a trained restorative justice practitioner familiar with the needs of crime victims in wrongful conviction cases and with the needs of exonerees. Also, every effort should be made to address and ensure real and perceived safety concerns of victims as they prepare to meet the exonerated person. This approach should be a form of the mediated dialogue process using restorative practices.

In conjunction with Healing Justice, the National Crime Victim Law Institute (NCVLI) released a position paper on crime victims' rights in a postconviction setting.[13] They point out that original crime victims' rights include rights to privacy and to treatment with respect, dignity, and fairness. In addition, crime victims' rights include being informed about the process throughout the postconviction process. Victims should have the choice to be present and have access to the information before journalists. And finally, postconviction aftermath care for original victims should include therapeutic services, financial compensation, and restorative-justice-based peer support, such as offered by Healing Justice.

Mitigating the harms of the exonerations for victims who are also family members to the exonerated wrongly convicted person ought to include an array of family supports, such as those outlined above and more. For the Wilhoit and Gauger families, their experiences included the violent murders of their loved ones and then the wrongful convictions of their beloved family members. They were not well served by the original investigation, the original trial, the wrongful convictions, and the sentences of death that they all endured. These survivors remained steadfast in their support of their wrongly convicted family members, which interrupted the grief process and their bereavement. These families should be seen as examples of strength and family support. Families in these situations may go into debt to pay for lawyers they should not have needed; those costs should be restored by the state to these families. These families lost out on valuable family time: birthdays, anniversaries, first days of school, family vacations, and holidays together. And they were prevented from building a family nest egg for college educations, elder care, and other investments in well-being. This should be acknowledged by the state, and families should be compensated through a meaningful financial settlement.

Reparations

In the post-exoneration process, original crime victims continue to have needs that often go unmet. The most immediate questions that arises is the identity of the actual perpetrators and if they will be prosecuted for those crimes. Every effort should be made to identify and hold accountable

the actual perpetrators. Beyond that, repairing the harms of wrongful convictions and exonerations may shift and evolve over time.

For some of the participants in this research, compensation to the exonerees is a form of reparations to themselves as well. This is especially apparent in Karen M.'s grief over the need for the exoneree in her case to receive
compensation; she advocated for it and is disheartened by the failure of the
state to provide it.[14] Also, prior to the exoneree being arrested on a subsequent and separate charge, Penny Beerntsen was actively involved in advocating for him to receive compensation from the state of Wisconsin. In the
Wilhoit family, compensation to the wrongly convicted would in fact have
been compensation to their family as victims. Nancy Wilhoit Vollertsen
says, "I think what would help. Compensation is so important and I think
from a victim's family standpoint it was all of our family who was harmed,
but I think I would help a victim." Sadly, Greg Wilhoit passed away without receiving compensation from the state of Oklahoma, and his family
members will not receive compensation for their own ordeal. Other crime
victims may be upset that the exonerated individuals received compensation
when they themselves did not.

Compensation to the victims directly for their pain seems equally logical and should be pursued. Victim compensation funds generally include
reimbursements for the costs of participating in the legal process but do not
extend to the postconviction process generally. The NCIIC covers the costs
for victims and survivors of the original crime to attend hearings and to be
informed of the proceedings. However, monetary reparations should be
allocated to original victims in these cases. Money cannot repair the damage done by trauma. But it can provide dependable access to resources that
can assist in repairing the harms such as therapy, medical care, lost wages for
missed workdays due to trauma or court proceedings, lost opportunities to
build a financial nest egg, lost opportunities for educational pursuits, and
other ordinary goals in life that have eluded many of these survivors. As
with exonerees, the idea of reparations should be expanded beyond merely
financial compensation to include efforts to restore a safe and secure life
(Baumgartner, Westervelt, et al., 2014).

Victims in this research whose actual perpetrators cannot be prosecuted
due to expired statutes of limitations advocate for reform on this issue. Debbie Jones and Karen M. remain frustrated that the men who actually raped
them decades earlier are not prosecuted for those crimes, even though DNA
evidence has identified them. From this perspective, the statute of limitations
expiring while the wrong person was incarcerated produces an evaporated
justice of "wrongful liberty" as described by Thompson and Baumgartner
(2018). And, of course, subsequent victimizations by the actual perpetrators

inflict immense damage on additional victims while the wrongly convicted person is in state custody. "LuAnn Mullis, Poole's last victim, commented recently to Jennifer: 'After finding out what had occurred in Ronald's and your case, . . . I became angry at the missed opportunity of the justice system to have removed Bobby Poole from society earlier. . . . If they had done it right then, what happened to me would not have occurred. . . . The first point of blame is the perpetrator; he did it. He showed no remorse. The second point of blame is the system'" (Thompson and Baumgartner, 2018).

Certainly an avenue for police reform would be to reinstate the authority to charge the actual perpetrators on the basis of the new evidence that helped to exonerate the wrongly convicted. State legislatures should consider this as a justice reform opportunity to support victims of crime in cases where wrongful convictions occurred. An original crime victim whose actual perpetrator cannot be charged is left with little confidence that the legal system is there to protect and serve them. Public safety also is better served when the actual perpetrators are brought to justice.

Institutional betrayal is a key aspect of the injuries experienced by the crime victims in the wrongful conviction cases shared in this research. Smith and Freyd (2014) outline a strategy for "institutional betrayal reparations" that includes "institutional self-examination" (p. 584). Their recommended process includes a careful institutional review of the processes that generated the flawed outcomes; to some extent, and to varying degrees, we have seen these internal examinations lead to open discovery reform, eyewitness–identification procedures reform, and other outcomes. And while these are good and necessary steps toward reforming the system, Smith and Freyd (2014) point out that these self-examinations should be a recurring process. The need for accuracy is vitally important in every case that is processed through the legal system, and that demands that the processes produce zero (or as close to zero as humanly possible) wrongful convictions of innocent suspects. In order for that aspiration to be realized, the system must continue to question itself and submit to being questioned vigorously by others. CRUs can play this role and have done so in several jurisdictions. And while it is important to do this on behalf of the wrongly convicted, it is equally important to do so on behalf of the original victims and subsequent victims of the actual perpetrators. Their parallel harms impose parallel needs for accuracy and institutional accountability.

FINAL THOUGHTS

Broken systems break people; system failures fail victims, defendants, and society. The traumagenic elements of the system are well documented. Broken people struggle toward healing and wholeness through the rest of their lives. Miscarriages of justice impose unbearable harms to the victims and survivors of the original crimes, to the wrongly convicted and incarcerated, to their families, and to subsequent victims of the actual perpetrators whose wrongful liberty is of surprisingly little concern to the system. Repairing the harms is complex and nuanced; it is individual, systemic, and structural. The role that institutionalized sexism and racism play in the legal process must be addressed. Raising awareness about the harms of victim blaming and sexism in general has been a goal of feminist criminologists for decades. We need to lean into it and continue the work. Raising awareness about the widespread harms of systemic racism in the legal system has been a major goal of human rights activists for centuries. We need to collaborate with others and shape a justice system around repairing the harms of crimes. When racism and sexism collide, as is seen in these cases, the devastation ripples throughout the lives of the direct victims, the exonerated, their families, and communities. The legal process crashes into their lives and often leaves them stranded. Justice is shattered. Justice should be about healing, and Healing Justice is inviting those who are harmed by wrongful convictions into the circle of concern. Tertiary trauma is complex.

Conjoined healing, exemplified by Janet Burke's meeting with the exoneree in her case, closes this book:

> At the end of the event, we walked downstairs, we were on the sidewalk in front of the building. I reached out my hand, I said something about not wanting his forgiveness but if he could ever just be able to *see me* you know? Just as a person that made a mistake or whatever. He said, "There's nothing to forgive you for. It was the system. And it was [the actual perpetrator] that caused this mess." And so I reached out my hand to say goodbye to him but he said, "No we're past that." And he hugs me and it was just like tears started flowing again.

Acknowledgments

I STARTED COLLECTING data for this research in June 2015 by interviewing Jennifer Thompson. At the time, she had just launched Healing Justice, where I am a founding member of the Board of Directors. The need for research on this topic was apparent to both of us. While I had some contacts with people impacted by wrongful convictions from previous work, this project was largely successful thanks to Jennifer's generous assistance in connecting with crime victims. I first met Jennifer at the Innocence Network conference in Charlotte, North Carolina, in 2013. At that conference, she participated in a panel moderated by Katie Monroe, with Christy Sheppard and Yolanda Thomas. Their stories were powerful and compelling and helped to inspire this research. Not many crime victims speak out publicly about their ordeals, so making contact would have been nearly impossible without Jennifer's assistance. Building a research project and helping to shape a nonprofit organization at the same time, collaborating on Jennifer's visions, has been one of the most rewarding experiences of my life. My deepest appreciation goes to Jennifer for trusting me and welcoming me in to this work. Watching Jennifer and executive director Katie Monroe build Healing Justice, which has become an organization defined by compassion and support, inspires me every day. You can follow Healing Justice on social media and sign up for their newsletter at www.healingjusticeproject .org. Furthermore, both Jennifer and Katie provided insightful feedback on an earlier draft of this book; their suggestions inevitably improved the quality of the finished product. Any weaknesses remain my own short-comings. I am enormously grateful to all who shared their experiences with me during this research project. This work is dedicated to the research participants.

Professor emerita Saundra Westervelt, with whom I wrote *Life After Death Row: Exonerees' Search for Community and Identity* (2012), has been my sounding board, my moral compass, and my trusted friend in all aspects of my life, and especially with this book. She offered very helpful feedback for organization and cohesion of this work. More than that, she offered weekends at her lake house, ice cream, boat rides, and shopping breaks. I appreciate her more than words can say; it's a special thing to be understood without having to say a word.

At Rutgers University Press, I am grateful for Peter Mickulas's support, guidance, and patience as I wrote this book, missed deadlines, and plodded along. I also am deeply grateful for the decades of friendship with Raymond Michalowski, series editor for Rutgers University Press. Though the pandemic has interfered with our customary annual visits, it has not dulled the sharp wit, keen insights, and goodwill from my dear friend. And Luis Fernandez has been a comrade and sage in the struggle for human rights and equity for as long as I have known him. Finally, the anonymous reviewer identified key elements of the book that needed improving. The peer review process works to our collective advantage as scholars, and that is certainly the case in this instance. They all have my deepest appreciation.

At UNCW, the Department of Sociology and Criminology offers a treasure trove of support: Mike Maume, Diane Levy, Jenn Vanderminden, Meg Rogers, Daniel Buffington, Jake Day, Justin Smith, Jill Waity, Kristin DeVall, Christina Lanier, Babette Boyd, Ann Rotchford, Angie Wadsworth, John Rice, Steve McNamee, Randy LaGrange, Menaka Raguparan, and Shannon Santana. University administrators also supported this research, including IRB members Lee Prete and Kristin Bolton, the Dean's office, including Jess Boersma, Kemille Moore, Michelle Scatton-Tessier, David Webster, Rich Ogle, and Daniella Murray, and the entire college staff. Their support included research leave and funding to cover the costs of travel, interviewing, and transcription. Thank you all so much. Our UNCW students have enriched this project by assisting with transcribing interviews and collecting research articles about specific topics. These students are every professor's dream: Wendy Austin, Karcin Vick Dunn, Kenyetta Corley, Christian Strickland, Cassius Hossfeld, and Ashley Parsons. Thank you all for working with me without complaint.

Criminology colleagues shaped the field of wrongful convictions research, feminist research, and intersectional analysis and provided much-needed inspiration: Alissa Ackerman, Jason M. Williams, James Ptacek, Robert Norris, Richard Leo, Sam Gross, Hilary Potter, Joanne Belknap, Jayne Mooney, Betsy Stanko, Lynn Chancer, Susan Miller, Denise Donnelly, Renee Lamphere, Lauren Silver, Jody Miller, Liz Webster, Walter DeKeseredy, and many more. I offer a special thanks to Mike Radelet, who inspired my early research on capital punishment, then facilitated our research with exonerated death row survivors, and has been a sounding board and mentor for over thirty years. And, to the readers who might engage with the topics inside this project, I hope you find it useful and illuminating. I am deeply grateful.

Writing during a pandemic is a blessing and a curse. In one sense, it provided time and space to devote to this work with fewer interruptions. In another sense, the pandemic was a stressful distraction from the intellectual and emotional needs of this project. Writing about trauma during collective traumas of the pandemic, racial injustices, and a painful political climate demanded self-care, discipline, and support of my family and friends. My son Greg has my deepest gratitude for sharing the meals he cooked, the yard work he did, the conversations we had, and the love of his cat. My parents in Maine, married for sixty-five years, are my roots and wings. My mother passed away with dementia and Covid. We miss her every day. My father is a cribbage savant, and I am glad he has the patience to teach me how to count my crib. As he recently said when he corrected my count: "you're just not a numbers person." Too true! My siblings, Carolee, Lea, Brian, and Rick, all contributed that special blend of compassion and humor that goes along with a complicated family. I appreciate them all.

Finally, I am grateful for beaches, sea turtles, piping plovers, binoculars, and sunshine any time of year. My birding life list stands at 304; I need more of these things.

NOTES

CHAPTER 1 INTRODUCTION

1. Some of the participants in that research, including Sabrina Butler, were convicted of crimes that never happened. Butler's nine-month-old son died of kidney failure, and she was accused of felony child abuse. See also Henry (2018, 2020).
2. Healing Justice, "From Harm to Healing" (2019), https://healingjusticeproject.org.
3. Saundra Westervelt and I are founding members of the Board of Directors for this nonprofit and helped to build the RJ program at Healing Justice; I continue to serve on the board. The research documented in this book would not have been possible without the access and credibility offered by Healing Justice. In two cases I interviewed family members of the exonerated death row survivors who participated in our previous research because they were first murder victims' family members (Westervelt and Cook, 2012).
4. National Registry of Exonerations, "About the Registry" (n.d.), https://www.law.umich.edu/special/exoneration/Pages/about.aspx.
5. For reasons that will be explained later, I identify this as a "flawed" process rather than a "mistake."
6. Readers might find it useful to bookmark this section for quick reference when reading the remaining chapters.

CHAPTER 2 SHATTERED LIVES

1. *Trigger warning*: This chapter contains graphic details of violent crimes.
2. Christie's use of hypothetical female victims is unproblematic for the purposes of this analysis.

CHAPTER 3 SHATTERED INVESTIGATIONS AND TRIALS

1. These data are accurate as of July 12, 2021.
2. PBS, "What Jennifer Saw" (February 1997), https://www.pbs.org/wgbh/pages/frontline/shows/dna/.
3. See also Phoebe Zerwick, "Excerpt: The Last Days of Darryl Hunt," *Triad City Beat*, May 7, 2017, https://triad-city-beat.com/last-days-da/.

CHAPTER 4 SHATTERED FAMILIES

1. Both of the exonerated family members, Greg Wilhoit and Gary Gauger, participated in the research previously conducted by Saundra Westervelt and me (Westervelt and Cook, 2012).

CHAPTER 5   SHATTERED JUSTICE

1. Both notifications help to inform best practices that were developed later and are explored in more depth in chapter 10.
2. Christy is referring to the trial of O. J. Simpson, who was acquitted of murdering his estranged wife, Nicole Brown Simpson, and her friend Ron Goldman in 1995. It was a highly publicized trial that marked the first high-profile use of DNA evidence.
3. Kate King, "For Victims' Families, the Torment of Exoneration," *Wall Street Journal*, November 7, 2016, https://www.wsj.com/articles/for-victims-families-the-torment-of-exoneration-1478482579
4. PBS, "What Jennifer Saw" (February 1997), https://www.pbs.org/wgbh/pages/frontline/shows/dna/photos/.
5. *Making a Murderer* (Netflix, 2018), https://www.netflix.com/title/80000770.

CHAPTER 6   SHATTERED SYSTEM

1. Private postconviction attorneys and attorneys at innocence organizations represent prisoners claiming innocence. Thus, their legal duty is to pursue investigation and litigation in their clients' best interests, even when those interests are contrary to the interests of the original victims. As such, a legal conflict of interest can arise and should be made transparent. While these attorneys can and should be sensitive to the needs of original victims in these cases, responsibility for providing initial notification and continuing legal information and support should fall to attorneys and trained victim advocates in systems-based agencies (prosecution, police, corrections, etc.) and community-based victim services organizations. (See the recommendations in chapter 10.)
2. According to their website, "The Innocence Network is an affiliation of organizations dedicated to providing pro bono legal and investigative services to individuals seeking to prove innocence of crimes for which they have been convicted, working to redress the causes of wrongful convictions, and supporting the exonerated after they are freed." Innocence Network, "Freeing the Innocent and Preventing Wrongful Convictions Worldwide" (2021), www.innocencenetwork.org.

CHAPTER 7   ELEMENTS OF TERTIARY TRAUMA

1. These data are accurate as of July 15, 2021.
2. "Duane Deaver, the SBI agent whose misconduct was central to Taylor's exoneration, has been fired for his actions in other cases." Joseph Neff and Mandy Locke, "N.C. Agrees to $12 Million Settlement for Two Wrongly Imprisoned Men," *McClatchy*, August 13, 2013, https://www.mcclatchydc.com/news/crime/article24751990.html.

CHAPTER 8   SHATTERED GRIEF, LOSS, AND COPING

1. Mayo Clinic, "What Is Grief?" (October 19, 2016), https://www.mayoclinic.org/patient-visitor-guide/support-groups/what-is-grief.
2. Clothesline Project, "Raising Awareness for Survivors of Assault and Abuse" (n.d.), http://www.clotheslineproject.info.
3. Iowa State University, "Dr. Gary Wells" (2021), https://psychology.iastate.edu/directory/dr-gary-wells.
4. Witness to Innocence, "It Could Happen to You" (n.d.), www.witnesstoinnocence.org.

5. Oklahoma Death Penalty Review Commission, "The Report of the Oklahoma Death Penalty Review Commission" (March 2017), https://www.courthousenews.com/wp-content/uploads/2017/04/OklaDeathPenalty.pdf.

CHAPTER 9   HEALING JUSTICE

1. Mr. Long was exonerated in North Carolina after forty-four years incarcerated for a crime he did not commit. His wrongful conviction was based on flawed witness identification procedures. He was released from prison in August 2020.
2. Personal communication and shared with permission from Professor Newman. Mr. Long is an exonerated client of the Duke University Wrongful Conviction Clinic.
3. U.S. Department of Justice, "Justice News" (April 21, 2015), https://www.justice.gov/opa/pr/justice-department-honors-12-individuals-and-teams-advancing-rights-and-services-crime.
4. Healing Justice, "From Harm to Healing" (2019), www.healingjusticeproject.org.
5. Beverly Monroe was exonerated from a wrongful conviction of a crime that never happened in Virginia (see Henry, 2020).
6. It is important to reiterate that the contacting of several original victims to participate in this research project was facilitated through Jennifer Thompson and Healing Justice. In the spirit of public sociology (Burawoy, 2004), I am a founding board member, and when I met with some participants not yet aware of Healing Justice, I shared with them a brochure and encouraged them to connect.
7. Witness to Innocence, "It Could Happen to You" (n.d.), www.witnesstoinnocence.org.
8. Travel and accommodations for participants are paid for by Healing Justice to ensure access irrespective of financial situation. My own interest in restorative justice began in 1999 when I applied for a Fulbright Fellowship to the Australian National University, hosted by Professor John Braithwaite. The Senior Scholar Award supported my time in Australia (January–June 2001), where I traveled and observed diversionary conferences (Cook, 2006; Cook and Powell, 2006) and a deliberative poll addressing Aboriginal Reconciliation (Cook and Powell, 2003). In 2004, I was trained in the circle process by Kay Pranis (2005) and became a certified facilitator. In addition to the training we received for Healing Justice, I have also participated in trainings by other organizations. Since that time, my work in restorative justice has continued mainly as community-involved facilitator, trainer, and advocate. Impact Justice, "Sujatha Baliga" (2021), https://impactjustice.org/people/sujatha-baliga/.
9. The "mask" and "walk a mile in my shoes" projects can be viewed online at the Healing Justice website, https://healingjusticeproject.org.
10. My involvement at the retreats is bound by confidentiality and is not the foundation for the findings reported in this research. Interested readers would find Bazelon's (2018) reportage illuminating.

CHAPTER 10   REPAIRING AND RESTORING JUSTICE

1. Christy Sheppard, "Richard Glossip Case: We Can't Be Cavalier about Death Penalty," *Oklahoman*, September 12, 2015, https://oklahoman.com/article/5446186/richard-glossip-case-we-cant-be-cavalier-about-death-penalty.
2. Witness to Innocence, "It Could Happen to You" (n.d.), www.witnesstoinnocence.org.

3. National Registry of Exonerations, "% Exonerations by Contributing Factor" (2021), http://www.law.umich.edu/special/exoneration/Pages/Exonerations ContribFactorsByCrime.aspx.

4. Innocence Project, "Eyewitness Identification Reform" (2021), https://www .innocenceproject.org/eyewitness-identification-reform/.

5. National Registry of Exonerations, "Exonerations by Year of Conviction and Type of Crime" (2021), http://www.law.umich.edu/special/exoneration/Pages /ExonerationConvictionYearCrimeType.aspx.

6. National Registry of Exonerations, "Conviction Integrity Units" (2021), http:// www.law.umich.edu/special/exoneration/Pages/Conviction-Integrity-Units .aspx.

7. North Carolina Innocence Inquiry Commission, "A Neutral, Fact-Finding State Agency Charged with Investigating Post-conviction Claims of Innocence" (2021), http://innocencecommission-nc.gov/.

8. Post-Conviction Survivor Resources, "Responding to Original Victims in Wrongful Conviction Cases" (n.d.), https://www.survivorservices.org/media/dvcpwfw1 /resources-for-practitioners_summary-project-report.pdf.

9. I served on the advisory committee for this project.

10. See Post-Conviction Survivor Resources, "Eight Guiding Principles" (n.d.), https://www.survivorservices.org/media/ks4jbced/practitioner-resources _guiding-principles_final.pdf; Post-Conviction Survivor Resources, "At a Glance: Guidelines for Practitioners" (n.d.), https://www.survivorservices.org/media /isioowtd/practitioner-resources_practitioner-guidelines_final.pdf; Post-Conviction Survivor Resources, "Sample Agency Policy" (n.d.), https://www.survivorservices .org/media/eaqdawk5/practitioner-resouces_sample-agency-policy_final.pdf; Post-Conviction Survivor Resources, "Resources for Crime Survivors & Victims' Families" (n.d.), https://www.survivorservices.org/crime-survivors-victims -families/.

11. Post-Conviction Survivor Resources, "Sample Agency Policy" (n.d.), https:// www.survivorservices.org/media/eaqdawk5/practitioner-resouces_sample -agency-policy_final.pdf.

12. The North Carolina Innocence Inquiry Commission (NCIIC) is a neutral government agency that investigates and adjudicates claims of innocence. It provides neutral, third-party victim support. The NCIIC is a unique agency that exists only in North Carolina. In other jurisdictions, victim notification, services, and support will likely flow from prosecution, police, and/or corrections agencies, ideally with the assistance of trained victim advocates therein.

13. National Crime Victim Law Institute, "Crime Victims Must Be Afforded Meaningful Notice When Offenders Claim Actual Innocence or Request DNA Testing as Part of Appellate Review" (October 2019), https://www.survivorservices .org/media/olahfm4n/legal-analysis-on-victims-rights.pdf.

14. This exoneree received compensation two years after my conversation with Karen M.

References

Ai, A. L., and Park, C. L. (2005). Possibilities of the positive following violence and trauma: Informing the coming decade of research. *Journal of Interpersonal Violence*, *20*(2), 242–250. https://doi.org/10.1177/0886260504267746.

Aldrich, H., and Kallivayalil, D. (2016). Traumatic grief after homicide: Intersections of individual and community loss. *Illness, Crisis and Loss*, *24*, 15–33. https:// doi.org /10.1177/1054137315587630.

Allen, M. (2018). *Non-Brady legal and ethical obligations on prosecutors to disclose exculpatory evidence*. National Registry of Exonerations. http://www.law.umich.edu /special/exoneration/Documents/NRE_Exculpatory_Evidence_Obligations_for _Prosecutors.pdf.

Baker, L. (2020). Introducing restorative practices at Leading Into New Communities (LINC). *Undergraduate Journal of Service Learning and Community-Based Research*, *10*, 47–68.

Bard, M., and Sangrey, D. (1986). *The crime victim's book* (2nd ed.). Brunner/Mazel.

Bath, H. (2008). The three pillars of trauma-informed care. *Reclaiming Children and Youth*, *17,3*, 17–21.

Baumgartner, F., DeBoef, S. L., and Boydstun, A. E. (2008). *The decline of the death penalty and the discovery of innocence*. Cambridge University Press.

Baumgartner, F., Grigg, A., Ramirez, R., Rose, K. J., and Lucy, J. S. (2014). *The mayhem of wrongful liberty: Documenting the crimes of true perpetrators in cases of wrongful incarceration*. Paper presented at the Innocence Network annual conference, Portland, OR, April 11–12.

Baumgartner, F., Westervelt, S. D., and Cook, K. J. (2014). Policy responses to wrongful convictions. In A. Redlich, J. Acker, R. Norris, and C. Bonventre (Eds.), *Examining wrongful convictions: Stepping back, moving forward* (pp. 251–266). Carolina Academic Press.

Bazelon, L. (2018). *Rectify: The power of restorative justice after wrongful convictions*. Beacon.

Bhattacharya, K. (2017). *Fundamentals of qualitative research: A practical guide*. Routledge.

Bordere, T. (2017). Disenfranchisement and ambiguity in the face of loss: The suffocated grief of sexual assault survivors. *Family Relations*, *66*, 29–54. https://doi.org /10.1111/fare.12231.

Boss, P. (1999). *Ambiguous loss*. Harvard University Press.

Boss, P. (2006). *Loss, trauma, and resilience: Therapeutic work with ambiguous loss*. Norton.

Bottomley, J. S., Burke, L. A., and Neimeyer, R. A. (2017). Domains of social support that predict bereavement distress following homicide loss: Assessing need and satisfaction. *OMEGA—Journal of Death and Dying*, *75*, 3–25. https://doi.org/10.1177 /0030222815612282.

Braga, A. A., and Dusseault, D. (2018). Can homicide detectives improve homicide clearance rates? *Crime & Delinquency 64*, 283–315. https://doi.org/10.1177/001112 8716679164.

Brown, B. (2006). Shame resilience theory: A grounded theory study on women and shame. *Families in Society, 87*(1), 43–52.

Brownmiller, S. (1975). *Against our will: Men, women, and rape.* Bantam Books.

Burawoy, M. (2004). Public sociologies: Contradictions, dilemmas, and possibilities. *Social Forces, 82*(4),1603–1618.

Campbell, R. (1998). The community response to rape: Victim's experiences with the legal, medical, and mental health systems. *American Journal of Community Psychology, 26*, 355–379.

Campbell, R., and Raja, S. (1999). Secondary victimization of rape victims: Insights from mental health professionals who treat survivors of violence. *Violence and Victims, 14*, 261–275.

Campbell, R., and Raja, S. (2005). The sexual assault and secondary victimization of female veterans: Help-seeking experiences with military and civilian social systems. *Psychology of Women Quarterly, 29*, 97–106.

Campbell, R., Sefl, T., Barnes, H. E., Ahrens, C. E., Wasco, S. M., and Zaragoza-Diesfield, Y. (1999). Community services for rape survivors: Enhancing psychological well-being or increasing trauma? *Journal of Consulting and Clinical Psychology, 67*, 847–858.

Campbell, R., Wasco, S. M., Ahrens, C. E., Sefl, T., and Barnes, H. E. (2001). Preventing the "second rape": Rape survivors' experiences with community service providers. *Journal of Interpersonal Violence, 16*, 1239–1259.

Caringella, S. (2009). *Addressing rape law reform in law and practice.* Columbia University Press.

Charmaz, K. (2014). *Constructing grounded theory* (2nd ed.). Sage.

Christie, J. (1977). Conflicts as property. *British Journal of Criminology, 17*, 1–15.

Christie, N. (1986). The ideal victim. In E. A. Fattah (Ed.), *From crime policy to victim policy: Reorienting the justice system* (pp. 17–30). St. Martin's.

Clark, S. E. (2011). Blackstone and the balance of eyewitness identification evidence. *Albany Law Review, 74*(3), 1105–1156.

Cole, S. (2014). The innocence crisis and forensic science reform. In M. Zalman and J. Carrano (Eds.), *Wrongful conviction and criminal justice reform: Making justice* (pp. 167–185). Routledge.

Collins, P. H. (1990). *Black feminist thought: Knowledge, consciousness, and the politics of empowerment* (2nd ed.). Routledge.

Collins, P. H. (2019). *Intersectionality as a critical social theory.* Duke University Press.

Cook, K. J. (1998). *Divided passions: Public opinions on abortion and the death penalty.* Northeastern University Press.

Cook, K. J. (2006). Doing difference and accountability in restorative justice conferences. *Theoretical Criminology, 10*, 107–124.

Cook, K. J. (2016). Has criminology awakened from its "androcentric slumber"? *Feminist Criminology, 11*(4), 334–353.

Cook, K. J. (Forthcoming). From battered woman to professor of criminology: a personal reflection. In Kimberly J. Cook, Renee Lamphere, Jason M. Williams, Stacy Mallicoat, and Alissa Ackerman (Eds). *Survivor Criminology: A Radical Act of Hope.* Rowman and Littlefield.

Cook, K. J., and Powell, C. (2003). Unfinished business: Aboriginal reconciliation and restorative justice in Australia. *Contemporary Justice Review, 6*, 279–291.

Cook, K. J., and Powell, C. (2006). Emotionality, rationality, and restorative justice. In W. S. DeKeseredy and B. Perry (Eds.), *Advancing critical criminology: Theory and application*. (pp. 83–100). Lexington Books.

Cook, K. J., and Westervelt, S. D. (2018). Power and accountability: Life after death row in the United States. In W. DeKeseredy and M. Dragiewicz (Eds.), *The Routledge Handbook of Critical Criminology*, (2nd Ed.), pp. 269–279. New York, NY: Routledge.

Cook, K. J., Westervelt, S. D., and Maruna, S. (2014). The problem of fit: Parolees, exonerees, and prisoner reentry. In A. Redlich, J. Acker, R. Norris, and C. Bonventre (Eds.), *Examining wrongful convictions: Stepping back, moving forward* (pp. 237–250). Carolina Academic Publishing.

Corr, C. A. (2002). Revisiting the concept of disenfranchised grief. In K. J. Doka (Ed.), *Disenfranchised grief: New directions, challenges, and strategies for practice* (pp. 39–60). Research Press.

Crenshaw, K. W. (1995). Mapping the margins: Intersectionality, identity politics, and violence against women of color. In K. W. Crenshaw, N. Gotanda, G. Peller, and K. Thomas (Eds.), *Critical race theory: The key writings that formed the movement* (pp. 357–383). New Press.

Crocker, D. (2015). Implementing and evaluating restorative justice projects in prison. *Criminal Justice Policy Review, 26*(1), 45–64. doi: 10.1177/0887403413508287.

Cutler, B. L., and Kovera, M. B. (2010). *Evaluating eyewitness identification*. Oxford University Press.

Cutler, B. L., and Penrod, S. D. (1995). *Mistaken identification: The eyewitness, psychology, and the law*. Cambridge University Press.

Daly, K. (2017). Sexual violence and victims' justice interests. In E. Zinsstag and M. Keenan (Eds)., *Restorative responses to sexual violence: Legal, social and therapeutic dimensions* (pp. 108–139). Routledge.

Dobash, R. E., and Dobash, R. (1979). *Violence against wives: A case against the patriarchy*. Free Press.

Doka, K. J. (2002). Introduction. In K. J. Doka (Ed.), *Disenfranchised grief: New directions, challenges, and strategies for practice* (pp. 5–22). Research Press.

Englebrecht, C. M., Mason, D. T., and Adams, P., J. (2016). Responding to homicide: An exploration of the ways in which family member react to and cope with the death of a loved one. *OMEGA—Journal of Death and Dying, 73*, 355–373.

Findley, K. A. (2012). Tunnel vision. In B. L. Cutler (Ed.), *Conviction of the innocent: Lessons from psychological research* (pp. 303–323). American Psychological Association.

Garrett, B. (2017). The crime lab in the age of the genetic panopticon. *Michigan Law Review, 115*, 979–999.

George, W. H., and Martinez, L. J. (2002). Victim blaming in rape: Effects of victim and perpetrator race, type of rape, and participant racism. *Psychology of Women Quarterly, 26*, 110–119.

Gonzales, T. (2012). Keeping kids in school: Restorative justice, punitive discipline, and the school to prison pipeline. *Journal of Law and Education, 41*, 281–335.

Goodmark, L. (2018). *Decriminalizing domestic violence: A balanced approach to intimate partner violence*. University of California Press.

Gould, J. B. (2014). Introduction. In M. Zalman and J. Carrano (Eds.), *Wrongful conviction and criminal justice reform: Making justice* (pp. 1–7). Routledge.

Grisham, J. (2006). *The innocent man: Murder and injustice in a small town*. Doubleday.

Gross, S. (2014). Investigative procedure and post-conviction review: Resetting incentives to separate the innocent from the guilty. In M. Zalman and J. Carrano

(Eds.), *Wrongful conviction and criminal justice reform: Making justice* (pp. 229–245). Routledge.

Gross, S. (2017). *Race and wrongful convictions in the United States*. National Registry of Exonerations.

Harrison, A. N. (2005). *The black butterfly*. Simply.

Henry, J. (2018). Smoke but no fire: When innocent people are wrongly convicted of crimes that never happened. *American Criminal Law Review, 55*(3), 665–704.

Henry, J. (2020). *Smoke but no fire: Convicting the innocent of crimes that never happened*. University of California Press.

Henry, T. S., and Jurek, A. L. (2020). Identification, corroboration, and charging: Examining the use of DNA evidence by prosecutors in sexual assault cases. *Feminist Criminology, 15*(5), 634–658. https://doi.org/10.1177/1557085120940795.

Herman, J. L. (1997). *Trauma and recovery*. Basic Books.

Irazola, S., Williamson, E., Stricker, J., and Niedzwiecki, E. (2013). *Study of victim experiences of wrongful conviction* (National Institute of Justice GS-23F-8182H). U.S. Department of Justice.

Johnson, M. B. (2021). *Wrongful conviction in sexual assault: Stranger rape, acquaintance rape, and intra-familial child sexual assaults*. Oxford University Press.

Johnstone, G. (2011). *Restorative justice: Ideas, values, debates*. Routledge.

Kelly, D. (1990). Victim participation in the criminal justice system. In A. J. Lurigio, W. G. Skogan, and R. C. Davis (Eds.), *Victims of crime: Problems, policies, and programs* (pp. 172–187). Sage.

Kessler, D. (2019). *Finding meaning: The sixth stage of grief*. Scribner.

Killias, M. (2013). Errors occur everywhere—but not at the same frequency: The role of procedural systems in wrongful convictions. In R. Huff and M. Killias (Eds.), *Wrongful convictions and miscarriages of justice: Causes and remedies in North American and European criminal justice systems* (pp. 61–76). Routledge.

King's County District Attorney's Office. (2020). *426 years: An examination of 25 wrongful convictions in Brooklyn, New York*. www.brooklynnda.org.

Kirshenbaum, J. M., Cabell, J. J., Moody, S. A., and Yang, Y. 2020. Life after exoneration: An overview of factors that affect exoneree reintegration. In M. K. Miller and B. H. Bornstein (Eds.), *Advances in psychology and law* (pp. 179–218). Springer. https://doi.org/10.1007/978-3-030-54678-6_6.

Kohm, S. A. (2009). Naming, shaming, and criminal justice: Mass-mediated humiliation as entertainment and punishment. *Crime Media Culture, 5*(2), 188–205.

Kubler-Ross, E. (1969). *On death and dying: What the dying have to teach doctors, nurses, clergy and their own families*. Macmillan.

Kubler-Ross, E., and Kessler, D. (2005). *On grief and grieving: Finding the meaning of grief through the five stages of loss*. Scribner.

LaFree, G. D. (1982). Male power and female victimization: Toward a theory of interracial rape. *American Journal of Sociology, 88*, 311–328.

Lane, R. K., and Felker, L. F. (2012). *From victim to victory: The story of Regina Lane, the Integon victim of Winston-Salem*. Running Angel Books.

LeBeau, J. L. (1988). Is interracial rape different? *Sociology and Social Research, 73*, 43–46.

Litvin, J. M., Kaminski, P. L., and Riggs, S. A. (2017). The complex trauma inventory: A self-report measure of posttraumatic stress disorder and complex posttraumatic stress disorder. *Journal of Traumatic Stress, 30*, 602–613. https://doi.org/10.1002/jts.22231.

Lloyd, M., and Ramon, S. (2017). Smoke and mirrors: U.K. newspaper representations of intimate partner domestic violence. *Violence Against Women, 23*(1), 114–139. https://doi.org/10.1177/1077801216634468.

Loftus, E. F. (1996). *Eyewitness testimony* (2nd ed.). Harvard University Press.

Lonsway, K. A., and Archambault, J. (2012). The "justice gap" for sexual assault cases: Future directions for research and reform. *Violence Against Women, 18*(2), 145–168. https://doi: 10.1177/1077801212440017.

Macmillan, R. (2001). Violence and the lifecourse: The consequences of victimization for personal and social development. *Annual Review of Sociology, 27*, 1–22.

Maercker, A., Neimeyer, R. A., and Simiola, V. (2016). Depressions and complicated grief. In J. Cook, S. Gold, and C. Dalenberg (Eds). *APA Handbook of Trauma Psychology*. American Psychological Association

Malavé, E. L., and Barkai, Y. (2014). Conviction integrity units: Towards prosecutorial self-regulation. In M. Zalman and J. Carrano (Eds.), *Wrongful conviction and criminal justice reform: Making justice* (pp. 189–206). Routledge.

Martin, P. Y., and Powell, R. M. (1994). Accounting for the "second assault": Legal organizations' framing of rape victims. *Law and Social Inquiry, 19*(4), 853–890.

Miethe, T. D., and Regoeczi, W. C. (2004). *Rethinking homicide: Exploring the structure and process underlying deadly situations*. Cambridge University Press.

Miller, K. S. (2006). *Wrongful capital convictions and the legitimacy of the death penalty*. LFB.

Miller, S. L. (2011). *After the crime: The power of restorative justice dialogues between victims and violent offenders*. New York University Press.

Miller, S. L. (2018). *Journeys: Resilience and growth for survivors of intimate partner abuse*. University of California Press.

Mooney, J. (2020). *The theoretical foundations of criminology: Place, time and context*. Routledge.

Mumma, C. C. (2014). The North Carolina Innocence Inquiry Commission: Catching cases that fall through the cracks. In M. Zalman and J. Carrano (Eds.), *Wrongful conviction and criminal justice reform: Making justice* (pp. 249–265). Routledge.

Newman, E., Risch, E., and Kassam-Adams, N. (2006). Ethical issues in trauma-related research: A review. *Journal of Empirical Research on Human Research Ethics, 1*(3), 29–46.

Norris, R. J. (2017). *Exonerated: A history of the innocence movement*. New York University Press.

Norris, R. J., Acker, J. R., Bonventre, C. L., and Redlich, A. D. (2020). Thirty years of innocence: Wrongful convictions and exonerations in the United States, 1989–2018. *Wrongful Conviction Law Review, 1*(1), 2–58.

Norris, R. J., Bonventre, C. L., and Acker, J. R. (2018). *When justice fails: Causes and consequences of wrongful convictions*. Carolina Academic Press.

Norris, R. J., Weintraub, J., Acker, J., Redlich, A., and Bonventre, C. (2020). The criminal costs of wrongful convictions: Can we reduce crime by protecting the innocent? *Crime and Public Policy, 19*, 367–388. https://doi.org/10.1111/1745-9133.12463.

Olney, M., and Bonn, S. (2015). An exploratory study of the legal and non-legal factors associated with exoneration and wrongful conviction: The power of DNA evidence. *Criminal Justice Policy Review, 26*(40), 400–420.

Petersen, N., and Ward, G. (2015). The transmission of historical racial violence: Lynching, civil rights–era terror, and contemporary interracial homicide. *Race and Justice, 5*(2), 114–143. https://doi.org/10.1177/2153368714567577.

Petro, J., and Petro, N. (2013). The prosecutor and wrongful convictions: Misplaced priorities, misconduct, immunity, and remedies. In C. R. Huff and

M. Killias (Eds.), *Wrongful convictions and miscarriages of justice: Causes and remedies in North American and European criminal justice systems* (pp. 91–109). Routledge.

Pierce, G. L., Radelet, M. L., Posick, C., and Lyman, T. (2014). Race and the construction of evidence in homicide cases. *American Journal of Criminal Justice, 39,* 771–786.

Pleck, E. (1987). *Domestic tyranny: The making of social policy against family violence from colonial times to the present.* Oxford University Press.

Posick, C., and Policastro, C. (2013).Victim injury, emotional distress, and satisfaction with the police: Evidence for a victim-centered, emotionally-based police response. *Journal of the Institute of Justice & International Studies, 13,* 185–196.

Potter, H. (2006). An argument for Black feminist criminology: Understanding African American women's experiences with intimate partner abuse using an integrated approach. *Feminist Criminology, 1*(2), 106–124.

Pranis, K. (2005). *The little book of circle processes: A new/old approach to peacemaking.* Good Books.

President's Council of Advisors on Science and Technology (PCAST). (2016). *Forensic science in criminal courts: Ensuring scientific validity and feature-comparison methods.* Executive Office of the President.

Rabil, M. (2012). My three decades with Darryl Hunt. *Albany Law Review, 75*(3), 1535–1577.

Rando, T. A., (1993). The increasing prevalence of complicated mourning: The onslaught is just the beginning. *OMEGA, 26,* 43–59.

Reeves, E. (2015). A synthesis of the literature on trauma–informed care. *Issues in Mental Health Nursing, 36*(9), 698–709. https//doi:10.3109/01612840.2015.1025319.Rheingold, A. A., and Williams, J. L. (2015). Survivors of homicide: Mental health outcomes, social support, and service use among a community-based sample. *Violence and Victims, 30*(5), 870–883. https://doi.org/10.1891/0886-6708.VV-D-14-00026.

Richards, T. N., Gillespie, L. K., and Smith, M. D. (2011). Exploring news coverage of femicide: Does reporting the news add insult to injury? *Feminist Criminology, 6,* 178–202.

Richardson, D., and May, H. (1999). Deserving victims? Sexual status and the social construction of violence. *Sociological Review, 47,* 308–331.

Rubin, L. B. (1976). *Worlds of pain: Life in the working-class family.* Basic Books.

Scheck, B., and Neufeld, P. (2002). DNA and innocence scholarship. In S. D. Westervelt and J. A. Humphrey (Eds.), *Wrongly convicted: Perspectives on failed justice* (pp. 241–252). Rutgers University Press.

Scheck, B., Neufeld, P., and Dwyer, J. (2000). *Actual innocence: When justice goes wrong and how to make it right.* Signet.

Schiff, M. (2018). Can restorative justice disrupt the "school–to–prison pipeline?" *Contemporary Justice Review, 21*(2), 121–139. https://doi.org/10.1080/10282580.201 8.1455509.

Sered, D. (2019). *Until we reckon: Violence, mass incarceration and a road to repair.* New Press.

Shakespeare-Finch, J., and Armstrong, D. (2010). Trauma type and posttrauma outcomes: Differences between survivors of motor vehicle accidents, sexual assault, and bereavement. *Journal of Loss and Trauma, 15,* 69–82.

Shlosberg, A., Nowotny, J., Panuccio, E., and Rajah, V. (2020). "They open the door, kick you out, and say, 'go'": Reentry challenges after wrongful imprisonment. *Wrongful Convictions Law Review, 1*(2), 226–252.

Simon, D. (2012). *In doubt: The psychology of the criminal justice system.* Harvard University Press.

Smith, C. P., and Freyd, J. J. (2013). Dangerous safe havens: Institutional betrayal exacerbates sexual trauma. *Journal of Traumatic Stress, 26*, 119–124.

Smith, C. P., and Freyd, J. J. (2014). Institutional betrayal. *American Psychologist, 69*, 575–587.

Smith, E. and Hattery, A. (2011). Race, wrongful conviction, and exoneration. *Journal of African American Studies, 15*, 74–94. https://doi:10.1007/s12111-010-9130-5.

Stanko, E. (1985). *Intimate intrusions: Women's experience of male violence.* Routledge.

Taylor, S. E. (2002). *The tending instinct: How nurturing is essential for who we are and how we live.* Times Books.

Tedeschi, R. G., and Calhoun, L. G. (2004). Posttraumatic growth: Conceptual foundations and empirical evidence. *Psychological Inquiry, 15*(1), 1–18.

Thompson, J. (2012). The unpredictable journey. *Albany Law Review, 75*(3), 1529–1533.

Thompson, J., and Baumgartner, F. (2018). *An American epidemic: Crimes of wrongful liberty.* Injustice Watch. https://www.injusticewatch.org/commentary/2018/an-american-epidemic-crimes-of-wrongful-liberty/#

Thompson-Cannino, J., Cotton, R., and Torneo, E. (2009). *Picking Cotton: Our memoir of injustice and redemption.* St. Martin's.

Tjaden, P. G., and Thoennes, N. (2000). *Full report of the prevalence, incidence, and consequences of violence against women: Findings from the National Violence Against Women Survey* (NCJ Rep. No. 183781). U.S. Department of Justice.

Vick, K., Cook, K. J., and Rogers, M. 2021. Lethal leverage: False confessions, false pleas, and wrongful convictions in death-eligible cases. *Contemporary Justice Review, 24*(1), 24–42. https://doi.org/10.1080/10282580.2020.1755845.

Vollum, S. (2014). Review of *Life after death row: Exonerees' search for community and identity* (2012; Rutgers University Press). *Contemporary Justice Review, 17*(4), 489–493.

Walker, L., and Hayashi, L. A. (2007). Pono Kaulike: A Hawaii criminal court provides restorative justice practices for healing. *Federal Probation, 71*(3), 18–24.

Walker, L., Sakai, T., and Brady, K. (2006). Restorative circles—A reentry planning process for Hawaii inmates. *Federal Probation, 70*(1), 33–37.

Walklate, S. (2012). Courting compassion: Victims, policy, and the question of justice. *Howard Journal, 51*(2), 109–121.

Walley-Jean, J. C. (2009). Debunking the myth of the "angry black woman": An exploration of anger among young African American women. *Black Women, Gender, and Families, 3*(2), 68–86.

Weathered, L., Wright, K., and Chaseling, J. (2020). Dealing with DNA evidence in the courtroom: A plain English review of current issues with identification, mixture and activity level evidence. *Wrongful Conviction Law Review, 1*(1), 59–73.

Webster, E. (2020). The prosecutor as a final safeguard against false convictions: How prosecutors assist with exonerations. *Journal of Criminal Law and Criminology, 110*(2), 245–305.

Wells, G. L., Kovera, M. B., Douglass, A. B., Brewer, N., Meissner, C. A., and Wixted, J. T. (2020). Policy and procedure recommendations for collection and preservation of eyewitness identification evidence. *Law and Human Behavior, 44*(1), 3–36. http://dx.doi.org/10.1037/lhb0000359.

Wemmers, J. (2009). Where do they belong? Giving victims a place in the criminal justice process. *Criminal Law Forum, 20*, 395–416.

Westervelt, S. D., and Cook, K. J. (2008). Coping with innocence after death row. *Contexts, 7*(4), 32–37.

Westervelt, S. D., and Cook, K. J. (2010). Framing innocents: The wrongly convicted as victims of state harm. *Crime, Law, and Social Change, 53*(3), 259–275.

Westervelt, S. D., and Cook, K. J. (2012). *Life after death row: Exonerees' search for community and identity.* Rutgers University Press.

Westervelt, S., and Cook, K. J. (2013). Life after exoneration: Examining the aftermath of a wrongful capital conviction. In C. R. Huff and M. Killias (Eds.), *Wrongful convictions and miscarriages of justice: Causes and remedies in North American and European criminal justice systems* (pp. 261–281). Routledge.

Westervelt, S. D., and Cook, K. J. (2018). Continuing trauma and aftermath for exonerated death row survivors. In J. Acker, H. Toch, and V. Bonventre (Eds.), *Living on death row* (pp. 301–329). American Psychological Association.

Wilkerson, I. (2020). *Caste: The origins of our discontents.* Random House.

Williamson, E. J., Stricker, J. M., Irazola, S. P., and Niedzwiecki, E. (2016). Wrongful convictions: Understanding the experience of the original crime victims. *Violence and Victims, 31*(1), 155–166. https://doi.org/10.1891/0886-6708.VV-D-13-00152.

Wright, J. S. (2019). Reintroducing life history methodology: An equitable social justice approach to research in education. In K. K. Strunk and L. A. Locke (Eds.), *Research methods for social justice and equity in education* (pp. 177–189). Palgrave.

Yoder, C. E. (2020). *The little book of trauma healing: When violence strikes and community security is threatened.* Good Books.

Zalman, M. (2014). The detective and wrongful conviction. In M. Zalman and J. Carrano (Eds.), *Wrongful conviction and criminal justice reform: Making justice* (pp. 147–163). Routledge.

Zehr, H. (2015). *The little book of restorative justice.* Good Books.

INDEX

abuse, 61–62, 69, 71–72
acceptance, 4, 5, 74, 127, 149
accuracy of original conviction:
doubts, 37, 53, 86, 99, 133, 138;
expectations of, 173–176; need for, 188
Acker, J., 174
activism, 148, 153, 170, 172
adversarial system, 25–26, 73, 100, 116,
158–159
Aldrich, H., 29
ambiguous loss, 18, 61, 68
analysis: inductive, 15, 73; intersectional feminist, 117
analytical units, 15
anger, 4, 97, 134–35, 139, 149
anguish, 3, 74, 84, 109, 136
anxiety, 180, 182
apology, apologize, 74, 100, 162,
164–166
Archambault, J., 30
attorneys, 90, 105–109, 165, 183;
defense attorneys, 2, 53–54, 56–58,
85, 99, 105, 107, 109, 174; district
attorneys, 42, 52, 55, 58, 83, 88, 90,
115, 122–23, 129, 168; postconviction attorneys, 87, 89–90, 99, 125,
180, 182–185
Avery, Steven, 20, 51–52, 82, 90, 93
avoidance strategies, 18, 135, 142–144

Baker, L., 160
Bard, M., 30, 98–99
Barkai, Y., 181
Bath, H., 7, 161

Baumgartner, F., 6, 14, 84, 110, 154,
172, 187–188
Bazelon, L., 31, 197
Beerntsen, Penny, 11, 20, 49–50, 51,
57, 82, 84, 93–94, 143, 148, 164
bereavement, 27, 75–76, 95, 135, 186.
See also grief
betrayal, 17–18, 84, 87, 90, 97, 104,
118–19, 125, 136. *See also* institu-
tional betrayal
Bhattacharya, K., 15, 73
Blossom, Ginger, 5, 37, 43, 49, 55, 62,
64, 110, 115, 138, 141, 144, 148. *See
also* Gauger family
Bonn, S., 173
Bordere, T., 135
Boss, P., 18, 61, 138, 167
Bottomley, J., 27, 29
Braithwaite, John, 158, 197n8
Brown, B. 127, 128, 166
Brownmiller, S., 32
Burke, Janet, 13–14, 20, 36, 38, 69–70,
75, 77, 79, 88, 92, 123–125, 142–143,
146, 156–157
Burton, Darryl, 99–100
Butler, Sabrina, 195n1 (chap. 1)

Calhoun, L., 135
Campbell, R., 32, 38–39, 40, 44,
53, 127
capital murder, 5, 28, 44, 60, 63–64
capital punishment, 120, 154, 170;
abolishing, 172; implementing, 170
Caringella, S., 38, 48, 53, 119, 123, 127

About the Author

Kimberly J. Cook is a professor of sociology and criminology at the University of North Carolina at Wilmington. She is the director of the Restorative Justice Collaborative at UNCW. She is co-author, with Saundra Westervelt, of *Life After Death Row: Exonerees' Search for Community and Identity* (2012).